ENHANCING EMOTIONAL INTELLIGENCE

Laura Delizonna, PhD
&
Ted Anstedt

Copyright © 2015 by Laura Delizonna and Ted Anstedt.

All rights reserved. Printed in the United States of America. Except as permitted under the United States copyright Act of 1976, no part of this publication may be reproduced or distributed in any form or by any means, or stored in a database or retrieval system, without prior written permission of the authors. Requests for permission should be directed to Dr. Laura Delizonna: laura@choosinghappiness.com.

ISBN—13: 978-1507750452

ISBN—10: 1507750455

Dedication

I dedicate this book
to my father, who taught me to dream big dreams, and
to my mother, who taught me to have the audacity to actually go after them.
- Laura

I dedicate this book to Suzanne, the light of my life, who has collaborated with me on many a book, and who continues to be my greatest source of happiness.
- Ted

Acknowledgments

We deeply appreciate the contributions from our stellar teaching and research team:
Bernie Wong, Andy Hyunh, Tiffany Chhay, and Paul Tran.
A special thanks to Tiffany for her contributions with our research studies and to Bernie for his leadership.

Your efforts improve this workbook,
your enthusiasm adds spark to the process,
and your support elevates all of us.

Thank you!

We would also like to say thank you to the thousands of Stanford students and Silicon Valley professionals who have shared your stories and experiences with us about your use of Emotional and Social Intelligence and how you have used the *Self-Coaching for Happiness® Process* to enhance your lives and your careers.

Your stories of personal and professional transformation
continue to inspire us all.

TABLE OF CONTENTS

Prologue ix

INTRODUCTION

What Is Emotional Intelligence? 4
      Definitions of Emotional intelligence
      Concepts of Emotional Intelligence
      Competencies of Emotional Intelligence
      Goleman's Emotional Skill Sets
      Benefits of Emotional intelligence

History Of Emotional Intelligence 11
      Mind Body Dualism—Isolating the Rational Mind
      Intelligence Tests—Focusing on the Rational Mind
      Multiple Intelligences—Accounting for Multiple Types of Success
      Descartes Error—Emotions are Necessary for Decision Making
      Emotional & Social Intelligence Become Popular Concepts
      Research on Emotional Intelligence

Mindfulness Based Emotional Intelligence 18
      Definition of Mindfulness
      Link Between Mindfulness and Emotional Intelligence
      Mindfulness Based Emotional Intelligence Programs

Theoretical Basis For Techniques—A Neuroscience Model 20
      The Triune Brain
      Increasing Emotional Intelligence—High Road & Low Road Strategies
      EI Emerges on the Middle Road—The Wise Mind

Meditation Rewires Neural Circuitry (Low Road Techniques) 24
      Research—Meditation, Neural Plasticity, and Wellbeing
      Meditation to Rewire Neural Circuitry
          Three Breaths Meditation Guide
          Three Breaths Tracking Log
      Additional Readings and Websites

Coaching Guidelines 34

SELF-AWARENESS

Introduction: Self-Awareness 38
      Mindfulness
      Mindlessness

Skill 1: **MONITOR THOUGHTS & BELIEFS** 39
      Information Processing Chain
      Benefits of Monitoring Thoughts & Beliefs
          Identifying Interpretations Worksheet & Tracking Log
          Journaling Worksheet
          Thought Labeling Meditation Worksheet & Tracking Log

Skill 2: **UNDERSTAND EMOTIONS** 51
      What is an Emotion?
      Five Components of the Emotion System
          Exercise: Five Components of an Emotion
      The Function of Emotions
      The Effect of Positive & Negative Emotions
          The Effect of Emotions Worksheet & Tracking Log

Skill 3: **OBSERVE BODILY SENSATIONS**.. 63
    Body Maps of Emotions
        Body Scan Meditation & Tracking Log

Skill 4: **DETECT EMOTIONS**.. 68
    Benefits of Detecting Emotions
    Research
    How to Detect Emotions
        Detect Emotions Worksheet

Skill 5: **IDENTIFY TRIGGERS AND REACTIONS**.. 73
    Emotional Equation
    Example: Anxiety, Anger, and Sadness
    A Different Type of Trigger—A Conditioned Response
    Triggers and Reactions of Emotions Chart
        Triggers & Reactions Worksheet & Tracking Log

Coaching Guidelines.. 83

SELF-MANAGEMENT

Introduction.. 88

SECTION ONE: MANAGE THOUGHTS... 90

Skill 6: **CHALLENGE THOUGHTS**... 93
    Challenge Thoughts, Perceptions, and Beliefs
    3 C's Technique
        3 C's Worksheet & Tracking Log

Skill 7: **DISENGAGE FROM THOUGHTS**.. 99
    How to Disengage from Thoughts
    When to Disengage from Thoughts
    Techniques for Disengaging from Thoughts
        Disengage from Thoughts Worksheet & Tracking Log
        Leaves in a Stream Meditation & Tracking Log

SECTION TWO: MANAGE EMOTIONS.. 110

Skill 8: **NEUTRALIZE EMOTIONS**... 113
    How to Neutralize Emotions
    Feel into the Emotion
        Feel into Your Emotions Meditation & Tracking Log

Skill 9: **PROCESS EMOTIONS**... 119
    How to Process Emotions—Take a S.E.A.T.
        Take a S.E.A.T. Worksheet
        Take a S.E.A.T. Meditation
        Take a S.E.A.T. Tracking Log

Skill 10: **SELF-COMPASSION**... 128
    Four Steps to Self Compassion
        Self-Compassion Worksheet & Tracking Log
        Self-Compassion Meditation & Tracking Log

Skill 11: **REDIRECT EFFORT**.. 141
    Techniques for Redirecting Effort
        Redirect Effort Worksheet & Tracking Log

Coaching Guidelines.. 147

SOCIAL AWARENESS

Introduction 152
    What is Social Awareness?
    Research—Interpersonal Neurobiology
    Mirror Neurons

Skill 12: **LISTEN MINDFULLY** 157
    Three Levels of Listening—Internal, Focused, Global
    Check Your Listening Style
    Signs of Mindless Listening
    How to Listen Mindfully
        Mindful Listening Worksheet & Tracking Log

Skill 13: **READING OTHERS' EMOTIONS** 166
    Three Step Process for Reading Emotions
    Research—Detecting and Understanding Emotions
    Gender Differences
        Three Steps to Reading Emotions Worksheet & Tracking Log
        Loving Kindness Meditation & Tracking Log

Skill 14: **NOTICE SIMILARITIES** 181
    Look for Similarities
    Consider Vulnerabilities
    Research—Empathy
        Notice Similarities Worksheet & Tracking Log
        Just Like Me Meditation & Tracking Log

Coaching Guidelines 193

RELATIONSHIP MANAGEMENT

Introduction 198
    Relationship Positivity Ratio

Skill 15: **BIDS FOR CONNECTION** 199
    How to Respond to Bids for Connection
    Examples of Responses to Bids for Connection
        Bid for Connection Worksheet & Tracking Log

Skill 16: **IDENTIFY CONFLICT ESCALATORS** 206
    Conflict Escalators—The Four Horsemen
        Identify Conflict Escalators Worksheet & Tracking Log

Skill 17: **CRAFT CONSTRUCTIVE CONFLICT** 212
    The Key to Crafting Constructive Conflict
    First, Do Your Homework
    How to Craft Constructive Conflict—Conflict De-escalators
        Craft Constructive Conversation Worksheet & Tracking Log

Skill 18: **DEEP DIVE CONVERSATIONS** 221
    Craft Deep Dive Conversations
    Craft Win-Win Solutions
        Deep Dive Conversations Worksheet & Tracking Log
    Gift of Relationship Meditation
        Gift of Relationship Meditation Guide & Tracking Log

Coaching Guidelines 231

STANFORD SERIES: Positive Psychology and the Keys to Sustainable Happiness 233

PROLOGUE

For 15 years I have been training people from the boardroom to the classroom to attain greater happiness and success. This professional work, however, was born from my own desire to thrive. My quest began early one morning, twenty-five years ago.

I had dropped out of University of Southern California to go soul-searching. Atop Mount Sinai where Moses is said to have seen the Burning Bush, I watched the sun rise. Gazing over a sea of golden mountain peaks, sunrays bursting into the pink sky, I had an epiphany. In my mind's eye, I saw myself trudging through life as if carrying a backpack full of rocks. A voice inside me said, "You are supposed to be dancing through life."

As tears streamed down my face, I made a vow: I would find my way to happiness, and when I arrived, I would teach what I had learned to others. I sealed my decision with a stack of stones and descended from the mountain. My journey began.

I studied under the world's best scholars. My mentors included top scientists at Stanford, Harvard, and Boston University. I listened to whomever had a nugget of wisdom, which included many unlikely geniuses—a French carpenter, Buddhist monks, a quirky suburban housewife, taxi drivers, Maasai warriors, Silicon Valley business titans, an old cowboy at a campfire, and countless other seekers.

What I discovered was a greater truth: Happiness is a choice. It emerges from our choices in what we focus on and act upon. We choose happiness when we turn toward the positive and possible—when we choose gratitude over greed, kindness over criticism, humor over hostility, faith over fear, or service over selfishness. No matter what we face, our challenge is to find the magic or the mystery of life. Flat tires, soft heartbreaks, and bruised knees still happen. Integral to the journey, they invite us to live wholeheartedly, define who we are, and rediscover love.

After earning a PhD and specializing in positive psychology, I began creating this happiness program. I distilled my personal insights and applied cutting edge research from neuroscience, positive psychology, and mindfulness. While teaching at Stanford, I had the incredible fortune to meet Ted Anstedt. For the past six years he and I have partnered in the service of our shared vision. We aim to positively impact society. This collaboration has tremendous synergy due to our passion, complementary skill sets, and diverse professional experiences. We design and deliver programs that empower individuals and organizations to reach extraordinary heights.

This program represents the current state of our understanding of how people thrive. We are motivated by the belief that when enough people live their best life, humanity will hit a tipping point. The result will be an unimaginable transformation in the world.

May you thrive,
Laura Delizonna

Three other books in the
Positive Psychology and the Keys to Happiness series:

Thrive: Self-Coaching for Happiness ® and Success

Elevate: Science-Based Strategies for Success and Happiness at Work

Mindful: Science-Based Strategies to Thrive at Work and in Life

Please visit the website for more information:

ChoosingHappiness.com

INTRODUCTION

*With realization of one's own potential and
self-confidence in one's ability,
one can build a better world.*

-Tenzin Gyatso, 14th Dalai Lama

INTRODUCTION

Enhancing emotional intelligence to increase thriving at work, in relationships, and in life.

Emotional intelligence is the capacity for monitoring and managing one's emotions, thoughts, motivations, and actions as well as monitoring and influencing others' emotions, thoughts, motivations, and actions. It is a skill set that has a direct impact on the ability to be effective in relationships, at school, at work, and in achieving personal goals. Research shows that people high in emotional intelligence enjoy multiple benefits, including greater success, improved health, overall life satisfaction, and strong relationships.

Emotional intelligence includes a set of skills that can be learned. This is a "how to" workbook that will teach you science-based skills of emotional intelligence and help you to use them to optimize your effectiveness across life domains. In this chapter, we present a model for emotional intelligence based upon the research of Positive Psychology. We review the definitions and components of emotional intelligence, the brief history of emotional intelligence, and the objectives of this emotional intelligence program.

INTRODUCTION

WHAT IS EMOTIONAL INTELLIGENCE?
- Definitions of Emotional intelligence
- Concepts of Emotional Intelligence
- Competencies of Emotional Intelligence
- Goleman's Emotional Skill Sets
- Benefits of Emotional intelligence

HISTORY OF EMOTIONAL INTELLIGENCE
- Mind Body Dualism—Isolating the Rational Mind
- Intelligence Tests—Focusing on the Rational Mind
- Multiple Intelligences—Accounting for Multiple Types of Success
- Descartes Error—Emotions are Necessary for Decision Making
- Emotional & Social Intelligence Become Popular Concepts
- Research on Emotional Intelligence

MINDFULNESS BASED EMOTIONAL INTELLIGENCE
- Definition of Mindfulness
- Link Between Mindfulness and Emotional Intelligence
- Mindfulness Based Emotional Intelligence Programs

THEORETICAL BASIS FOR TECHNIQUES—A NEUROSCIENCE MODEL
- The Triune Brain
- Increasing Emotional Intelligence—High Road & Low Road Strategies
- EI Emerges on the Middle Road—The Wise Mind

MEDITATION REWIRES NEURAL CIRCUITRY (LOW ROAD TECHNIQUES)
- Research—Meditation, Neural Plasticity, and Wellbeing
- Meditation to Rewire Neural Circuitry
  - *Three Breaths Meditation Guide*
  - *Three Breaths Tracking Log*
- Additional Readings and Websites

Coaching Guidelines

WHAT IS EMOTIONAL INTELLIGENCE?

Emotional Intelligence is a term that has come in to more common use since the publication in 1996 of Daniel Goleman's book, *Emotional Intelligence, Why IQ is Not Enough.* Peter Salovey at Yale University and John Mayer were the leading researchers of the construct since 1990. The term was first mentioned in the early 1900's and to reflect the idea that there is a different kind of intelligence from that measured by IQ tests.

DEFINITIONS

There are a variety of definitions relating to the emotional domain, reflecting emotions' highly abstract and subjective nature. In this workbook, we use the following working definitions.

Emotion—*A basic physiological state characterized by identifiable bodily changes and subjective sensory experience. Each emotion has a distinctive biological signature and plays a unique role in our emotional and behavioral repertoire.*

Each emotion prepares the body for a very different kind of response. For example, with *fear*, blood goes to the large skeletal muscles, such as in the legs, making it easier to flee and making the face blanch as blood is moved away from it. At the same time, the body freezes, if only for a moment, perhaps allowing time to gauge whether hiding might be a better reaction. Circuits in the brain's emotional centers trigger a flood of hormones that put the body on general alert, making it edgy and ready for action. Attention fixates on the threat at hand, the better to evaluate what response to make.

Feeling—*The internal, subjective state associated with an emotion.*

An emotion elicits a subjective feeling. For most people, fear, anxiety, frustration, and other negative emotions are associated with pain or discomfort. The physiological responses may be similar, for example fear and exhilaration, but the subjective feeling is different between these two highly activating emotional states. Fear is uncomfortable, while exhilaration is generally enjoyable.

Intelligence—*The ability to learn, understand, or respond effectively with new or challenging situations.*

In psychology, the term may be more specifically used to denote the ability to apply knowledge to manipulate one's environment or to think abstractly as measured by objective criteria such as the IQ test.

Intelligence Quotient (IQ)—*This is a number intended to represent a measure of relative intelligence as determined by the subject's responses to a series of test problems.*

The IQ was originally computed as the ratio of a person's mental age to his or her chronological (physical) age, multiplied by 100, but use of the concept of mental age has been largely discontinued, and IQ is now generally assessed on the basis of the statistical distribution of scores. The most widely used intelligence tests are the Stanford-Binet test (1916) for children, and the Wechsler test (1939), originally for adults but now also for children.

Emotional Intelligence—*Emotional Intelligence (EI) is a term that describes the ability, capacity, skill or a self-perceived ability, to identify, assess, and manage the emotions of one's self, others, and groups.*

Emotional intelligence is often defined in terms of attention to, and discrimination of, one's emotions, accurate recognition of one's own and others' moods, mood management and control over emotions. It includes emotional empathy and a response with appropriate (adaptive) emotions and behaviors in various life situations, especially to stress and difficult situations. It considers a balancing of honest expression of emotions against courtesy, consideration, and respect (possession of good social skills and communication skills).

Additional qualities may include selection of work that is emotionally rewarding to avoid procrastination, self-doubt, and low achievement also known as good self-motivation and goal management. It may also include the ability to balance between work, home, and recreational life.

Emotional Quotient (EQ)—*When measured, emotional intelligence is often referred to as an Emotional Intelligence Quotient, comparable to Intelligence Quotient.*

CONCEPTS OF EMOTIONAL INTELLIGENCE

There are several general concepts associated with the idea of emotional and social intelligence. One of the most widely accepted general models of EI competencies is the one that Daniel Goleman developed based on Howard Gardner's *intra*personal and *inter*personal intelligences. We have adapted portions of this model for our approach to enhancing emotional intelligence. There are four major categories to the model, which includes self-awareness, self-management, social awareness, and relationship management. This model is outlined below.

EMOTIONAL & SOCIAL INTELLIGENCE CONCEPTS

	INTRAPERSONAL (Internal)	INTERPERSONAL (Relationships)
MONITOR	**Self-Awareness of:** Physical Sensation. Emotion, Trigger, & Reaction. Thought & Perception. Personal Resources.	**Social-Awareness** Empathy. Attunement. Empathic Accuracy. Social Cognition. Service Orientation. Group Awareness.
MANAGE	**Self-Management of:** Physical Reactions. Emotions & Reactions. Thoughts & Reactions. Situations & Reactions. Personal Resources. Positivity.	**Relationship Management** Synchrony. Self-Presentation. Concern. Influence. Change Catalyst. Conflict Resolution. Supporting Others. Collaboration & Teamwork. Inspirational Leadership.

COMPETENCIES OF EMOTIONAL INTELLIGENCE

There are a number of competencies associated with each of the four categories.

1. Self-Awareness—*What are the emotions I am feeling, what are my beliefs, what are my action patterns and triggers?* This is the ability to read one's own emotions and recognize their impact on oneself and others. It is also the ability to use "gut feelings" to guide decisions. Self-Awareness means knowing your emotions and their effects. Individuals differ in their ability to perceive their own emotions. This includes the ability to identify one's own emotions.

The skill of perceiving emotions represents a basic aspect of emotional intelligence, as it makes all other processing of emotional information possible. Understanding emotions includes the ability to be aware of minor variations between emotions, and the ability to recognize and describe emotional states.

2. Self-Management—*How can I best manage these emotions, thoughts, and actions?* This is the ability to govern one's emotions and impulses. It is also the ability to adapt to changing circumstances. Self-Management includes knowing how to manage your emotions, how to keep disruptive impulses in check, and being flexible and comfortable with new ideas.

The emotionally intelligent person can prevent the emotional hijacking that can occur and use them as guides to help her or him to achieve intended goals. Goleman also includes such characteristics as Integrity, Adaptability, Initiative, Optimism, and Achievement in his model of self-management.

3. Social Awareness—*What are other people feeling, thinking, wanting, needing, and motivated by?* This is the ability to sense, understand, and react to the emotions of others. It is also the ability to comprehend social relationships and social networks. Social awareness is an ability to listen, to be persuasive, to collaborate, and to nurture relationships.

The ability to regulate emotions in both ourselves and in others is also important. It can be difficult to detect and decipher emotions in faces, pictures, and voices. Accurate detection of another's emotional state is the first step to effectively connecting and interacting with others.

4. Relationship Management—*How can I best manage the relationships I have with others?* This is the ability to persuade, influence, and inspire others. It is also includes the ability to manage conflict.

Relationship management is an ability to influence others, handle conflict, develop, lead and work with others. Seeing similarities along with taking another's perspective are the roots of empathy, compassion, and fostering interpersonal connection. It also depends upon having insight to one's own emotional states and responses.

GOLEMAN'S EMOTIONAL SKILL SETS

SELF-AWARENESS—Awareness of one's own internal states, preferences, resources and intuitions.

Internal Awareness—Recognizing one's internal states and their effects.

Accurate Self-Assessment—Knowing one's strengths and limits.

Self-Confidence—A strong sense of one's self-worth and capabilities.

SELF-MANAGEMENT—Managing one's own internal states, impulses, and resources.

Internal Self-Control—Keeping disruptive internal states and impulses in check.

Integrity—Acting congruently with one's values.

Adaptability—Flexibility in handling changing circumstances.

Initiative—Readiness to act on opportunities.

Optimism—Persistence in pursuing goals despite obstacles and setbacks.

Achievement—Striving to improve or meeting a standard of excellence.

SOCIAL AWARENESS—Awareness of others' feelings, needs, & concerns; how to handle relationships.

Empathy—Sensing others' feelings & perspective, and taking active interest in them.

Service Orientation—Anticipating, recognizing, and meeting needs of others.

Group Awareness—Reading a group's emotional currents and power relationships.

RELATIONSHIP MANAGEMENT—Inducing desirable responses in others.

Influence—Persuading others through effective communication.

Change Catalyst—Initiating or managing change through effective persuasion.

Conflict Resolution—Negotiating and resolving disagreements.

Supporting Others—Sensing the needs of others, and bolstering their abilities.

Collaboration & Teamwork—Developing group synergy.
    Working with others toward collective goals.

Inspirational Leadership—Inspiring and guiding individuals and groups.

BENEFITS OF EMOTIONAL INTELLIGENCE

Emotional intelligence benefits individuals, as well as families, communities, and society at large. An individual high in emotional intelligence often will be more able to make decisions that take into account the likely consequences of a behavior on her/himself and/or others. For example, hospital staff with higher emotional intelligence had fewer incidents of workplace violence than those with lower emotional intelligence.

Research suggests that emotionally intelligent people enjoy many benefits over their less emotionally intelligent peers. Some of the benefits of emotional intelligence include the following:

BENEFITS OF EMOTIONAL INTELLIGENCE

HIGHER LEVELS OF RESILIENCY
- Have more effective coping skills
- Overcome adversity easier
- Bounce back quicker

BETTER PHYSICAL HEALTH
- Bolstered immune system
- Lowered stress levels
- Less pain
- More vitality, energy, and flow
- Longer life

LARGER SOCIAL REWARDS
- More satisfying marriages
- Longer marriages
- More friends
- Stronger social support
- Richer social interactions

SUPERIOR WORK OUTCOMES
- Greater productivity
- Higher quality of work
- Higher incomes

"Having great intellectual abilities may make you a superb fiscal analyst or legal scholar, but a highly developed emotional intelligence will make you a candidate for CEO or a brilliant trial lawyer."
--Daniel Goleman

RESEARCH—BENEFITS OF EMOTIONAL INTELLIGENCE

Research shows that people high in emotional intelligence enjoy multiple benefits, including greater success, improved health, overall life satisfaction, and strong relationships. A study on quality of social interaction and emotional intelligence showed that the emotion regulation is connected to positive social interactions in both self- assessment and peer assessment. Higher levels of emotion regulation abilities are associated with greater interpersonal sensitivities and pro-social tendencies (Lopes et al, 2005).

Lopes, P., Salovey, P., Côté, S., Beers, M., Petty, R. (2005, March). Emotion Regulation Abilities and the Quality of Social Interaction. *Emotion*, 5(1), 113-118.

INTRODUCTION

Emotional intelligence is a significant predictor of health, well-being, academic achievement, and work-related outcomes such as performance and productivity. However, individuals with high emotional intelligence could be using certain techniques to internally isolate emotions, so that they do not hinder task performance (Lam & Kirby, 2002). Since people with high emotional intelligence are better able to control their emotions, as well as the emotions of those around them, they are less likely to become stressed during negative situations and have the capability to channel positive emotions during these times. This further leads to increased productivity and engagement amongst individuals surrounded by high EI individuals (Lam & Kirby, 2002).

Nelis, D., Quoidbach, J., Mikolajczak, M., & Hansenne, M. (2009). Increasing emotional intelligence: (How) is it possible?. *Personality and Individual Differences*, 47(1), 36-41.

Lam, L.T., & Kirby, S.L. (2002). Is emotional intelligence an advantage? An exploration of the impact of emotional and general intelligence on individual performance. *The Journal of Social Psychology*, 142(1), 133-143.

Dulewicz and Higgs (2004) addressed the questions of whether emotional intelligence is learnable and if there is a critical period for this. Unlike previous articles, this article categorized emotional intelligence into seven elements: self-awareness, emotional resilience, motivation, inter-personal sensitivity, influence, intuitiveness, and conscientiousness. After the training intervention, intuitiveness and conscientiousness did not show highly significant improvements, while self-awareness, sensitivity, and influence did. The training intervention consisted of lectures, discussions, and videos once a week for four weeks amongst middle managers at a retail company. "It focused on the development of self-awareness, detachment, regulation of emotions, recognition of emotions in others and the impact of one's behaviour on others". The authors concluded that the seven elements of emotional intelligence lie on a continuum ranging from easy to develop through difficult to develop.

Dulewicz, V. & Higgs, M. (2004). Can emotional intelligence be developed?, *The International Journal of Human Resource Management*, 15(1), 95-111.

The research indicates that emotional intelligence can be enhanced through learning and practice. That is a major objective of this workshop. In a study aimed at assessing the effectiveness of emotional intelligence training programs researchers evaluated a newly implemented program to increase emotional intelligence in MBAs. Results from self-assessment and peer-assessment showed increases in twenty-one skills; most of which are directly related to emotional intelligence. From these results it can be deduced that emotional intelligence can be increased and can be taught with specific programs.

Boyatzis, R., Stubbs, E., Taylor, S. (2002). Learning Cognitive and Emotional Intelligence Competencies through Graduate Management Education. *Academy of Management Learning and Education*, 1(2), 150–162.

RESEARCH—Impact of Emotional Intelligence

Staff underwent a four-month long training program focusing on EI. The experimental group showed significant increases in emotional intelligence as assess by the Dutch version of the Bar-On EQ-i. Results indicated that EI can be learned.

Zijlmans, L. J. M., Embregts, P. J. C. M., Gerits, L., Bosman, A. M. T. and Derksen, J. J. L. (2011), Training emotional intelligence related to treatment skills of staff working with clients with intellectual disabilities and challenging behaviour. *Journal of Intellectual Disability Research*, 55: 219–230. doi: 10.1111/j.1365-2788.2010.01367.x

In a UK study on sixty managers, results showed increase in emotional intelligence as well as health and well-being at completion of EI training.

Slaski, M., Cartwright, S. (2003) Emotional Intelligence Training and Its Implication for Stress, Health, and Performance. *Stress and Health*, 19(4), 233–239

Study assessed the relationship between EI characteristics of perception, control, use and understanding of emotions and physical and mental health. Self-assessment of 577 individuals showed a negative correlation between high levels of EI and poor health including cigarette smoking. EI was positively correlated with exercise and well-being.

Tsaousis, I. Nikolaou, I. (2005, April). Exploring the relationship of emotional intelligence with physical and psychological health functioning. *Stress and Health, 21(2), 77–86*.

Study tested a sample of forty-four staff members of a financial department to see whether EI is related to positive work outcomes. Study used MSCEIT to measure EQ-i, administered performance tests, used peer and supervisor ratings and company data to evaluate subjects.

Results showed that increased EI was related to increased job performance, interpersonal skills, and affect and attitude at the work place. Job performance criteria consisted of salary, merit increase, and company status. Interpersonal skills included interpersonal sensitivity, sociability, positive interactions, contribution to positive work environment, and liking. The affect and attitude category measured job satisfaction, mood, and stress tolerance.

Lopes, P. N., Grewal, D., Kadis, J., Gall, M., & Salovey, P. (2006b). Evidence that emotional intelligence is related to job performance and affect and attitudes at work. *Psicothema*, 18, 132–138

HISTORY OF EMOTIONAL INTELLIGENCE

The Western intellectual tradition has made a major distinction between rational thinking and emotional behavior. Western philosophy has historically ascribed some type of Dualism to the mind and body/emotion. An extreme Dualism sees emotional behavior as antithetical to rational behavior. Descartes has often been credited (or vilified) for separating mind and body.

MIND-BODY DUALISM—Isolating the Rational Mind

The philosopher *Rene Descartes* (1596-1650) developed a method of reasoning that is based upon the proposition that if we think, we must exist. His most famous statement is: *Cogito ergo sum* (I think, therefore I am; or I am thinking, therefore I exist—*Je pense, donc je suis*). A simple meaning of the phrase is that if one is skeptical of existence, then that is in and of itself proof that he does exist. Descartes helped to establish the mind-body dualism by separating the workings of the body from the workings of the mind.

The Body. Descartes suggested that the body works like a machine. The body has the material properties of extension and motion, and it follows the laws of physics. The emotions, which Descartes called animal passions, are resident in the body.

The Mind. Descartes described the mind or soul as a nonmaterial entity, which lacks the material properties of extension and motion. It does not follow the laws of physics. He argued that only humans have minds, and that the mind interacts with the body at the pineal gland. The mind controls the body. The body can also influence the otherwise rational mind, such as when people act out of passion (emotion).

Cartesian dualism set the agenda for philosophical discussion of the mind-body problem for many years after Descartes' death and continues to this day. It also helped to move early psychology in the direction of the separation of mind, body, and emotions.

INTELLIGENCE TESTS—Focusing on the Rational Mind

Alfred Binet was a French psychologist (1857-1911) who was the inventor of the first usable intelligence test, which is the basis of today's IQ test. He was interested in the workings of the normal mind rather than the pathology of mental illness, and focused on ways to measure how we think and reason, separately from education in any particular field.

Intelligence Quotient (IQ). He developed a test in 1905 in which children had to do tasks such as follow commands, copy patterns, name objects, and put things in order or arrange them properly. Binet administered his test to Paris schoolchildren, and then created a standard based on the data he collected. If 70 percent of 8-year-olds, for example, could pass a particular test, then success on the test represented the 8-year-old level of intelligence. The phrase "intelligence quotient," or "IQ" become popular due to Binet's work. IQ is the ratio of mental age to chronological age with 100 being the average. For example, the 8 year old who passes the 10-year old's test would have an IQ of 10/8 x 100, or 125 IQ.

Early in the century Alfred Binet warned against the exclusive use of quantitative intelligence tests as a predictor of life success. Since the 1980's a number of scientists have picked up this idea. Some of the important milestones in the rediscovery of other forms of "intelligence" include the work by Howard Gardner, Antonio Damasio, Peter Salovey and John Mayer.

MULTIPLE INTELLIGENCES—Accounting for Multiple Types of Life Success

In his book *Frames of Mind: The Theory of Multiple Intelligences* (1983), Howard Gardner proposed the theory of multiple intelligences. Gardner challenged some of the earlier definitions of "intelligence" and tried to more accurately define the concept of intelligence. The idea of multiple intelligences suggests that there are many different types of human intelligence.

In his initial work, Gardner identifies seven types of intelligences.
1. Linguistic
2. Logic-mathematical
3. Musical
4. Spatial
5. Bodily Kinesthetic
6. Interpersonal
7. Intrapersonal

Gardner maintains that each individual manifests varying levels of the different intelligences, and each person has a unique cognitive profile.

Diverse Human Abilities. Gardner's theory argues that the traditional idea of intelligence does not sufficiently encompass the wide variety of human abilities. He points out that a child who masters multiplication easily is not necessarily more intelligent overall than a child who struggles to master multiplication. The second child may be stronger in another type of intelligence and may excel in a field outside of mathematics. The second child may also learn the same material quickly if a different kind of approach is used, and may even be looking at the multiplication process at a fundamentally deeper level that hides a potentially higher mathematical intelligence than in the one who easily memorizes the concept.

Implications for Education. Gardner's theory has significant implications for education. The traditional emphasis in schools has been on the development of logical intelligence and linguistic intelligence—mainly reading, writing, and arithmetic. There are many students who function well in this environment, but there are those that do not, yet still go on and have successful lives. Gardner argues that many students would be better served by a broader vision of education in which teachers use different methodologies, exercises, and activities to reach all of the students. His work has had a great impact on the theory of learning and its application in the classroom.

DESCARTES' ERROR

In 1994, neurologist Antonio R. Damasio, published a book entitled *Descartes' Error: Emotion, Reason, and the Human Brain*. Damasio points out that "Descartes' error" was the dualist separation of mind and body, and the creation of the artificial dichotomy between rationality and emotion. Damasio discusses the controversial "mind/body" relationship. He traces the evolutionary role that emotions have played in effective decision-making. Rather than emotion being something entirely separate from reason, he argues that emotion and reason are quite dependent on one another for decisions.

Now we know emotions are crucial for effective decision-making.

Damasio argues that the body/brain is the origin of thought, and he examines the physiological processes that contribute to the functioning of the mind. He suggests that thinking is inherent to a body in which no spirit exists, and he suggests that rationality does not function without emotional input. He uses a number of case studies to make his point about thought, emotion, and decision-making.

Damasio points to the famous case of Phineas Gage as an example of the role of emotion in decision-making. After the spike penetrated the front part of his brain in an accident in 1848, Gage thought and behaved differently. Before the accident, he had been a railroad foreman who had made complicated decisions and managed himself and others effectively. After the accident, his personality changed radically, and the previously tactful, emotionally steady man became rude and erratic. He made what appeared to be irrational decisions. Although his cognitive intelligence remained intact after the accident, he became severely handicapped because his emotions were no longer engaged in the process of decision-making.

In another case study, Elliot, the importance of emotions in decision making was revealed. Elliot was a young man of high IQ who appeared to have undergone a major change in his personality after developing, and having surgery to remove a brain tumor. One of the most dramatic consequences of this damage was Elliot's loss of feelings—his own subjective sense of emotion. Elliot could no longer make a rational decision. He could discuss the pros and cons of various scenarios, and his rational ability and IQ appeared to be intact. But he could no longer *choose* between options. It appears that without emotions, he could not weigh, evaluate, judge, and make a choice. This decision-making difficulty was most pronounced in the social and personal realms.

Bodily Senses, Emotions, & Rationality. Damasio argues that rationality stems from our emotions, and that our emotions stem from our bodily senses. Our feeling or state of mind is merely a reflection of the state our body. Feeling is an indispensable ingredient of rational thought. Damasio presents the *somatic-marker hypothesis* (SMH), which proposes a mechanism by which emotional processes can guide or bias behavior, particularly decision-making.

EMOTIONAL & SOCIAL INTELLIGENCE BECOME POPULAR CONCEPTS

In 1995, Daniel Goleman published a book entitled *Emotional Intelligence: Why it Matters More than IQ*. In 1998, he followed up with a book called *Working With Emotional Intelligence*, which focused on practical applications of EI in the workplace. The books and subsequent articles popularized the idea of emotional intelligence. Goleman has frequently written for the New York Times on behavioral science, and has his PhD in psychology from Harvard. He is a founder and co-chairman of the Rutgers University based *Consortium for Research on Emotional Intelligence*.

Goleman challenges the traditional view of IQ by drawing on research in neuroscience, as well as evolutionary psychology and cultural anthropology. He looked closely at the research on how the brain evolved, and how the brain works. Approaching the problem from the standpoint of neuroscience, he also saw the "error" in Descartes' dualism, and provides insights into the physical structure and workings of the brain to demonstrate his theory. He also uses Gardner's concept of multiple intelligences to explain the concept of emotional intelligence. Goleman points out that high IQ is not necessarily a prerequisite for having a successful and/or a happy life. In his books on EI, he identifies many people who were brilliant academically, but were failures in social or corporate life. He also identifies others who were not distinguished in academic terms, but who had highly successful personal lives.

Evolution of Intelligence. Goleman draws upon the findings of evolutionary psychology to explain how the brain has evolved to make us successful within our society and culture. The brain has adapted to increasingly complex environments. Goleman describes how the evolution of the brain has implications for our emotions and behavioral responses. The brain has evolved over millions of years, and has come to comprise three main areas that influence our emotional response—the brain stem, the hippocampus, and the neo-cortex.

Brain Stem. This is the most primitive part of the brain and is located at the base of the brain and the top of the spinal cord. It controls bodily functions and instinctive survival responses.

Hippocampus. The hippocampus and the amygdala evolved after the brainstem. It is located just above the brain stem. It is here where the brain stores emotional, survival-linked responses to visual and other inputs. The amygdala can catalyze the kind of impulsive action that overpower rational thought and the capacity for considered reactions. This is the source of "emotional hijackings."

Neo-cortex. This is the large, well-developed, top region of the brain, which comprises the center of our thinking, memory, and reasoning functions.

Evolution builds upon the past. It works with what is already there and adds to it. Our most primitive emotions evolved first as powerful survival mechanisms. Our higher order cognitive functions evolved much later. Due to the course of evolution, our emotions and our thinking intelligence are situated in separate areas of the brain.

Our emotional centers receive input before our thinking centers and can react strongly and quickly in emotionally charged situations. When people first confront stimuli that prompt extreme fear, anger, frustration, or disgust, their first impulse to active response comes from the amygdala. Unless some intelligent control is exerted, the brain moves into survival mode and stimulates instinctive actions of fight or flight. The emotional reaction might seem emotionally right for the situation, but it may turn out to be wrong for the social context.

Instinctive reactions may be wise in certain circumstances and successfully perform their original survival functions. However, we usually do not have a need to fight or run away from dangers of the kind faced by our prehistoric ancestors. We need to be aware of how the primitive response in the brain's emotional center precedes all rational evaluation and response.

Emotional intelligence is in part about understanding the emotional brain. We will explore this process at greater length in module one on the emotional brain. Emotional intelligence is also about our ability to control and manage the process. We will explore a number of tools and techniques to monitor and manage the processes in modules two through five.

Social Intelligence. Goleman has continued to develop his theories based upon neuroscience research that has emerged since the publication of EI in 1995. In his book entitled *Social Intelligence, The Revolutionary New Science of Human Relationships*, he draws on neuroscience that indicates that our brain's very design makes it sociable. Our brains have evolved to make a brain-to-brain linkup whenever we engage with another person. This neural bridge allows us to impact the brain and the body of everyone that we interact with, and allows them to do the same to us.

Relationships influence biology. Our relationships not only influence our relationships with others, but they impact our biology. Even our most routine encounters act as regulators in the brain, and act to prime emotions within us. Our social interactions can act like modulators or interpersonal thermostats to the functioning of our brain and our emotions. Our feelings are influenced by the feelings and behavior of others just as we influence them. These feelings send out hormones that regulate biological systems from our heart to our immune cells and stressful relationships appear to even impact the very operation of specific genes that regulate the immune system.

Goleman suggests that the brain-to-brain link allows our strongest relationships to shape our biology. Relationships that are nourishing can have a beneficial impact on our health. Relationships that are *toxic* can function as a poison in our bodies and even impact the production of T-cells.

Emotional Competencies. Goleman identified a number of behaviors or competencies that are indicative of emotional intelligence. He initially grouped these into five categories, which were later reduced to four. The original five categories are self-awareness, self-regulation, motivation, empathy, and social skills.

Measuring Emotional Competencies. Goleman believes that the abilities involved with emotional intelligence can be assessed and developed over a period of time. In association with the Hay Group, he developed an Emotional Competence Inventory (ECI) to use in assessing emotional competencies at work.

RESEARCH—EMOTIONAL INTELLIGENCE ACROSS CULTURES

Researchers examined the effect of culture on an individual's level of emotional intelligence. Individualistic cultures stress the importance of the self, while collectivistic cultures places emphasis on one's relationship with others. They found that culture is an antecedent of emotional intelligence. In individualistic cultures, the emotional state of the individual is emphasized, whereas in collectivistic cultures the individual emotional state is of less importance than the communal emotional state.

Jordan, P. J., Ashkanasy, N. M., Hartel, C. E., & Hooper, G. S. (2002). Workgroup emotional intelligence: Scale development and relationship to team process, effectiveness, and goal focus. *Human Resource Management Review, 12*, 195–214.

RESEARCH—EI INTERVENTIONS

Improving emotional intelligence and self-efficacy. In a teaching intervention for university students focused on developing emotional intelligence and emotional self-efficacy, researchers found significant increases to levels of emotional self-efficacy and certain aspects of EI ability. The findings are examined in the context of graduate employability and suggests that increasing EI may have a positive effect on graduate marketability.

Dacre Pool, L., & Qualter, P. (2012). Improving emotional intelligence and emotional self efficacy through a teaching intervention for university students. *Learning and Individual Differences*, 22(3), 306-312.

Increasing EI in 6 Weeks. In a systematic, controlled study utilizing four group EI trainings (two hours and a half each), Delphine Nelis, Michel Hansenne, and colleagues found a significant increase in emotion identification and emotion management abilities in the EI training group in comparison to the control group. Follow-up assessments after 6 months continue to indicate that these improvements were persistent, suggesting that EI can be developed through training and sustained.

Nelis, D., Quoidbach, J., Mikolajczak, M., & Hansenne, M. (2009). Increasing emotional intelligence:(How) is it possible?. *Personality and Individual Differences*, 47(1), 36-41.

Social and Emotional Learning Impacts Academics. Through a meta-analysis of 213 school-based, universal social and emotional learning (SEL) programs with 270,034 students (kindergarten through high-school), researchers found that SEL participants demonstrated significant improvement in social and emotional skills, attitudes, behaviors, and academic performance, reflecting an 11-percentile-point gain in achievement. Their empirical findings further underscore the value of SEL programming in education.

Durlak, J. A., Weissberg, R. P., Dymnicki, A. B., Taylor, R. D., & Schellinger, K. B. (2011). The impact of enhancing students' social and emotional learning: A meta‐analysis of school‐based universal interventions. *Child development*, 82(1), 405-432.

EI Interventions Increase Student Success. Researchers led a study in which they modified a college Technology Career Essentials course to include curriculum related to improving emotional and social competencies. They compared the emotional and social competency levels of students in the modified course to the levels in a control group and found higher levels of psychological mindedness (i.e. self-awareness) in students that underwent EI training.

Bond, B. & Manser, R. (2009) Emotional Intelligence Interventions to Increase Student Success. Toronto: Higher Education Quality Council of Ontario.

RESEARCH—A PILOT STUDY OF OUR 4-WEEK EI WORKSHOP AT STANFORD

Our course entitled "Enhancing Emotional Intelligence" focuses on building fundamental personal and interpersonal skills for happiness and success. Students learn how to monitor and manage their emotions, monitor and manage their thoughts, monitor others, and manage relationships.

We assessed whether the self-reported pre- and post- assessment scores would show a change. We hypothesize that all participants would experience an increase in their level of happiness, personal outlook, and workplace outlook. We predicted that participants who took the course for credit or a grade have more motivation to succeed and have to put more work into the course would show more improvement. Participants who enrolled in the course for credit must complete 4 assignments, while participants who enrolled in the course for a grade must complete 8 assignments. Participants who enrolled in the course for no credit were not obligated to turn in any assignments.

We were interested whether exposure to the course material was enough to raise a participant's level of happiness, personal outlook, and workplace outlook or if engagement in the worksheets (and how much effort has to be put into these) effects levels of well-being and happiness.

We also tested demographic variables, hypothesizing that European American students would benefit more than the Asian American students. Many of the practices and activities are geared towards

In line with our hypotheses, the mean scores from all the assessments showed a positive increase after taking the course, except for a decrease on the PANAS Negative Affect assessment. There were significant effects for subjective, chronic happiness; trait emotional intelligence; and attitudes and beliefs. There were insignificant effects for levels of positive and negative affect. All assessments were moderately to strongly correlated with one another as expected.

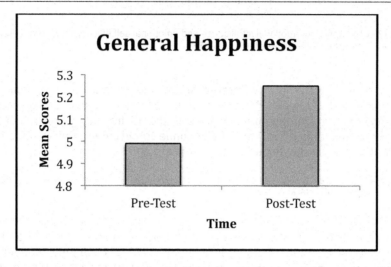

The difference between pre-test and post-test was statistically significant (*p-value* < 0.05).

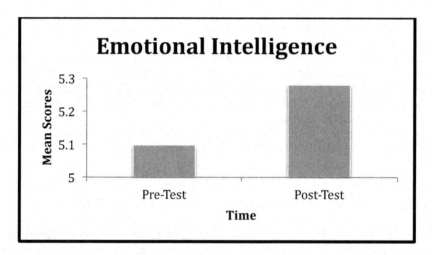

The difference between pre-test and post-test was statistically significant (*p-value* < 0.01).

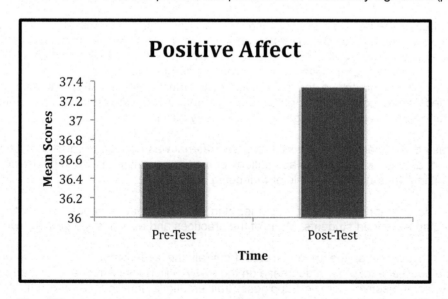

The difference between pre-test and post-test was not statistically significant (*p-value > 0.05)*.

Ethnicity Effects. Asian Americans experienced a decrease in their mean scores for all measures, except for the PANAS Negative Affect assessment. There were insignificant effects for subjective, chronic happiness; trait emotional intelligence; feelings of positive affect; and feelings of negative affect. All pre- and post-assessments were very correlated; the small sample size may explain the insignificance.

European Americans experienced an increase in their mean scores for all measures, except for the PANAS Negative Affect assessment. There was a significant effect for subjective, chronic happiness and trait emotional intelligence. However, there were insignificant effects for feelings of positive and negative affect. All pre- and post-assessments were moderately to very strongly correlated. In line with Tiffany's expectations, European Americans experienced more significant effects from this course than Asian American students.

MINDFULNESS-BASED EMOTIONAL INTELLIGENCE

Since 2006, our programs have been designed to develop higher levels of mindfulness. We see mindfulness as the foundational ability upon which all emotional intelligence skill sets are built. Over the years, we have seen the benefit of practices that directly target mindfulness as a way of being and have increasingly integrated these practices. We present a variety of mindfulness techniques such as mindfulness meditation as powerful tools to increase emotional intelligence.

DEFINITIONS OF MINDFULNESS

While mindfulness is growing in popularity, its definitions differ significantly. Ellen Langer, a social psychologist at Harvard University who has studied mindfulness for 40 years, defines mindfulness as a state characterized by (1) presence and openness to new developments or information; (2) flexibility in mindsets, perspective, and understanding; and (3) growth. Her definition was developed in social psychology. Initially, she studied its opposite, mindlessness. This line of research examined how we tend to get locked into mindsets and fail to revise them. Instead, we follow them like actors following a script.

Langer's research demonstrates that mindfulness is the mechanism of action that drives effectiveness across life domains. Mindfulness is the root of emotional intelligence.

Mindfulness is a way of being or a mental state, comprised of three essential components:

1. Openness to new information
2. Taking multiple perspectives
3. Revising mindsets

A similar definition of mindfulness has been popularized by Jon Kabat-Zinn, Professor of Medicine at University of Massachusetts. He is credited as bringing the concept and practice of mindfulness to the medical world and beyond with his program called Mindfulness-Based Stress Reduction. This program has been highly researched, showing the strongest positive impact on reducing chronic pain and anxiety. His definition has roots in Buddhist philosophy. He defines mindfulness as a state that is characterized by:

1. Paying attention on purpose,
2. In the present moment,
3. Non-judgmentally

Many people including professionals in the field confuse definitions of mindfulness, misusing the term and lacking precision in its use. The term mindfulness can refer to any of the following three domains: (1) a technique (e.g., mindfulness meditation), (2) a state (i.e., temporary psychological state), or (3) a trait (i.e., a way of being). In the popular media, the term mindfulness commonly refers to a technique, especially mindfulness meditation, or a state as in Jon Kabat-Zinn's definition. These definitions are not contradictory. To eliminate confusion between the Kabat-Zinn and Langerian definitions, note the similarities:

LANGERIAN MINDFULNESS	**KABAT-ZINN MINDFULNESS**
Openness to new information	Paying attention on purpose In the present moment
Taking multiple perspectives Revising mindsets	Non-judgmental

We define mindfulness as a mental state characterized by being present, noticing new information, and revising mindsets. Our approach blends traditional (Kabat-Zinn) and modern (Langerian) views of mindfulness.

THE LINK BETWEEN MINDFULNESS AND EMOTIONAL INTELLIGENCE

Mindful people are naturally high in emotional intelligence. Not surprisingly, research demonstrates that mindful people just like emotionally intelligent people enjoy many advantages in wellbeing, vitality, and success.

According to Ellen Langer, emotional intelligence as a subset, or an application of mindfulness (when defined as a trait or way of being). Mindfulness applied to different realms of experience allows the conditions from which emotional intelligence naturally emerges. When being mindful of inner experience, the EI competency Self-Awareness emerges; when mindfully regulating emotions, thoughts and reactions, the EI competency Self-Regulation improves. Mindfulness toward others is referred to as Social Awareness, and when applied toward relationships, this is the concept of Relationship Management.

At the heart of emotional intelligence is choosing what aspect of experience to attend to. Mindfulness practices help us build this muscle. As Philippe Goldin, researcher at University of California at Davis, says, mindfulness fosters the capacity to volitionally redirect attention. Regardless of the situation, when in a mindful state, attention can be turned to the most important aspects of a situation.

MINDFULNESS-BASED EMOTIONAL INTELLIGENCE PROGRAMS

In the last ten years there has been an upwelling of mindfulness-based emotional intelligence and positive intelligence programs. The leading expert is Robert Weissberg at the Center for Academic and Social and Emotional Learning. Their social and emotional intelligence programs have been well-researched and are highly respected. Since adding mindfulness practices to their programs, they state they have seen even greater benefits. The MindUp Curriculum created by the actor Goldie Hawn's The Hawn Foundation has demonstrated strong advantages for children learning this mindfulness-based emotional intelligence program.

Search Inside Yourself, an emotional intelligence program developed at Google, is based in mindfulness practice. This program has been taught to thousands of Googlers around the world. Its mission is to train enlightened leaders worldwide in order to create the conditions for world peace. In the service of this mission, since 2013, this program has been delivered in major companies outside of Google. We provided Chade-Meng Tan, the mastermind behind the program, with an earlier version of this *Enhancing Emotional Intelligence* workbook when he was developing Search Inside Yourself and writing his book of the same name. Laura Delizonna is a lead trainer for Search Inside Yourself.

Daniel Goleman, who popularized emotional intelligence and recently released his latest book entitled *Focus*, describes mindfulness as a foundational skill that enables emotional intelligence to emerge. Annie McKee, co-author of *Resonant Leadership and Primal Leadership*, also emphasizes the importance of mindfulness in emotional intelligence. She calls mindfulness an essential factor in resonant, or highly effective, prosocial leadership.

RESEARCH—MINDFULNESS-BASED EMOTIONAL INTELLIGENCE PROGRAMS

Mindfulness Education (ME) program. ME facilitates the development of social and emotional competence and positive emotions. Students engaged in mindful attention training three times a day. A total of 246 pre- and early adolescent students in the 4th to 7th grades (six ME program classrooms and six comparison wait-list control classrooms) completed pretest and posttest self-report measures assessing optimism, general and school self-concept, and positive and negative affect. Teachers rated pre- and early adolescents on dimensions of classroom social and emotional competence. Results revealed that pre- and early adolescents who participated in the ME program, compared to those who did not, showed significant increases in optimism from pretest to posttest. Similarly, improvements on dimensions of teacher-rated classroom social competent behaviors were found.

Schonert-Reichl & Stewart-Lawlor (2010). The Effects of Mindfulness-Based Education Program on Pre- and Early Adolescents' Well-Being and Social and Emotional Competence, Mindfulness(1) 137-151.

MindUP Curriculum. Kimberly Schonert-Reichl at University of British Columbia evaluated the effectiveness of MindUP™ on students in grades 4 and 5, based on evidence centered on neuroendocrine regulation, executive functions and self and peer reports of pro-social behaviors.

Improved Optimism and Self- Concept:
  82% of children reported having a more positive outlook
  81% of children learned to make themselves happy
  58% of children tried to help others more often

Healthy Neuroendocrine Regulation:
  Measurement of salivary cortisol revealed MindUP™ children maintained a healthy, regulated diurnal pattern.

Increased Executive Function:
  Children demonstrated faster reaction times while performing tests such as Dr. Diamond's "Flanker Fish" trials. The correlates to heightened self-regulatory ability.

Positive Teacher Response:
  100% reported that MindUP™ positively influenced classroom culture and that students were significantly more attentive.

Academic Achievement:
  15% of students improved their math achievement scores

Schonert-Reichl, K. A. and Lawlor, M. (2010). The Effects of a Mindfulness- Based Education Program on Pre- and Early Adolescents' Well-Being and Social and Emotional Competence. Mindfulness and

Schonert- Reichl, K. A., Oberle, E., Lawlor, M. S., Abbott, D., Thomson, D., Oberlander, T., & Diamond, A. (2011). Enhancing cognitive and social- emotional competence through a simple-to- administer school program.

THEORETICAL BASIS FOR TECHNQUES—A NEUROSCIENCE MODEL

"The brain is fundamentally a lazy piece of meat. It doesn't want to waste any energy."
—Gregory Burns, Neuroscientist

Neuroscientists refer to a general model for the brain regions that shape emotional response. Although it is an oversimplification to say that a specific brain region is responsible for complex phenomena such as an emotional response, it is helpful for non-neuroscientists to use basic models. The major regions of the brain are sometimes referred to as the "Triune Brain", including the Reptilian complex, the Limbic system, and the Neo-cortex. Below describes these regions' gross functions.

Reptilian Complex. This primitive part of the brain is located at the base of the brain and the top of the spinal cord. It controls bodily functions and instinctive survival responses.

Limbic System. The hippocampus and the amygdala evolved after the brainstem. Emotional, survival-linked responses to visual and other inputs are stored in this region. The amygdala is known for catalyzing impulsive action and overpowering slower thought processing and considered reactions. This is the source of "emotional hijackings."

Neo-cortex. This large, well-developed, top region of the brain comprises the center of our thinking, memory, and reasoning functions.

TRIUNE BRAIN

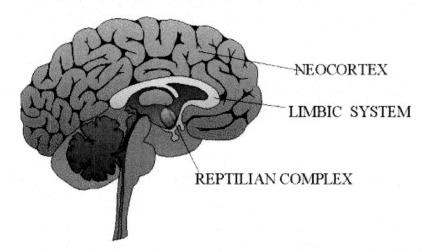

As Daniel Goleman states, "The brain is an elegant machine for survival and has been shaped by what works in survival." Our most primitive emotions evolved first as powerful survival mechanisms. Our higher-order cognitive functions evolved much later. Due to the course of evolution, our *emotions* and our *thinking* are situated in *separate areas* of the brain.

Role of the Amygdala. The amygdala is primarily responsible for our ability to "act fast, think later." This almond-shaped mass of gray matter resides bilaterally in the anterior portion of the temporal lobe and specializes in threat and fear. The amygdala operates on a hairpin trigger, sounding the alarm bells to recruit other areas of the brain to ignite the fight-or-flight system. The amygdala floods the body with hormones designed to activate systems involved in the protective fight-or-flight response. The tense muscles, increased blood pressure and respiration rates, and shunting of blood away from the gut to the muscular system (among others) are part of this exquisitely synchronized cascade of reactions.

Role of the Cortex. As information slowly makes its way to the cortex, the cortex perceives the difference between the stick and the snake. It finally says, *"It's only a stick."* Once the discriminating cortex has determined that there is no call for panic, it sends a message to the amygdala, quieting the fear response.

INCREASING EMOTIONAL INTELLIGENCE—HIGH ROAD & LOW ROAD STRATEGIES

Goleman posits that individuals are born with a general emotional intelligence that determines their potential for learning emotional competencies. He suggests that these competencies can be learned and that they need to be developed by each one of us in order to become happier and more successful in personal and professional pursuits. Most people have the potential to develop higher levels of emotional intelligence through training, coaching, and practice.

We designed this program with two types of strategies that can be used to build the skills of emotional intelligence. These map onto the Triune Brain regions.

In his book *Social Intelligence,* Daniel Goleman refers to the brain processes as falling into two general types of circuitry, which he calls the *High and Low Roads.* Although this oversimplifies the complex circuitry of the brain, his metaphor is helpful for understanding at a gross level how the brain operates at emotional and logical levels. The *Low Road* represents our automatic response system. The *High Road* represents our voluntary response system.

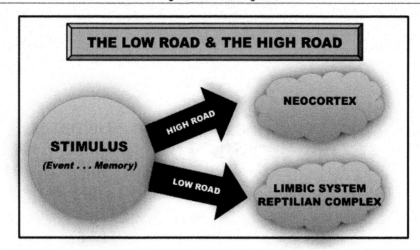

High Road. These strategies employ analytical and cognitive reasoning to consciously take different perspectives and challenge existing mindsets to arrive at a different or more complex understanding. This can be thought of as activating the neocortex functions.

The High Road represents the conscious response system. It operates more slowly than the automatic response system and with voluntary control. It requires effort and conscious intent. High Road circuitry activates when automatic process are interrupted by novelty, unexpected events, a mistake, or a threat, among other stimuli. Consciously engaging with thoughts and concepts also occurs within this system. High-level and abstract thinking, such as problem solving, considering ideas, reflecting and other types of cogitation, occurs here. This system includes the anterior cingulate cortex, lateral prefrontal cortex, posterior parietal cortex, and hippocampus, among others.

Low Road. These strategies are more experiential. They build muscle memory to create habits at the nonverbal or subconscious level and recondition emotional, mental, and behavioral reactions. These experiential techniques activate the emotional and memory centers, attempting to recondition and build new associations between stimuli and response. The Low Road relates to the automatic response system. It operates automatically at high speeds and outside of awareness.

The Low Road is the "default" mode of the brain. Countless automatic brain processes perform crucial functions below our awareness. Structures comprising these regions are the amygdala, basal ganglia, lateral temporal cortex, ventromedial prefrontal cortex, and dorsal anterior cingulate cortex.

The Low and High Road systems often work concurrently. For example, as you read this, you are engaging High Road functions to direct attention and reflect on the meaning and implications of this content. At the same time, numerous Low Road functions perform the countless supporting functions of recognizing patterns, decoding syntax, and so on. Goleman speculates that there may be no purely High Road mental functions, but there are many purely low road functions.

High Road processing can override the automatic processing at the Low Road level. This capacity allows for conscious choice and is occurring when we manage emotions, thoughts, and behavior.

Example: Fear on the Low Road and High Road. Fear is among the evolutionary oldest and most primitive emotions. Two parallel routes process fear. Low-level processing is prioritized due to its quick, automatic circuitry that helps us stay safe.

Imagine you are on a nature hike, and suddenly at the corner of your eye, your brain perceives a thin black curvy object. Instinctively, you freeze, your heart rate and respiration spike, and your eyes widen, fixated on the object. All of this happens in milliseconds, outside of conscious processing. You then realize it is a stick. Heart and respiration rates slow, and you continue walking. What happened? We have evolved to fear snakes and our automatic, or Low Road system, is vigilant and reactive to threats.

INTRODUCTION

EMOTIONAL INTELLIGENCE EMERGES ON THE MIDDLE ROAD—THE WISE MIND

Marsha Linehan, a leading researcher in the development of innovative and effective psychotherapy interventions, developed a metaphor for effective thinking and action. Her metaphor maps onto Goleman's High and Low Road model.

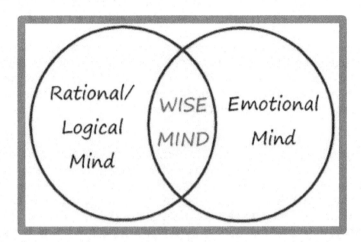

The emotional mind processes stimuli based on feeling, not logical reasoning. This "mind" helps us know what feels good or bad to us, what we like and don't like. This is similar to the hot, Low Road system where emotions and impulses reside.

The logical mind processes stimuli based on logical reasoning. This "mind" helps us consider the past and future, determine cause and effect, and develop working models of the world. This relates to the cool, High Road system where high-level abstract and rational thinking resides.

The wise mind represents the combination of the rich information provided by the emotional mind and logical mind. The wise mind can help you to employ more effective thoughts and engage in more effective actions. The cognitive exercises and meditations in this workbook are designed to further develop your ability to access the wise mind, drawing from the best of the emotional mind and the logical mind. This, we refer to as the Middle Road—sourcing the intelligence of the emotional mind and logical mind. This is where emotional intelligence resides—utilizing both analytical, logical thinking and emotional information.

MEDITATION REWIRES NEURAL CIRCUITRY

"Meditation refers to a family of mental training practices that are designed to familiarize the practitioner with specific types of mental processes."
-Brefczynski-Lewis, 2007

Meditation is a practice that can operate at the Low Road level and can rewire the neural circuitry. Meditation is simply directing attention with intention and then intending to sustain that attention. Meditation is a fundamental aspect of this emotional intelligence program due to a growing body of research findings. Research has shown that meditations increase happiness, well-being, decrease loneliness and anxiety, and improve health. Strikingly, meditation can change the neural circuitry in the brain.

Mindful awareness of internal experience has scientific support as a means to reduce stress, improve attention, boost the immune system, reduce emotional reactivity, and promote a general sense of health and well-being. Researchers' interest in mindfulness practice has steadily increased as studies continue to reveal its beneficial effects. Current research is examining how the brain responds to mindfulness practice and the benefits reaped for relationships, and physical and mental health. A burgeoning amount of research reveals that mindful awareness enhances many aspects of well-being.

A number of studies have related meditation practice to positive changes to the brain. One of the best-known studies in 2005, led by Sara Lazar, indicated that meditation experience is associated with increased cortical thickness.

Richard Davidson, a neuroscientist at the University of Wisconsin, has worked with the Dalai Lama and other experienced meditators on meditation and its effects on the brain. His results suggest that meditation practice causes different levels of activity in brain regions associated with such qualities as anxiety, depression, anger, fear, attention, and the ability of the body to heal itself. These changes in function may be caused by changes in the physical structure of the brain.

The meditations presented here are simply structured visualizations and exercises for focusing attention to sensations and other internal experiences. There is nothing mystical or religious about meditation. Many people associate meditation with religion, but this is simply because focusing inward in the form of contemplative practices has been used in many religions including Christianity (prayer), Eastern Religions (e.g., Zen meditation, Buddhism, Hinduism), Judiasm, tribal religions, and more.

RESEARCH—MEDITATION, NEUROPLASTICITY, & WELLBEING

Neurons that fire together wire together.

Below are abstracts from a selection of research studies on meditation. These studies have been conducted in respected research institutions and are published in peer reviewed scientific journals.

Rewire the Brain. A number of studies have indicated that meditation helps to rewire the brain. A recent study at Yale University, for example, indicates that the brains of experienced meditators may actually work differently that the brains of non-meditators. The study provides evidence that meditation changes the way that the brain works and could give meditators an advantage when it comes to dealing with life issues and stress.

Brain Changes with Mindful Awareness.
Mindful awareness practices are associated with physiological changes in the brain. After 2 months of participation in a mindfulness meditation-training program, participants showed changes in brain and immune functioning. The brain changes were in areas associated with positive emotions.

"Changes in brain function with mindfulness meditation" by Davidson, et al. (2003).

INTRODUCTION

A recent study involving long-term mindfulness meditators showed increases in theta band activity and coherence in frontal areas of the brain during deep meditative states. Increase in theta activity in this region suggests an increase in attentional processing and working memory operations. This increase was accompanied by deactivation in theta activity in parietal-occipital areas signifying a reduction in the processing associated with self, space, and time (Baijal et al, 2010).

Baijal, S. & Srinivasan, N. (2010). Theta activity and meditative states: Spectral changes during concentrative meditation. *Cognitive Processing*, 11(1), 31-38.

Thirty-minutes of meditation for 8 weeks changes the brain. A recent study shows that practicing thirty minutes of mindfulness meditation a day for eight weeks can improve the brain. This study shows that areas of the brain involved in memory, sense of self, empathy, stress, and emotion regulation all showed increases in density of gray-matter after the trial period. The study also found a decrease in gray-matter in the amygdala pointing to a decreasing stress and anxiety.

Holzel, B., Carmody, J., Vangel, M., Congleton, C., Yerramsetti, S., Gard, T., Lazar, S. (2011, January) Mindfulness practice leads to increases in regional brain gray matter density. *Psychiatry Research Neuroimaging*. 191(1). 36-43.

Meditation and Attention. Four short sessions of meditation training has been shown to reduce fatigue and anxiety, and significantly improve visuo-spatial processing, working memory, and executive function.

Zeidan, F., Johnson, S. K., Diamond, B. J., David, Z., & Goolkasian, P. (2010). Mindfulness meditation improves cognition: Evidence of brief mental training. Consciousness and Cognition

The attentional component of mindfulness has been associated with better task performance and fewer cognitive failures. (e.g. forgetting, distraction, blunders, etc.) .

Dane, E. (2010). Reconsidering the trade-off between expertise and flexibility: A cognitive entrenchment perspective. *Academy of Management Review*, 35, 579–603.

Workers who practiced mindfulness meditation reported less emotional exhaustion and greater job satisfaction compared to workers who did not practice mindfulness meditation.

Hulsheger, U. R., Alberts, H. J., Feinholdt, A., & Lang, J. W. (2012). Benefits of Mindfulness at Work: The Role of Mindfulness in Emotion Regulation, Emotional Exhaustion, and Job Satisfaction. *Journal of Applied Psychology*.

Brain and immune function changes. For an 8-week period, 25 employees were trained in a well-known mindfulness meditation program and data were collected on brain changes using an EEG. There were 16 control subjects who were not given the program and EEG data was also recorded. At the end of the 8 weeks, both groups were given the influenza vaccine. Results show an increase in left-sided anterior brain activation (pattern associated with positive affect) in the meditators, as well as a significant increase in antibody titers compared with the control group. Most importantly, the magnitude of left-sided activation predicted the magnitude of antibody titer found in the bodies of meditators. These findings demonstrate that meditation can change brain and immune function in a positive way.

Davidson, R J. (2003). Alterations in brain and immune function produced by mindfulness meditation. *Psychosomatic medicine*, 65(4), 564-570.

Psychological Functioning. A study of long-term meditators and non-meditators showed that long-term meditators have higher levels of psychological functioning. Long-term meditators showed decreased rumination, lower avoidance of emotion, and increases in adaptive functioning and emotional regulation.

Lykins, E. L. B., & Baer, R. A. (2009). Psychological functioning in a sample of long-term practitioners of mindfulness meditation. *Journal of Cognitive Psychotherapy*, 23(3), 226-241.

Decreased stress, improved immune response. Many studies have shown that months or years of intensive meditation training can improve attention. However, in this study, after only 5 days of mind-body meditation training for 20 minutes, meditators showed significantly better attention and control of stress compared to the control group who received relaxation training. More specifically, meditators showed greater improvement in conflict scores on the Attention Network Test, lower anxiety, depression, anger, and fatigue, and higher vigor on the Profile of Mood States scale, significant decrease in cortisol and increase in immunoreactivity.

> Tang, Y., et al. (2007). Short-term meditation training improves attention and self-regulation. PNAS,104(43), 17152-17156.

Meditation and Health. This review examined the link between meditative practices and whether or not there is a long lasting impact on physical health. Meditation induces psychological changes, which further results in improvements to one's immune and cardiovascular health. The mind-body interaction is strongly linked and can be changed through meditative practices.

> Kok, B.E., Waugh, C.E., & Fredrickson, B.L. (2013). Meditation and health: The search for mechanisms of action. *Social and Personality Psychology Compass, 7(1),* 27-39.

Meditation and Healing. In an early study by Jon Kabat-Zinn, the data revealed that mindfulness can greatly accelerate the healing of psoriasis (a skin condition). All participants were given the usual PUVA or UVB treatments, but for half of them, tapes of John Kabat-Zinn's meditation instructions were played to the participants during the treatment. Just playing the tapes significantly accelerated the rate of skin clearing.

Improve Concentration and Ability to Cope with Stressors. Research suggests that meditation increases awareness, improves concentration, and provides meditators with a better ability to deal with the cognitive and emotional stresses of contemporary life. Dr. Judson Brewer, the medical director of the Yale Therapeutic Neuroscience Clinic, conducted a study during which experienced meditators and people with no meditation experience practiced three basic meditation techniques— *concentration, loving-kindness,* and *choice-less awareness.* fMRI (functional magnetic resonance imaging) was used to observe the participants' brain activity when they were practicing the meditative techniques and when they were asked to not think of anything in particular. The experienced meditators had decreased activity in an area of the brain call the "default mode network," a region that is usually at work when the mind wanders. Even when the meditators were not meditating, this area of the brain was much calmer than that of the inexperienced meditators. When the "default mode" networks of the experienced meditators were active, so too were the brain regions that are associated with self-monitoring and cognitive control.

Researchers concluded that one of the things that meditation and basic mindfulness appear to be doing is to quiet down this "default mode" region of the brain, which is the self-monitoring region. Brewer suggests that this may indicate the neurological basis for the many benefits reported by meditators. It is worth noting that a psychological hallmark of many forms of mental illness—anxiety, depression, post-traumatic stress disorder, and schizophrenia—is a fixation on one's own negative thoughts. A series of studies have linked these disorders with over-activity or faulty neurological wiring in the "default mode" network.

Meditation Relieves Negative Emotions. Fred Luthans and colleagues examined randomized clinical trials to determine the effectiveness of mindfulness meditation in improving psychological stress. They found that mindfulness meditation had a moderate positive impact on anxiety, depression, and pain and underscore the importance of further studies to explore how meditation may improve the positive aspects of mental health.

> Luthans, F., Avolio, B. J., Avey, J. B., & Norman, S. M. (2007). Positive psychological capital: Measurement and relationship with performance and satisfaction. Personnel Psychology, 60(3), 541-572.

Mindfulness and Positivity. A mindfulness-based stress reduction study explored whether healthy college-students could decrease psychological distress through a 6-week adapted mindfulness-based stress reduction (MBSR) intervention. Compared to the control group, study participants self-reported a significant reduction in psychological distress and a marked increase in mindful awareness by beginning mindfulness practices, suggesting that MBSR can bring a wide range of positive benefits in a relatively short time.

> Canby, N. K., Cameron, I. M., Calhoun, A. T., & Buchanan, G. M. (2014). A Brief Mindfulness Intervention for Healthy College Students and Its Effects on Psychological Distress, Self-Control, Meta-Mood, and Subjective Vitality. *Mindfulness,* 1-11.

Greater empathy. A study researching experienced meditators found that seasoned practitioners have greater levels of empathy. The study showed that mindfulness meditators had stronger activation in temporal parietal junctures when exposed to the sound of suffering indicating a higher empathic response.

Lutz, A., Brefczynski-Lewis, J., Johnstone T., Davidson,RJ. (2008, March) Regulation of the neural circuitry of emotion by compassion meditation: effects on meditative expertise. PLoS One. 26;3(3).

Reduced Social Anxiety. In a study using Mindfulness Based Stress Reduction (MBSR), a cognitive therapy program utilizing principles of mindfulness, people with social anxiety disorder completed therapy in order to determine its effects on emotion reactivity and regulation on negative self-beliefs. Fourteen patients underwent MRI scans while completing 3 tasks: reacting to negative self-beliefs, emotion regulation using breath-focused attention, and emotion regulation using distraction-focused attention. Results for people who completed MBSR showed: improved self-esteem, as well as depression and anxiety symptoms; decreased negative emotion experience; reduced amygdala activity (amygdala is the fear center of the brain); and increased activity in brain areas involved in attention.

Goldin, P R.; Gross JJ. (2010). Effects of mindfulness-based stress reduction (MBSR) on emotion regulation in social anxiety disorder. *Emotion*, 10(1), 83-91.

ADDITIONAL INFORMATION

For information on fMRI studies on mindfulness meditation:

- Gollub Neuroimaging Lab projects or the recently studies on Tibetan meditation practices at the University of Wisconsin.
- Harvard Medical School Neuroimaging Lab, www.mgh.harvard.edu/depts/neuroimaging/gollublab
- Health Emotions Research Institute, Scientifically Determining How Emotions Influence Health, University of Wisconsin, www.healthemotions.org

Erisman, S. M. & Roemer, L. (2010). A preliminary investigation of the effects of experimentally induced mindfulness on emotional responding to film clips. *Emotion*, 10(1), 72-82.

Epel, E. (2009). Can meditation slow rate of cellular aging? Cognitive stress, mindfulness, and telomeres. Longevity, regeneration, and optimal health: Integrating Eastern & Western perspectives, 34-53.

Birnie, K., Garland, S. N. and Carlson, L. E. (2010), Psychological benefits for cancer patients and their partners participating in mindfulness-based stress reduction (MBSR). *Psycho-Oncology*, 19: 1004–1009.doi: 10.1002/pon.1651

Evans, D. Baer, R. Segerstrom, S. (2009, September) The effects of mindfulness and self-consciousness on persistence. *Personality and Individual Differences*, 47(4), 379-382.

Other Meditation Sources. There are many online sources for meditations. You can find recordings of the meditations in this workbook at ChoosingHappiness.com. Several additional sources are listed below.

- ChoosingHappiness.com. Go to the Shop webpage for guided meditations.
- UCLA Mindful Awareness Research Center (marc.ucla.edu)
- The Guided Meditation Site (www.the-guided-meditation-site.com)
- Insight Meditation Society (www.dharma.org)
- Guided Meditation (www.healthjourneys.com)

THREE BREATHS MEDITATION

One of the simplest and most effective meditations that you can use is simply taking a few conscious breaths. It is quick, easy, and powerful. We stop, breathe, observe, and connect with inner and outer experience.

This basic Low Road technique increases awareness of the body and gets the attention away from thought so that calmness and clarity can potentially arise. This technique can be used at any point during the day and incorporated into other practices.

During all the meditations, try to let go of expectations about how the practice is supposed to feel or what is supposed to happen. Your job is to do two things. First, observe sensations in your body with a nonjudgmental, explorative manner. Second, each time your mind wanders, turn your attention back to sensations in your body.

INSTRUCTIONS
(1 minute)

1. FOCUS INWARD: Breathe and Center

- **Center**—Close your eyes and turn your attention inward.
- **Anchor in Your Breath**—Feel your breath fill and release your body. Breathe deeply with a slower exhale and natural inhale. Place your hand on your abdomen to feel your diaphragm rise and fall.

2. DIRECT ATTENTION: Three Breaths

- *First Breath:* **Feel Your Breath**—Feel the air flowing in and out of your chest, down into your lungs and diaphragm. Feel your chest rising and falling. We have some 20,000 breaths per day. Notice these breaths in this moment. Breath is one of the constants in life. From the moment life begins to the moment life ends there is breath.

- *Second Breath:* **Feel Your Body**—Notice the sensations in your body.

- *Third Breath:* **Connect with Calm, Joy or Centeredness**—Experiment with summoning a momentary sense of calm, joy, or simply feeling centered in your body and mind.

3. REFLECT ON INSIGHTS: Reflect

- Reflect on the insights or benefits you gained during this meditation.

4. MAINTAIN INNER AWARENESS: Soft Gaze and Stay with Awareness

- Slowly open your eyes and keep your gaze soft, directed downward, settling on a neutral object.
- Stay with the awareness you gained during the meditation.

THREE BREATHS MEDITATION WORKSHEET

After you have completed the meditation, jot down observations about what you experienced, observed, thought, or felt during your meditation.

1. FOCUS INWARD.

To what extent were you able to focus inward and turn your attention away from what was going on around you?

_____
_____

To what extent were you able to center yourself in this time and place?

_____
_____

To what extent did you turn your attention back to the meditation when thoughts came into your mind?

_____
_____

2. DIRECT ATTENTION.

What was it like to feel the sensations in your breath anchor point?

_____
_____

What was it like to feel the sensations in your body?

_____
_____

What was it like to attempt to summon feelings of calm, joy, or centeredness?

_____
_____

3. INSIGHTS AND BENEFITS. What insights or benefits did you gain from this meditation?

_____
_____

How might you use or modify this meditation to increase your ability to thrive?

_____
_____
_____
_____

THREE BREATHS TRACKING LOG

DAY	APPLICATION How did I use Three Breaths meditation? When and where?	IMPACT What was the impact of this meditation on me, others, and/or my situation?
Day 1		
Day 2		
Day 3		
Day 4		

THREE BREATHS TRACKING LOG

DAY	APPLICATION How did I use Three Breaths meditation? When and where?	IMPACT What was the impact of this meditation on me, others, and/or my situation?
Day 5		
Day 6		
Day 7		

INSIGHTS - What benefits or patterns emerged?

_____
_____
_____
_____
_____
_____

ADDITONAL READINGS—BOOKS ON EMOTIONAL INTELLIGENCE

There are many books related to emotional intelligence written by top research psychologists. A few are listed below:

Damasio, Antonio. *Descartes' Error: Emotion, Reason, and the Human Brain*. 2005.

Ekman, Paul. *Emotions Revealed, Recognizing Faces and Feelings to Improve Communication and Emotional Life*. 2007.

Ekman, Paul, and Dali Lama. *Emotional Awareness: Overcoming the Obstacles to Psychological Balance and Compassion*. 2008.

Elias, Maurice (Editor), and Arnold, Harriett (Editor). *The Educator's Guide to Emotional Intelligence and Academic Achievement: Social-Emotional Learning in the Classroom*. 2006.

Goleman, Daniel. *Focus*. 2014.

Goleman, Daniel. *Emotional Intelligence, Why It Can Matter More Than IQ*. 1996.

Goleman, Daniel, Boyatzis, Richard. *Primal Leadership: Learning to Lead with Emotional Intelligence*. 2004.

Goleman, Daniel. *Social Intelligence, The New Science of Human Relationships*. 2006.

Hughes, Marcia. *Emotional Intelligence In Action: Training and Coaching Activities for Leaders and Managers*. 2005.

LeDoux, Joseph. *The Emotional Brain: The Mysterious Underpinnings of Emotional Life*. 1998.

Nelson, Darwin B., and Low, Gary R. *Emotional Intelligence: Achieving Academic and Career Excellence in College and in Life*. 2010.

Pink, Daniel. *A Whole New Mind: Why Right-Brainers Will Rule the Future*. 2006.

INTERNET RESOURCES ON EMOTIONAL INTELLIGENCE

Choosing Happiness, Dr. Laura Delizonna, www.choosinghappiness.com

Authentic Happiness, University of Pennsylvania, http://www.authentichappiness.sas.upenn.edu

Center for Positive Organizational Scholarship, Stephen M. Ross School of Business, University of Michigan, www.bus.umich.edu/Positive/

Laboratory for Affective Neuroscience, http://psyphz.psych.wisc.edu/

Emotional Intelligence Information, http://www.unh.edu/emotional_intelligence/

Foundation for Education in Emotional Literacy, http://www.eq.org/

Consortium for Research on Emotional Intelligence in Organizations, http://www.eiconsortium.org/

Daniel Goleman, http://danielgoleman.info/

Professor Sonja Lyubomirsky, UC Riverside, www.faculty.ucr.edu/~sonja

Pew Research Center, Are We Happy Yet?, http://pewresearch.org/pubs/301/are-we-happy-yet,

Positive Emotion and Psychophysiology Lab, University of North Carolina, Chapel Hill, www.unc.edu.peplab

Positive Psychology Center, University of Pennsylvania, www.ppc.sas.upenn.edu

Reflective Learning, www.reflectivelearning.com

University of Pennsylvania, Positive Psychology News Daily, www.pos-psych.com

Values in Action VIA Strengths, Values in Action Institute, www.viastrengths.org

COACHING GUIDELINES

Use the self-coaching process and coaching tools to create long-term change. For maximum effectiveness, focus on one skill at a time. For each skill, take an *assessment* if one is available, complete a *coaching worksheet*, practice high road and low road techniques, and track your application of the skill over a seven day period using a *Tracking Log*.

Select one skill. It is easier to build new habits if you focus on one change at a time. Consider which skill would make the greatest difference in your current life circumstances if you used it more frequently and effectively. Identify reasons why this particular skill would improve your emotional intelligence. Select which skill in this chapter is your priority:

- Three Breaths

STEP 1. ASSESS. Assess your current mastery level of the skill. Use an online assessment tool if one is available for the skill. The Coaching Worksheet will also help you assess your need and benefits of using the skill.

Assessments—Questionnaires that assess your current skill level and provide data on your progress.

STEP 2. PLAN. To create an action plan, understand how a technique can help you build greater mastery of a skill. Next, consider how you can apply it to your own situations.

Coaching Worksheets—Tools for learning and creating an action plan for practicing the techniques.

STEP 3. PRACTICE. During the following seven days, apply the skill daily. Use both High Road techniques and Low Road techniques to practice the skill.

Tracking Logs—Habit forming tools to help guide your efforts as you practice the techniques for seven days.

- Three Breaths Meditation Tracking Log

Meditation Guides—Low Road techniques to build the skill at the emotional or non-verbal level.

- Three Breaths Meditation

STEP 4. TRACK RESULTS. In addition to structuring your practice of the techniques, *Tracking Logs* provide a place to note the impact of the skill on your experience. Tracking Logs can help you become more aware of behaviors and patterns in yourself. They are a source of feedback so you can modify a technique to make it more effective.

SELF-AWARENESS

*I have been and still am a seeker,
but I have ceased to question stars and books;
I have begun to listen to the teaching my blood
whispers to me.*

~Hermann Hesse

SELF-AWARENESS

Pause to observe, identify, analyze, and understand internal states.

Self-Awareness is the ability to mindfully observe one's physical sensations and emotions from a distance, take internal inventory, draw connections between internal experience and external circumstances, and develop a sophisticated understanding of internal states.

Individuals differ in their ability to perceive, identify and manage their thoughts and emotions. Like other skills, mastery of the skills that involved in Self-Awareness can be learned and strengthened regardless of current mastery level.

OUTLINE

Introduction: Self-Awareness
- Mindfulness
- Mindlessness

Skill 1: **MONITOR THOUGHTS & BELIEFS**
- Information Processing Chain
- Benefits of Monitoring Thoughts & Beliefs
    - *Identifying Interpretations Worksheet & Tracking Log*
    - *Journaling Worksheet*
    - *Thought Labeling Meditation Worksheet & Tracking Log*

Skill 2: **UNDERSTAND EMOTIONS**
- What is an Emotion?
- Five Components of the Emotion System
- *Exercise: Five Components of an Emotion*
- The Function of Emotions
- The Effect of Positive & Negative Emotions
    - *The Effect of Emotions Worksheet & Tracking Log*

Skill 3: **OBSERVE BODILY SENSATIONS**
- Body Maps of Emotions
    - *Body Scan Meditation & Tracking Log*

Skill 4: **DETECT EMOTIONS**
- Benefits of Detecting Emotions
- Research
- How to Detect Emotions
    - *Detect Emotions Worksheet*

Skill 5: **IDENTIFY TRIGGERS AND REACTIONS**
- Emotional Equation
- Example: Anxiety, Anger, and Sadness
- A Different Type of Trigger—A Conditioned Response
- Triggers and Reactions of Emotions Chart
    - *Trigger & Reactions Worksheet & Tracking Log*

Coaching Guidelines

INTRODUCTION

Self-Awareness refers to a range of abilities, including being able to detect and describe one's cognitive, affective, and physical states; recognizing broader patterns of functioning and responding; knowing sources of meaning, priorities, and values; and recognizing self-perceptions, viewpoints, strengths, and limitations. Self-Awareness is the fundamental building block of emotional intelligence, because all the other competencies depend on this complex knowledge. It is a very difficult skill set to master, and we all have blind spots in our self-awareness. Like the other emotional intelligence competencies, we can only aspire to cultivate high levels of self-awareness, and this is an ongoing process of growth.

MINDFULNESS AND SELF-AWARENESS

Self-Awareness emerges when we are mindful of ourselves across domains and on a moment-to-moment basis. In this program, all the skills aim to build mindfulness. Self-Awareness is mindfulness directed at the self. We use this term mindfulness in a very specific way, based on Ellen Langer's 40 years of research at Harvard University.

Langer's research demonstrates that mindfulness is the mechanism of action that drives effectiveness across life domains. Mindfulness is the root of health, happiness, satisfying relationships, and success. Curiosity is a way to conceptualize this active mental state. When we are curious we easily find growth opportunities. This enables us to create our experiences.

Mindfulness is a way of being, comprised of three essential components:

1. Presence—Openness to new information
2. Non-judgmental—Taking multiple perspectives
3. Growth—Revising mindsets

MINDLESSNESS

Langer defines mindlessness as a state of mind characterized by rigid mindsets or lack of awareness in the present moment. After decades of research on mindlessness and mindfulness, Langer emphasizes that we have a tendency to "look but not see". When mindless, we stop noticing, learning, and asking questions. Her research suggests that mindlessness is the cause of problems, unhappiness, failures, accidents, and even poor health.

Often we lose curiosity with the familiar and predictable. This is natural because minds are designed to get easily accustomed to circumstances where change is slow or subtle. The problem, however, is that change is always happening whether we realize it or not. Without noticing changes, we fall under the illusion that there is nothing more to learn or gain, that we know all there is to know in a situation. When this happens the quality of our attention changes. We tune out. We become mindless. This is why Self-Awareness is a difficult competency to master. We can never be fully mindful of ourselves across domains in every moment and from every perspective. Thus, true self-awareness is impossible.

The skills presented in this chapter aim to build Self-Awareness. We have selected skills that tend to be challenging for many. While important, we have elected not to present skills related to strengths, values, or deeper motivations, for example. Instead, we present skills that are less intuitive such as monitoring thoughts and beliefs, understanding emotions, tuning into bodily sensations, detecting emotions, and identifying triggers and reactions.

SKILL 1. MONITOR THOUGHTS & BELIEFS

"I will use my thoughts wisely. I will respect their power." –Deepak Chopra

Some estimate that we have at least 30,000 thoughts per day. If that is correct, then calculations suggest we have 210,000 thoughts per week, 10,920,000 thoughts per year, and by the time we are fifty years old we have had approximately 546,000,000 thoughts. While it is impossible to accurately approximate the number of thoughts, indisputably, our minds rarely take a break from thinking.

Just like a fish does not realize it is swimming in water, we don't realize we are swimming in thoughts. We go about our days remembering, predicting, interpreting, strategizing, explaining, judging, regretting, and so on typically without considering the content of this mental activity. The mind is essentially a word generating machine. It cannot help itself. Even during sleep, the mind generates thoughts, images, and stories.

The fact that the mind constantly generates thoughts warrants pausing to think about thinking. Psychologists call this "metacognition," which is defined as stepping back from thoughts, monitoring cognitive state, and reflecting on the content and quality of thinking. The ability to monitor mental content and quality of thinking is important for Self-Awareness. Although it is not necessary to monitor mental activity throughout the day, this ability enables cultivating presence, intentional way of being, and effective response. It is especially critical when things go wrong or we want something different. Thus, it represents a cornerstone of emotional intelligence.

When we take a step back from the mind and notice the content of thoughts, what becomes evident is that the mind is constantly creating relationships and attributions, determining patterns, and making snap judgments. Cognitive scientists explain that the mind is designed to make sense of things, to determine cause and effect, to explain why something happened and predict what will happen next. In the evolutionary sense, there was and still is tremendous survival benefit to a mind that can deftly monitor and understand complex environments in order to minimize threat and optimize opportunity. The mind's job, then, is to create stories.

INFORMATION PROCESSING CHAIN

We refer to the process of formulating these attributions and their subsequent effects on emotional states and actions as the Information Processing Chain. Essentially, all bits of information get processed in this predictable manner.

First, an event occurs and is perceived through the sensory system.

Second, the mind interprets that event.

Third, this interpretation triggers an emotion, and finally the interpretation and emotion are used to formulate a plan and motivate action.

The process happens in milliseconds and is the same in simple as well as highly complex situations.

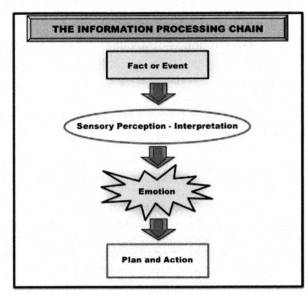

For example:

- **Fact or Event**—*a coiled dark object lies between sticks in the forest where you are hiking.*

- **Perception**—*Your eyes detect something coiled and black on the ground.*

- **Interpretation**—*It's a snake!*

- **Emotion**—*Fear.*

- **Action**—*Jump back.*

Another example:

- **Fact or Event**—*An email arrived in my inbox from Lisa. She said she could not make the meeting I arranged. I had asked everyone on the team to attend.*

- **Interpretation**—*She does not want to meet with me, because she does not respect me. She is not going to cooperate with me and will undermine my ability to do well on this project.*

- **Emotion**—*Frustration, Anxiety, Anger.*

- **Action**—*I write back and tell her firmly that she needs to attend this meeting. I remind her that our boss is very concerned about this project.*

BENEFITS OF MONITORING THOUGHTS AND BELIEFS

It can be revealing to observe the constantly changing conditions of mind. Increased awareness of one's current mind state can help increase objectivity and insights, which can then pave the way for managing one's internal state or taking action to affect external circumstances. Monitoring thoughts and beliefs has three main benefits:

- **Awareness**. Increases awareness about a psychological state. With this awareness, we are better positioned to make sense of situations and respond effectively.

- **Understanding**. Fosters understanding about which thoughts and emotions are showing up and why.

- **Foundation**. Provides a foundation for many other aspects of both Self-Awareness and Self-Management.

HOW TO MONITOR THOUGHTS

Three techniques for monitoring thoughts and beliefs are presented below, including Identify Thoughts and Interpretations, Journaling, and Label Thoughts Meditation.

Identify Thoughts and Interpretations. Awareness of one's mental state begins with getting specific about what content the mind is generating. As discussed with the Information Processing Chain, we all make interpretations about facts or events that we witness whether we realize it or not. Interpretations cause emotions and inform actions. They are central to our experience and yet, they are changeable and very much within our control.

Identify thoughts by simply putting the words in front of the thought, "I am having the thought that..." This practice is simply articulating. Identifying thoughts might seem like a senseless exercise in semantics, but after practicing it, most discover the benefit. Articulating the current thought brings tremendous specificity and depth of understanding of one's cognitive state.

In this simple process, state the specific thought and withhold judgment about the thought.

Say aloud or write on a piece of paper: ***"I am having the thought that..."*** And then state the thought.

For example:

"I am having the thought that *this meeting is not going to go well.*"

"I am having the thought that *Lisa thinks I am not as competent as she is.*"

Journaling. Get in touch with what you believe about yourself, your experiences, and how you relate to various topics in life. Journaling can be a powerful way to increase Self-Awareness. One way to do this is by writing about the first associations that come to mind. Sometimes this is referred to as a "mind dump." In this worksheet, several prompts are provided. Simply write whatever comes to mind without censoring, judging, or over-thinking.

Categorize the Thought—Labeling Thoughts Meditation. This technique brings awareness of the mind's activity. This non-judgmental and non-analytical approach to monitoring the thoughts involves simply observing and labeling the type of thought it is. It refrains from evaluating thoughts as good or bad, right or wrong, helpful or unhelpful. It is like taking inventory of the mind. In this meditation, watch thoughts come up and then label every thought that emerges according to which category of thought it falls into.

Common categories of thought are:
- Judging,
- Worrying,
- Predicting,
- Desiring,
- Regretting.
- Rehearsing
- Remembering
- Analyzing

IDENTIFY INTERPRETATIONS WORKSHEET

As discussed in the Information Processing Chain, we all make interpretations about facts or events that we witness whether we realize it or not. A crucial ability in emotional intelligence is to identify which interpretations we have formed. Interpretations cause emotions and inform actions. They are central to our experience and yet, they are changeable and very much within our control. The purpose of this worksheet is to identify interpretations you have made about facts or events.

For example:
- **Fact or Event**—*An email arrived in my inbox from Lisa. She said she could not make the meeting I arranged. I had asked everyone on the team to attend.*

- **Interpretation**—*She does not want to meet with me, because she does not respect me. She is not going to cooperate with me and will undermine my ability to do well on this project.*

- **Emotion**—*Frustration, Anxiety, Anger.*

- **Action**—*I write back and tell her firmly that she needs to attend this meeting. I remind her that our boss is very concerned about this project.*

1. IDENTIFY A FACT OR EVENT. What is a fact or event I recently perceived? (Who, What, Where)

_____

_____

_____

2. INTERPRETATION. What was my interpretation of the fact or event? Why do I think it happened or what significance did I attribute to it?

_____

_____

_____

_____

3. EMOTIONS. What did I feel as a result of this interpretation? (Ex: Anxiety, Disappointment, Frustration, Pride, Joy, or Love)

_____

_____

4. ACTIONS. What actions did I take that related to my interpretation? What action followed?

_____

_____

_____

_____

IDENTIFY INTERPRETATIONS TRACKING LOG

Situation #1

FACT OR EVENT
WHO, WHAT, WHERE

MY INTERPRETATION
WHY DID THIS EVENT HAPPEN? WHAT'S THE SIGNIFICANCE OF IT?

EMOTIONS
WHAT DID I FEEL? WHAT EMOTIONS EMERGED?

ACTIONS
WHAT DID I DO? WHAT ACTION FOLLOWED MY INTERPRETATION OR EMOTION?

Situation #2

FACT OR EVENT
WHO, WHAT, WHERE

MY INTERPRETATION
WHY DID THIS EVENT HAPPEN? WHAT'S THE SIGNIFICANCE OF IT?

EMOTIONS

WHAT DID I FEEL? WHAT EMOTIONS EMERGED?

ACTIONS

WHAT DID I DO? WHAT ACTION FOLLOWED MY INTERPRETATION OR EMOTION?

Situation #3

FACT OR EVENT

WHO, WHAT, WHERE

MY INTERPRETATION

WHY DID THIS EVENT HAPPEN? WHAT'S THE SIGNIFICANCE OF IT?

EMOTIONS

WHAT DID I FEEL? WHAT EMOTIONS EMERGED?

ACTIONS

WHAT DID I DO? WHAT ACTION FOLLOWED MY INTERPRETATION OR EMOTION?

SELF-AWARENESS

JOURNALING WORKSHEET

Get in touch with what you believe about yourself, your experiences, and how you relate to various topics in life. Journaling can be a powerful way to increase Self-Awareness. One way to do this is by writing about the first associations that come to mind. Sometimes this is referred to as a "mind dump." In this worksheet, several prompts are provided. Simply write whatever comes to mind without censoring, judging, or over-thinking. You could write a phrase to complete the sentence or you could use the prompt as a topic of a longer journaling session. If you choose to journal about a specific prompt, you might find it useful to journal for a designated amount of time, perhaps 5 or 10 minutes.

The purpose of this worksheet is to explore your beliefs in various realms of life. The mind dump journaling approach can result in increased Self-Awareness and insights.

1. WRITING PROMPTS—Write down whatever comes to mind when you read the following prompts.

My goal in life is _____

I think I am _____

What gets me angry is _____

I am envious of _____

What I want more of in life is _____

My most frequent emotion is _____

What I love is _____

My deepest fear is _____

My deepest need is _____

My greatest strengths are _____

My weaknesses are _____

To me, death is _____

My view of money is _____

Friendships are _____

Falling in love is _____

What I value most in others is _____

I feel most at home when _____

Someone I admire most is _____

I feel weak when _____

When I am my best self, I _____

When I am my worst self, I _____

The best thing about the opposite sex is _____

The worst thing about the opposite sex is _____

My experience with romantic relationships has been _____

What I want more of in my life is _____

2. REFLECT ON INSIGHTS. What insights or benefits did I gain in doing this mind dump journaling exercise?

_____
_____
_____
_____
_____
_____
_____

3. APPLICATION. How and which journaling prompts could I use to increase my Self-Awareness?

_____
_____
_____
_____
_____
_____
_____

THOUGHT LABELING MEDITATION

The mind is word generating machine. It can be revealing to observe the constantly changing conditions and content of the mind. The benefit of Thought Labeling is increased awareness of your current mind state and the busyness of the mind's chatter. This can help you gain objectivity, take thoughts less literally and seriously, and improve your ability to manage your internal state and external circumstances.

In this technique, simply label the type of thought, as if you are taking inventory of each category of thought that the mind generates.

For example:
- If you have the thought, "I want to rest", label the thought: "desiring".
- If you have the thought, "He is wrong for doing that", label the thought "judging."

Common categories of thought are:

- Judging,
- Desiring,
- Remembering
- Worrying,
- Regretting.
- Analyzing
- Predicting,
- Rehearsing

INSTRUCTIONS

(2 to 3 minutes)

1. FOCUS INWARD: Breathe and Center

- **Close your eyes**—Close your eyes to better focus your attention inward.

- **Feel Your Breath**—Focus attention by feeling your breath enter and exit your body. Breathe deep into your abdomen. Place your hand on your abdomen to feel your diaphragm rise and fall. Slowly exhale and naturally inhale.

- **Set your Intention**---To direct your attention in this time, place, and to the objective of this meditation.

2. DIRECT ATTENTION to thoughts.
- **Notice** the thoughts that emerge in your mind.

- **Label the Type of Thought.** As thoughts come through your mind, label the category of thought. When another thought emerges, label it, and repeat this process.

3. REFLECT ON INSIGHTS: Breathe and Reflect

- Come back to your breath.
- Reflect on the insights or benefits you gained during this meditation.

4. MAINTAIN YOUR INNER AWARENESS: Soft Gaze and Stay with It

- Slowly open your eyes and keep your gaze soft, directed downward, and settling on a neutral object.
- Stay with the awareness you gained during the meditation.

Enhancing Emotional Intelligence

THOUGHT LABELING MEDITATION WORKSHEET

After you have completed the meditation, jot down observations about what came up during your meditation. Make note of thoughts you had, feelings you experienced, bodily sensations you felt, and/or detours that you took.

1. FOCUS INWARD: Breathe and Center. Were you able to concentrate inward and turn your attention back to your intention for this exercise?

_____

_____

2. DIRECT ATTENTION: Label the Thoughts. What thoughts came up and which labels did you use (Judging, Worrying, Predicting, Desiring, Regretting)?

Predicting. What predicting did you identify?

_____

_____

_____

Judgments. What judgments did you identify?

_____

_____

_____

Worries. What worries did you identify?

_____

_____

_____

Desires. What desires did you identify?

_____

_____

_____

Regrets. What regrets did you identify?

_____

_____

_____

3. REFLECT ON INSIGHTS: Breathe and Reflect. What insights or benefits did you gain in the meditation?

_____

_____

_____

THOUGHT LABELING MEDITATION TRACKING LOG

DAY	APPLICATION What thoughts did I notice? Which thought categories did I label?	IMPACT What was the impact of doing Thought Labeling on my emotional, mind, and/or body state?
Day 1		
Day 2		
Day 3		
Day 4		

THOUGHT LABELING MEDITATION TRACKING LOG

DAY	APPLICATION What thoughts did I notice? Which thought categories did I label?	IMPACT What was the impact of doing Thought Labeling on my emotional, mind, and/or body state?
Day 5		
Day 6		
Day 7		

INSIGHTS - What patterns or benefits emerged?

_____
_____
_____
_____
_____

SKILL 2. UNDERSTAND EMOTIONS

The artist is a receptacle for emotions that come from all over the place: from the sky, from the earth, from a scrap of paper, from a passing shape, from a spider's web. –Pablo Picasso

WHAT IS AN EMOTION?

Although poetic descriptions of emotions abound, from a scientific perspective, they are defined concretely and have essential, specific evolutionary functions. According to a leading neuroscientist, Daniel Schacter, an emotion is a positive or negative experience that is associated with a particular pattern of physiological activity. It is an emergent state comprised of physiological, mental, and qualitative elements. Emotions are characterized by basic, predictable physiological states with associated bodily and mental changes.

Emotions are complex, evolutionarily adaptive, involuntary reactions to a stimulus. They are triggered involuntarily when a salient external or an internal stimulus, real or imagined, is perceived.

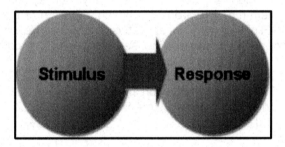

Six Universal Emotions. There are six primary emotions that are universal to all humans. There are four negative emotions (fear, anger, sadness, disgust), one positive emotion (joy), and surprise is the one neutral emotion (i.e., it can be negative or positive). Cross-cultural research by Paul Ekman, a leading authority on emotional expression, and other emotion researchers demonstrate that these six emotions are wired into the hardware that makes us human.

These primary emotions are experienced in all cultures, and each is expressed in a biologically universal manner. We do not know what the total number of emotions is since there are innumerable blends of emotions, and these differ across cultures.

SIX PRIMARY EMOTIONS
Surprise
Fear
Anger
Sadness
Disgust
Joy

FIVE COMPONENTS OF THE EMOTIONAL SYSTEM

Emotions serve an evolutionary function by operating five components of the emotional system.

FIVE COMPONENTS OF THE EMOTIONAL SYSTEM
1. Physiological State
2. Motivation
3. Cognitive Orientation
4. Feedback
5. Communication Signal

1. Physiological State

Emotions ready the body for action. The two main modes are referred to as "Fight or Flight" or "Broaden and Build". They mobilize cognitive and physical systems to react. Generally, the parasympathetic nervous system (i.e., low arousal, calming, relaxing) or the sympathetic nervous system (i.e., high arousal, Fight or Flight system) is activated. Emotions are associated with hormones and neurotransmitters such as dopamine, noradrenaline, serotonin, oxytocin, cortisol, and GABA.

There are predictable physiological and autonomic changes for each emotion. That is, every emotion has a distinct physiological thumbprint. Each emotion prepares the body for a very different kind of response.

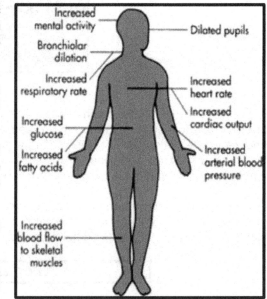

For example, you see a coiled snake when on a hike. Fear fills your body. Fear stimulates physiological changes:

• *Blood Pressure.* Blood goes to the large skeletal muscles, such as in the legs, making it easier to flee. The face blanches and digestive organs shutdown as blood is shunted to muscles that help us fight or flee.

• *Action Impulse or Tendency.* The body freezes allowing time to gauge whether hiding might be a better reaction.

• *Hormones.* Circuits in the brain's emotional centers trigger a flood of hormones that put the body on general alert, making it edgy and ready for action.

• *Attention.* These psychophysiological reactions change the quality of attention. Attention fixates on the threat with increased vigilance for sudden movement.

2. Motivation

Emotions are the driving force behind motivation. The Latin root of the word emotion is *movere*, meaning "to move". All emotions have a valence, a qualitative experience on spectrum of unpleasant and pleasant subjective experience.

It is said that pain is the ultimate motivator. From this perspective, it is not surprising that we often experience emotional pain in similar ways to physical pain. A neuroimaging study found that areas of brain activated during emotionally inflicted pain are the same as those activated during physically induced pain. This explains the physical pain sensations often associated with emotional distress.

<small>Panskepp, J. (2003). Feeling the pain of social loss. *Science* 10 October 2003: Vol. 302 no. 5643, pp. 237-239.</small>

The job of distressing emotions is to provoke action to mitigate, avoid, or otherwise eliminate undesirable stimuli. Likewise, positive emotions are reinforcing. Their job is to provoke approach to desirable stimuli. These are referred to as action tendencies or impulses.

The second motivational component is level of activation. Intense subjective experience of an emotion provokes action with greater urgency and attention. The degree of motivation corresponds to both valence and activation. Together, these properties provide an exquisitely precise system for provoking appropriate action for survival or thriving. Below is a graphic illustrating common emotions along two axes: Activation—Deactivation and Unpleasant—Pleasant.

	Activation	
Tense		alert
Nervous		excited
Stressed		elated
Upset		happy
Unpleasant		**Pleasant**
Sad		contented
Depressed		serene
Bored		relaxed
Fatigued		calm
	Deactivation	

3. Cognitive Orientation

Emotions influence the nature and flow of thinking, attention, memory and other cognitive processes. They orient the mind toward salient aspects of experience. Thinking can be fast and scattered or slow and flowing; attention can range from narrow to open. For example, when you feel anxious, you may notice that your mind is busy with thoughts, worry, and focus on the challenge and doubt. There may be a hyper focus on the subject of the stressor. In contrast, when you are feeling curious, you may notice free flowing thoughts and relaxed attention.

Emotions also affect memory formation and consolidation. Fear provoking, highly salient and negative events get encoded more vividly and are durable over time compared to delight provoking, low salience, positive events.

4. Feedback

The physical sensations associated with emotions provide feedback to help us evaluate experiences. At a very basic level, this feedback is simply do we like this or dislike this? Is this safe or dangerous? This information is conveyed through the bodily sensations. This information allows us to evaluate and draw distinctions within an experience, which is referred to as a cognitive appraisal.

Daniel Goleman refers to "the wisdom of emotions." In his new book entitled *Focus*, he emphasizes that decision-making depends on emotions. Emotions inform decision making by providing subtle bodily sensations that both cause and result from cognitive appraisal. For example, Should I marry this person? Move to another city? Search for a new job or make the best of this one? "Intuition" may simply be low level bodily reactions associated with emotions triggered by a real experience or imagined future.

5. Communication Signal

Emotions communicate intention and reaction to others. They express themselves through body language, vocal tone, facial expressions, and micro-expressions. These verbal and nonverbal signals of emotions reveal to others what an individual is experiencing. This highly efficient system provides a tremendous amount of emotional data in milliseconds, which is highly adaptive. For example, tears signal the need for support and care; smiles signal friendliness and safety; tense facial expressions signal alarm and cause others to become alert for threat to safety.

These five components of the emotional system synchronize to navigate our highly complex internal and external worlds. They work together to form an exquisitely complex ability to experience and respond to life's dangers and opportunities. A recent example of a highly emotionally charged situation Laura experienced demonstrates these five components of the emotional system. The overriding emotion was fear.

Just as I was walking into a meeting I received a call. In a panicked voice, my sister informed me that a large uncontained wildfire was swiftly approaching my mother's rural home in the dry California hills. Flames quickly engulfed oak trees on the edge of the property as my mother rushed to gather her dog, some family photo albums, and escape. A flood of fear overcame me. As I imagined her in harm's way, this fear activated my Fight or Flight mode. My focus narrowed, heart rate speeded, and hands trembled as adrenaline flooded my body. I immediately canceled the meeting, grabbed my keys and wallet, and drove to San Jose where my mother's house was located. As I drove, I fought to concentrate on the road. My focus was pulled into thoughts and images of our family home in flames. A deluge of fearful thoughts about my mom's safety overtook my mind. Fear hijacked my amygdala, making higher order thinking a struggle. Finally an hour and a half later, I arrived at the local high school where Red Cross set up a disaster relief station. Thankfully, the skillful coordination of ground and aircrew firefighters saved our home.

Physiological State: Fight or Flight response activated, including spiked Adrenaline and heart rate.

Motivation: I canceled the meeting and immediately drove to be with my family.

Cognitive Orientation: My mind was on my mom's safety and the possibility that the house was in flames. It was challenging to focus on driving…and keeping to the speed limit.

Communication Signal: My sister's vocal tone alerted me to the seriousness of the situation. The look on my face told the person with whom I was to meet that I had an emergency situation.

EXERCISE: FIVE COMPONENTS OF AN EMOTION

Bring to mind a situation where you experienced or witnessed strong positive or negative emotion. Reflect on how you experienced or observed the five components of emotion in that experience.

Describe the Situation

Briefly, what was the situation (Who, What, Where)?

Jeb basejumping and having a catastrophic crash

Which emotions were present?

alert, shock, frightened → relief & happiness

1. Physiological State

What were the physiological changes you experienced/witnessed?

increased HR, muscles tightening

2. Motivation

What was the valence (i.e., unpleasant or pleasant) and intensity (i.e., high activation or low activation)?

unpleasant → high activation

In what ways were behaviors affected? Was there an approach toward something positive or an action to avoid or mitigate an aversive experience (i.e., a feeling of being drawn in, wanting more of a positive; a feeling of being turned off, wanting to get less of, or get away from something negative)?

3. Cognitive Orientation

In what ways did the quality or direction of attention change? (ex: focused, distracted, narrow, chaotic or calm?)

_____
_____
_____
_____
_____
_____
_____

4. Feedback

The physical sensations associated with emotions provide feedback to help us evaluate experiences. Did you (or another) like or dislike the situation? At a basic level, did it feel safe or dangerous (or, where on the spectrum of security and danger did it fall)?

_____
_____
_____
_____
_____
_____
_____

5. Communication Signal

How did emotions communicate intention and reaction? Were there signs expressed through body language, vocal tone, or facial expressions?

_____
_____
_____
_____
_____
_____
_____

SELF-AWARENESS

THE FUNCTION OF EMOTIONS—To Help Us Thrive and Survive

Emotions have an essential evolutionary function, which is to help navigate our environment to avoid danger and attain desirable outcomes. They each have a unique adaptive value to help us to survive and thrive. They help us to meet immediate challenges, solve important problems, and plan for the future. They are fundamental for learning, growth, and orientation.

Over millions of years of evolution, emotions may have evolved to help us to survive and thrive. The chart below is adapted from *The Human Brain Book* by Rita Carter. This chart lists typical stimuli and the adaptive responses associated with several common emotions.

EMOTION	STIMULUS	ADAPTIVE RESPONSE EXAMPLE
FEAR	A threat from a source of danger.	• A fight response to attack the threat. • A flight response to circumvent the threat. • An attempt to avoid the threat.
ANGER	Injustice and a threat.	• A fight response. • A dominant and threatening posture or action.
SADNESS	Loss of something or someone of value.	• A passive response. • Backward-looking state of mind and passivity. • Avoid additional challenge while vulnerable.
DISGUST	Unwholesome Object (Unclean environment, rotting meat, sewage, etc.)	• An aversion response. • Remove oneself from the disgusting situation.
SURPRISE	Novel experience. Unexpected event.	• An attention response. • Focus attention on item of surprise. • Ensure maximum input to guide next actions.

NEGATIVE EMOTIONS

Negative emotions help us survive. They are designed to ensure safety. Survival as a species has depended upon them. Distressing emotions orient us to avoid aversive circumstances.

FIGHT, FLIGHT, OR FREEZE EFFECT OF NEGATIVE EMOTIONS

The classic effect of most negative emotions is some form of the Fight, Flight, or Freeze response. The fight response helps us attack or destroy the threat, the flight response helps us get out of harms way, and the freeze response can help us avoid the threat until it passes or otherwise transforms.
Negative emotions motivate us through pain or distress to decrease an aversive stimulus or to avoid something that may cause physical harm or mental distress. They focus our attention on what's wrong. From an evolutionary perspective, the tendency to feel negative emotions more strongly than positive

emotions is highly adaptive. This can be quite beneficial, especially when dealing with a simple threat. A recent study showed that depressed people are better at focusing on simple, concrete problems and solving them. Like the keel on a sailboat, negative emotions help keep us upright during stormy weather.

Negative emotions:
- Help us mobilize for defense or aggression
- Enhance focus on problems
- Make us feel unsafe and inhibit further risk
- Cause us to retreat from others
- Help us reflect on setbacks, losses, and danger
- Repel others and make us feel threatening to them
- Help us conserve resources and focus attention on needs and security
- Protect us from others who may do harm

ROLE OF POSITIVE EMOTIONS

Positive emotions help us thrive. These "approach" emotions motivate us through pleasant feelings to get more of something or to do it again. They feel rewarding, satisfying, or pleasurable. They also encourage others to come along and join us.

Like the sail on a sailboat, positive emotions drive us toward our objectives, hopes, dreams, and goals. They are the fuel behind aspirations.

THE BROADEN AND BUILD EFFECT OF POSITIVE EMOTIONS

Simply by sailing in a new direction
you could enlarge the world.
-Allen Curnow

Research shows positive emotions don't just feel good, they also are good for us. Positivity builds upon itself to create an upward spiral of growth and enjoyment. Psychologists refer to these benefits as the Broaden and Build Theory of Positive Emotions, established by Barbara Fredrickson at University of North Carolina, Chapel Hill. Positive emotions *broaden* our vision and help us to *build* resources and grow as individuals.

Positive emotions:
- Help us see new possibilities
- Enhance creativity
- Make us feel more secure and help us take moderate risk
- Enhance connections to others
- Help us bounce back from setbacks
- Attract others and make others seem attractive
- Increase generosity, interest, and cooperation with others

THE EFFECT OF POSITIVE & NEGATIVE EMOTIONS WORKSHEET

All emotions have a job to do. From an evolutionary perspective, negative emotions are designed to help us survive, while positive emotions are designed to help us thrive. Both roles are crucial to well-being and success. Operating with this knowledge is a fundamental aspect of emotional intelligence.

The purpose of this worksheet is to help you deepen your understanding of the function of emotions you experience. In this exercise, the objective is not to change the emotions or assess whether they are bad or good. Instead, it is to observe the evolutionary role of emotions in everyday situations.

THE EFFECT OF NEGATIVE EMOTIONS

Bring to mind a difficult or distressing situation where you experienced or witnessed a negative emotion. Reflect on how the negative emotions served an adaptive purpose (i.e., even if not entirely beneficial, identify how the negative emotion attempted to help you or another avoid or mitigate unwanted circumstances).

DIFFICULT OR DISTRESSING SITUATION. Briefly, what was the situation (Who, What, Where)?

_____

_____

_____

_____

IDENTIFY NEGATIVE EMOTIONS. Which negative emotions were present?

_____

_____

_____

_____

FLIGHT, FIGHT, OR FREEZE EFFECT OF NEGATIVE EMOTIONS. How did negative emotions have a protective effect on me, my thinking or attention, my actions, and/or the circumstances? How did the negative emotions help me or another avoid an aversive circumstance or threat (i.e., to "survive")?

_____

_____

_____

_____

_____

_____

_____

THE EFFECT OF POSITIVE EMOTIONS

Bring to mind a situation where you experienced or witnessed a positive emotion. Reflect on how the positive emotions had a broadening and building effect on you, your mind, your actions, and the circumstances.

POSITIVE SITUATION. Briefly, what was the situation (Who, What, Where)?

_____
_____
_____
_____

IDENTIFY POSITIVE EMOTIONS. Which positive emotions were present?

_____
_____

BROADEN AND BUILD EFFECT OF POSITIVE EMOTIONS. How did the positive emotions help me broaden my perspective and/or build resources including connect with others? How did they help me attain or engage in a desirable circumstance (i.e., to "thrive")?

Broadening Effect of Positive Emotions. To what extent did positive emotions help me widen my perspective, energize me, motivate creative thinking, etc.?

_____
_____
_____
_____

Building Effect of Positive Emotions. To what extent did positive emotions help me build resources, connect with others, motivate me to be generous or collaborative, motivate, inspire a new plan, etc.?

_____
_____
_____
_____

INSIGHTS. What insights did I gain by considering the role of positive and negative emotions in my well-being and success?

_____
_____
_____
_____

THE EFFECT OF EMOTIONS TRACKING LOG

DAY	APPLICATION Which positive and negative emotions did I experience? How did the positive emotion have a Broaden and Build Effect on me? How did the negative emotion have a Fight, Flight, or Freeze Effect?	IMPACT What was the impact of looking at the effect of emotions on my understanding of my experience?
Day 1		
Day 2		
Day 3		
Day 4		

THE EFFECT OF EMOTIONS TRACKING LOG

DAY	APPLICATION Which positive and negative emotions did I experience? How did the positive emotion have a Broaden and Build Effect on me? How did the negative emotion have a Fight, Flight, or Freeze Effect?	IMPACT What was the impact of looking at the effect of emotions on my understanding of my experience?
Day 5		
Day 6		
Day 7		

INSIGHTS - What patterns or benefits emerged?

_____
_____
_____
_____

SKILL 3: OBSERVE BODILY SENSATIONS

An initial step in Self-Awareness is to check in with the body. The body can tell us a lot about what is going on in our internal experience—what we feel, think, and what we need. Often we tune-out of our bodily sensations, however.

Emotions are fundamentally bodily experiences. Emotion is a complex, subjective internal experience that involves physiological changes as a preparation for action. Observing bodily sensations activates the brain region of the insula, which is involved in understanding the self as well as others.

BODY MAPS OF EMOTION

In 2013, Lori Nummenmaa and her team of Finnish researchers induced different emotions in 701 participants. Participants then colored in a body map to illustrate where they felt increasing or decreasing activity. Participants were from both Western European countries and from East Asia. Despite the cultural differences, people showed remarkable similarities in responses. Below are the body maps for several of the emotions that the researchers examined. Yellow indicates the highest level of activity, followed by red. Black is neutral, while blue and light blue indicate lowered and very low activity, respectively. The authors explain:

"Most basic emotions were associated with sensations of elevated activity in the upper chest area, likely corresponding to changes in breathing and heart rate. Similarly, sensations in the head area were shared across all emotions, reflecting probably both physiological changes in the facial area as well as the felt changes in the contents of mind triggered by the emotional events."

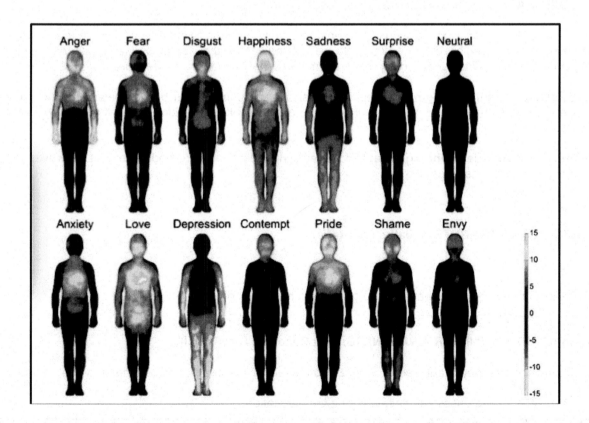

BODY SCAN MEDITATION

An initial step in Self-Awareness is to tune-in to the body. The body can tell us a lot about what is going on in our internal experience—what we feel, think, and what we need. Often we tune out of our bodily sensations, however. This meditation provides an opportunity to systematically tune-in to current bodily sensations. For some this is relaxing, for others it might stir up negative emotions.

The objective in this meditation is simply to observe without an agenda. One never knows what will show up when turning attention to internal experience. As with all meditations, your job is simply to observe. Each time your mind wanders, turn your attention back to the sensations of your body. This meditation activates the brain region of the insula, which is also involved in understanding others.

INSTRUCTIONS
(5 to 10 minutes)

1. FOCUS INWARD: Breathe and Center

- **Close your eyes**— Close your eyes to let your attention turn inward.

- **Feel Your Breath**—Focus attention by feeling your breath enter and exit your body. Breathe deeply with a slower exhale and natural inhale. Place your hand on your abdomen to feel your diaphragm rise and fall.

- **Set your Intention**---Direct your attention to this time, place, and the objective of this meditation.

2. DIRECT ATTENTION: Scan Your Body for Sensations.

- **Feel bodily sensations**—Observe the sensations in your body. Systematically, move the spotlight of attention to each region of your body. Notice the nature of the sensations and observe neutrally, objectively. Perhaps the sensation is prickly, warm, pinching; sensations of pressure or contraction.

- **Experience without judgment**—Feel the physical sensations in your body. Release the judgment of the sensation as bad or good, pleasant or painful. Take a break from asking yourself whether you like or don't like the sensations.

- **Acknowledge the changing nature of sensation**—Sensations are body events. Like waves rolling onto shore, sensations come and go.

3. REFLECT ON INSIGHTS: Breathe and Reflect

- Come back to your breath.

- Reflect on the insights or benefits you gained during this meditation.

4. MAINTAIN YOUR INNER AWARENESS: Soft Gaze and Stay with It.

- Slowly open your eyes and keep your gaze soft, directed downward, and settling on a neutral object.

- Stay with the awareness you gained during the meditation.

BODY SCAN MEDITATION WORKSHEET

After you have completed the meditation, jot down observations about what came up during your meditation. Make note of thoughts you had, feelings you experienced, and bodily sensations you felt.

1. FOCUS INWARD: Breathe and Center. Were you able to concentrate inward and turn your attention back to your intention for this exercise?

yes

2. DIRECT ATTENTION: Scan Your Body for Sensations. What did you experience when you scanned your body?

Feel bodily sensations. What sensations did you feel (e.g., prickly, warm, pinching; sensations of pressure or contraction)

warm

Experience without judgment. To what extent did you release your judgment of pleasant or unpleasant? What was the effect?

pleasant

Acknowledge the changing nature of sensation. To what extent could you sense the ever-changing nature of sensation?

3. REFLECT ON INSIGHTS: Breathe and Reflect. What insights or benefits did you gain in the meditation?

BODY SCAN TRACKING LOG

DAY	APPLICATION How did I do the Body Scan? What sensations did I observe?	IMPACT What was the impact of the Body Scan Meditation on my emotional, mind, and body states?
Day 1		
Day 2		
Day 3		
Day 4		

BODY SCAN TRACKING LOG

DAY	**APPLICATION** How did I do the Body Scan? What sensations did I observe?	**IMPACT** What was the impact of the Body Scan Meditation on my emotional, mind, and body states?
Day 5		
Day 6		
Day 7		

INSIGHTS—What patterns or benefits emerged?

_____
_____
_____
_____

SKILL 4: DETECT EMOTIONS

Labeling emotions is a seemingly simple process, but it requires accurate emotional perception and a nuanced understanding of the distinctions between emotions. It also requires a robust vocabulary of emotions and precision in emotional labeling. It results in the ability to discriminate between similar emotions, such as knowing the difference between jealousy and envy or frustration and annoyance.

Individuals differ in their ability to perceive, categorize, and articulate their own emotions, but like other skills, reading emotional states can be learned and strengthened regardless of current mastery level.

BENEFITS

Increase Self-Knowledge or Intuition about a Situation. Often internal signals are subtle. People often speak of knowing something intuitively. *Intuition* describes subtle emotions that communicate important information that does not make it into explicit thoughts. An initial step to increasing emotional intelligence is turning up the volume on your emotions and learning to read them more effectively.

Some emotions scream loudly while others whisper softly. Loud emotions such as anger often overshadow more subtle emotions such as disappointment. For example, you may notice that you feel angry that your reservation at a special restaurant was dropped, but it might require closer examination to identify the disappointment that you will not be able to celebrate your anniversary the way you imagined.

Move from Low Road to High Road. Simply labeling an emotion lowers its intensity. Translating diffuse, abstract emotional states into concrete categories of information transforms the emotional experience. The cooler, logical mind can take over with its planning and problem solving capabilities. Activating the language centers in the brain may promote integration of cognitive and emotional processing, thereby relaxing the highly reactive "Reptilian" brain center.

EXAMPLE

The following is a description from a former workshop participant who learned this technique. Her experience demonstrates the power of simply labeling emotions, which helped her move from the Low Road to the High Road.

"I had a very difficult conversation with one of my team members. She is a very needy person, and our calls are not that productive most of the time. I realized before the call even started that I was tense. Needless to say the call ended on a bad note. After, I found myself reacting emotionally. I stopped and used the technique of labeling my emotions. In this case they were anger, frustration, anxiousness. As soon as I did this, I found myself physically relaxing.

It always amazes me how well this works. I have had a lifetime of emotions playing such a central role that it seems almost impossible to believe that they don't have to have such a death grip. In the heat of the moment, I realized that I didn't have to wait for the outside world to validate my experience with her, or my emotional reactions. I could do it for myself."

RESEARCH—Labeling Emotions

A growing body of research shows that simply naming an emotion can diminish the intensity of the feeling of the emotion.

Research at UCLA has shown that when people are asked to label an angry or frightened expression, their regional cerebral blood flow (rCBF) decreases in both sides of the amygdala and their rCBF increases in the right prefrontal cortex. This is important because the amygdala is a region in the brain that responds to fear related stimuli, whereas the right prefrontal cortex is associated with regulating emotions. This research suggests that labeling emotions helps people decrease their fear related responses and regulate their emotions more effectively.

Creswell, J. David, Way, Baldwin M., Eisenberger, Naomi I., Lieberman, Matthew. (2007). Neural correlates of dispositional mindfulness during affect labeling. *Psychosomatic Medicine*, 69(6), 560-565.

HOW TO LABEL EMOTIONS

Be Specific. Bringing specificity to emotional states can be challenging. For example, when attempting to label emotions commonly people identify feeling "stressed." "Stressed" however, is not an emotion. This is a nonspecific state that generally it refers to a combination of distressing emotions. Sometimes emotions are difficult to identify. It may feel like general stress, but is the emotion anxiety or is it excitement? You may know you feel mad, but is the emotion anger or is it frustration? What is the difference between shame and guilt?

Labeling the emotions that comprise feeling stressed might include differentiating between combinations of emotions such as anxiety, frustration, annoyance, and surprise. Likewise, feeling "upset" is not an emotion. It may refer to a combination of emotions such as anger, frustration, and disappointment. This precision in emotional perception creates a foundation for all the skills.

We generally have a sense of what we are feeling. In this practice, however, we aim for a more sophisticated articulation of emotional states. The chart below expands these categories of primary emotions. This list can be helpful when making distinctions between subtle emotional states.

EIGHT FAMILIES OF EMOTIONS

Surprise:	shock, astonishment, amazement, and wonder
Fear:	anxiety, apprehension, nervousness, concern, consternation, misgiving, wariness, qualm, edginess, dread, fright, terror and in the extreme cases phobia and panic.
Anger:	fury, outrage, resentment, wrath, exasperation, indignation, vexation, acrimony, animosity, annoyance, irritability, hostility, and perhaps these are manifest in the extreme as hatred and violence.
Sadness:	grief, sorrow, cheerlessness, gloom, melancholy, self-pity, loneliness, dejection, despair, and depression in the extreme case.
Disgust:	contempt, distain, scorn, abhorrence, aversion, distaste, and revulsion
Shame:	guilt, embarrassment, chagrin, remorse, humiliation, regret, mortification, and contrition.
Enjoyment:	happiness, joy, relief, contentment, bliss, delight, amusement, pride, sensual pleasure, thrill, rapture, gratification, satisfaction, euphoria, whimsy, and ecstasy.
Love:	acceptance, friendliness, trust, kindness, affinity, devotion, adoration, infatuation, and agape.

LABEL AND DESCRIBE EMOTIONS

Try labeling your emotions and observe if you, like the research participants in the UCLA brain imaging study, experience any decrease in the intensity of your emotional experience. It's a simple process: Label which specific emotion, describe the sensations associated with it, and withhold judgment about having the emotion.

1. Label the Emotion. Identify emotions by simply putting the "notice phrase" in front of the emotion and say which emotion.

"I am having the emotion of " _____ *"*

For example: *"I am having the emotion of frustration." "I am having the emotion of joy."*

This simple semantic structure facilitates an implicit understanding that emotions are transitory and increases the sense that we relate to emotions rather than being defined by them. This allows us to relate to our emotions more objectively rather than saying that "I am frustrated". Feel the difference for yourself.

2. Describe Sensations. Describe the sensations associated with the emotions.

Describe. Describe the emotion by noting what is going on in your body and your mind.

Location: Identify the location in your body where you feel the emotion-associated sensations.

Intensity: Rate the intensity level of the emotion (1-10, with 10 being an intolerable level of the emotion):

1   2   3   4   5   6   7   8   9   10

3. Withhold Judgment. It is important to be non-judgmental about the emotions that you observe and label. The practice of labeling refrains from evaluating emotions as good or bad, right or wrong, helpful or unhelpful until you have done some analysis. The practice is designed to bring specificity to interpretations and the mind's activity.

IS IT A THOUGHT OR AN EMOTION?

Many people confuse thoughts and emotions. Common phrases for describing internal experience reveal this tendency or lack of ability to discriminate between thoughts and emotions. In conversation it is common to call thoughts emotions and refer to emotions as thoughts. Have you ever said, *"I feel like...."* when you actually mean *"I think..."*?

Consider the statement, *"I feel like you don't understand."*

Is that a statement about thoughts or emotions? Technically, that is a thought reference—a statement is about an interpretation or a cognitive appraisal. The emotion might be disappointment, frustration or sadness.

More accurately spoken would be *"I think you don't understand."*

If the speaker wanted to describe an emotional state, a more accurate statement might be: *"I feel hurt [or disappointed], because I think you don't understand."*

The difference might seem like semantics, but this imprecision can diminish understanding of emotional experience. Most people gain increased emotional clarity when they precisely label their emotional state and differentiate emotions from interpretations or appraisals.

SELF-AWARENESS

DETECT EMOTIONS WORKSHEET

Detecting emotions is an important ability in Self-Awareness. The following process can be used to help you improve your emotion detection accuracy. Use the Eight Basic Families of Common Emotions list to help you identify which emotion.

EIGHT FAMILIES OF COMMON EMOTIONS

Surprise:	shock, astonishment, amazement, and wonder
Fear:	anxiety, apprehension, nervousness, concern, consternation, misgiving, wariness, qualm, edginess, dread, fright, terror and in the extreme cases phobia and panic.
Anger:	fury, outrage, resentment, wrath, exasperation, indignation, vexation, acrimony, animosity, annoyance, irritability, hostility, and perhaps these are manifest in the extreme as hatred and violence.
Sadness:	grief, sorrow, cheerlessness, gloom, melancholy, self-pity, loneliness, dejection, despair, and depression in the extreme case.
Disgust:	contempt, distain, scorn, abhorrence, aversion, distaste, and revulsion
Shame:	guilt, embarrassment, chagrin, remorse, humiliation, regret, mortification, and contrition.
Enjoyment:	happiness, joy, relief, contentment, bliss, delight, amusement, pride, sensual pleasure, thrill, rapture, gratification, satisfaction, euphoria, whimsy, ecstasy, and at the far edge, mania.
Love:	acceptance, friendliness, trust, kindness, affinity, devotion, adoration, infatuation, and agape.

SITUATION ONE: BRIEFLY DESCRIBE AN EMOTIONAL SITUATION

_____

_____

1. LABEL. USE THE PHRASE: *"I AM HAVING THE EMOTION OF _____."*

(There is added benefit by using this simple semantic structure. It facilitates an implicit understanding that emotions are transitory and increases the sense that we relate to emotions rather than being defined by them. This allows us to relate to our emotions more objectively rather than saying that "I am frustrated". Feel the difference for yourself.)

"I am having the emotion of _____."

2. DESCRIBE. DESCRIBE YOUR PHYSICAL EXPERIENCE OF THE EMOTION.

Describe: Briefly describe what you notice about the emotion.

_____

_____

_____

Locations: Identify locations in your body where you are feeling the emotion.

_____

_____

_____

Intensity: Rate the intensity level of the emotion (1-10, with 10 being an intolerable level of the emotion):

    1   2   3   4   5   6   7   8   9   10

SITUATION TWO: BRIEFLY DESCRIBE AN EMOTIONAL SITUATION

_____
_____

1. LABEL. USE THE PHRASE: *"I AM HAVING THE EMOTION OF _____."*

"I am having the emotion of _____."

2. DESCRIBE. DESCRIBE YOUR PHYSICAL EXPERIENCE OF THE EMOTION.

Describe: Briefly describe what you notice about the emotion.

_____
_____
_____

Locations: Identify locations in your body where you are feeling the emotion.

_____
_____
_____

Intensity: Rate the intensity level of the emotion (1-10, with 10 being an intolerable level of the emotion):

    1   2   3   4   5   6   7   8   9   10

SITUATION THREE: BRIEFLY DESCRIBE AN EMOTIONAL SITUATION

_____
_____

1. LABEL. USE THE PHRASE: *"I AM HAVING THE EMOTION OF _____."*

"I am having the emotion of _____."

2. DESCRIBE. DESCRIBE YOUR PHYSICAL EXPERIENCE OF THE EMOTION.

Describe: Briefly describe what you notice about the emotion.

_____
_____

Locations: Identify locations in your body where you are feeling the emotion.

_____
_____

Intensity: Rate the intensity level of the emotion (1-10, with 10 being an intolerable level of the emotion):

    1   2   3   4   5   6   7   8   9   10

SKILL 5: IDENTIFY TRIGGERS & REACTIONS

Self-Awareness involves understanding the origins, consequences, and purpose of emotions. This can help develop a deeper understanding of experience, which is the first step in managing our emotional experience and discovering how we intentionally choose to respond.

EMOTIONAL EQUATIONS

Each emotion has a distinctive biological signature, and each plays a unique role in our emotional repertoire. We can think of every emotion as having a predictable equation that produces it.

There are three main causes and effects of each emotion:

- Triggers
- Action Impulses
- Bodily Reactions

Triggers. A trigger is the event or stimulus that elicits an emotional response. Emotions have predictable origins, which is tied to the interpretation of an event or stimulus. For example, a perception of some form of threat and an injustice results in anger; sadness is triggered when something valued is lost; disappointment is triggered when an expected positive event fails to occur.

EMOTIONAL EQUATIONS

DISTRESSING EMOTIONS

EMOTIONS		TRIGGERS
Anger	➔	Injustice/Violation + Threat
Fear / Panic	➔	Present Threat
Anxiety	➔	Challenge + Doubt
Frustration	➔	Effort + Lack of Success
Disappointment	➔	Unfulfilled Positive Expectation

PLEASANT EMOTIONS

EMOTIONS		TRIGGERS
Joy	➔	Pleasant Experience
Excitement	➔	Anticipation of Positive Experience
Love	➔	Intimacy + Respect
Contentment	➔	Satisfaction with Present
Hopefulness	➔	Positive Future Potential

The intensity of the trigger typically parallels the intensity of the emotion. Imagine the minor annoyance of a short traffic jam on your way to work. It is mildly annoying and you wish you were doing something else. The intensity level of those emotions (e.g., annoyance, frustration) is mild. In contrast imagine getting caught in a heavy traffic jam as you are rushing to the hospital with a loved one who has broken their arm and is writhing in pain. The perceived threat is large, and correspondingly, the emotion's intensity will be significantly distressing.

Action impulses. An emotion's action impulse is the urge to react in a certain as a result of an emotion. Every emotion has not only a unique trigger, but it also has an associated action impulse. Emotions ignite an impulse. For example, anger creates an impulse to attack while disappointment evokes an impulse to give up.

Bodily Reactions. The bodily reaction serves the action impulse, readying the body for a particular action. Each emotion has a signature effect on the body's physical and mental systems. Mental effects include the emotion's impact on narrowing or expanding attention, alertness or sluggishness, vigilance or tuning out, and so on. The effect a particular emotion has on the body matches the action impulse.

For example, anger's action impulse is to attack, therefore the body moves into attack mode by shunting blood to the muscles, adrenaline rush to create a surge of energy, narrowing of attention on the perceived threat, and so on.

EXAMPLES—ANXIETY, ANGER, & SADNESS

Below are descriptions of the triggers, action impulse, and the bodily reactions for three emotions.

ANXIETY

Trigger: Perception of an imminent threat, anticipation of a negative event, or concern that an unwanted situation will occur in the future. In our evolutionary past, the threat might have been a tiger hiding behind a bush. These days the "threat" may be the possibility of fumbling during a presentation in a board meeting, the expectation of negative response from a loved one, or the arrival of a bill that is larger than the balance of your checking account.

Action Impulse: The "Fight or Flight" response is associated with anxiety. This adaptive reaction enhances the ability to overcome a challenge or ward off a threat.

Bodily Reaction: The body readies itself to fight or flee with acute and automatic mobilization of resources need for intense attention, physical agility, and burst of strength.
- Increased heart rate, respiration, and blood flow prepare the muscles for action.
- Adrenaline rushes through the body to mobilize for immediate action.
- Attention narrows, vigilance heightens, muscles tighten and perspiration increases.

Example: Awaiting the test results from a biopsy, my sister experienced anxiety. The possibility of a malignant tumor was the imminent threat and the lack of control over this unwanted outcome together gave rise to anxiety.

In our modern environment, the Fight or Flight response can help us focus on a report that is imminently due or prepare for a difficult meeting. When anxiety is too strong or chronic, however, it becomes maladaptive. Loss of sleep, nervousness, and incessant worry are examples of counterproductive reactions associated with anxiety.

ANGER

Trigger: A perception of a violation or injustice in addition to a perception of threat.

Action Impulse: To get rid of a threat to well-being and correct the injustice.

Bodily Reaction: Activates Sympathetic Nervous System (the Flight or Flight reaction), energy spikes, adrenaline excreted, attention narrows, thought takes on an obsessive quality, and vigilance increases.

Example: When I moved across the country I sent several boxes via train. Apparently, there was theft during transit. The items had been insured, but the theft report I filed in the station was never recorded, apparently the result of foul play. Due to an apparent cover-up, I was unable to rectify the damage and my appeals rejected. I had the emotion of anger emerge as a result of the injustice of the theft and of the apparent cover-up.

SADNESS

Trigger: Losing something that was deemed valuable. This is highly functional, because it facilitates learning from unwanted experiences and/or helps us honor the loss. For example, mourning can be thought of as a way of honoring the deceased.

Action Impulse: To rest and reflect. Associated with introspection, closing out others, slowing down to reflect.

Bodily Reaction: A general slowing down of the physiology. Lethargy, tiredness, apathy, and decreased appetite are common.

Example: When my ex-boyfriend died suddenly, I experienced sadness and grief for some time. The role of sadness was to get me to slow down and focus on the tragic loss so that I could reflect and, ultimately, honor the love I felt for him. When sadness arose, I would say to myself:

"Sadness is a way of honoring the good times and the positive role that Ron had in my life. Of course I miss him, because I valued him so much. My sadness is a way of honoring all the good that he was to me."

A DIFFERENT TYPE OF TRIGGER—A CONDITIONED RESPONSE

Emotions follow behavioral psychology rules of conditioning such as reinforcement and reward, punishment, and extinction. The power of conditioning explains why we can feel distressed seemingly for no reason, out of the blue, in what seems to be benign circumstances.

Conditioned Stimulus → Reaction

Classical Conditioning. You have probably heard of Pavlov's famous dog research. The dogs associated a bell with getting fed meat. Initially, this inadvertently occurred because there was a bell that sounded every time a lab technician opened the door to the laboratory where they were caged at feeding time. Soon they became "conditioned" to the ringing of bell and would salivate upon hearing the bell even in the absence of the feeding. The once benign, meaningless bell became associated with meat (a naturally rewarding stimulus) and therefore the bell gained the power to elicit the same response as meat. From these experiments Pavlov developed the concept of Classical Conditioning.

Emotions can become conditioned to a stimulus. When this happens the mere presence of that stimulus will trigger the emotion. Fear as a reaction to a fire alarm, anxiety at the sight of a police officer walking up to your car, anticipation at the ping of a new email, and anticipated joy with the hissing of an espresso machine are all examples of conditioned responses. Other examples of conditioning is the feeling of elation triggered by the ring tone of a lover, the feeling of anxiety when walking into a boss's office, or annoyance upon hearing a co-worker with whom you have conflict say, "Hello, good morning!" to the receptionist outside your office.

Priming—a Conditioned Thought. Thoughts as well as emotions can appear merely because of previous associations. Psychologists call this type of classical conditioning "priming." Consider the following priming examples. Watch your thoughts emerge simply because previous word associations:

Priming examples:

Blondes have more ____.

Mary had a little ____.

Tick tock it's ten ____.

Operant Conditioning. Learning history, expectations, previous experience, and one's understanding of situations create operant conditioning of emotions. Operant conditioning defined as the shaping of future actions by past reward and punishment experiences. In other words, it is the associations that emerge after repeated patterns of cause and effect. A behavior that is reinforced will increase and a behavior that is met with aversive consequences (i.e., punishment) will decrease. When a behavior that was previously reinforced is met with neither reward nor punishment it will (i.e., extinguish) eventually decrease. Our minds reflexively determine the cause and effect of our experiences. Emotions can be influenced from the *expectation* or *interpretation* of cause and effect.

• If you were *praised* for expressing your needs and opinions as a child, you would likely feel confident and reasonably certain that good things will happen if you express yourself as an adult.

• If you were *punished* (e.g., scolded; shamed in some way; told that you were rude, entitled) for expressing your needs and opinions as a child, you would likely avoid direct expression for fear of punishment (e.g., being told you are rude, entitled, etc.).

It is important to be aware of one's emotional conditioning, because it can help explain why emotions emerge in certain circumstances but not others and why emotional reactions can be extremely resistant to change.

TRIGGERS OF EMOTIONS AND REACTIONS TO EMOTIONS CHART

The *Triggers and Reactions* Chart describes primary emotional families and some typical triggers, bodily reactions, and action impulses. On side one of the chart are emotions that help us to survive. Side two outlines emotions that help us thrive.

TRIGGERS & REACTIONS
SURVIVAL EMOTIONS

EMOTION	TRIGGER	BODILY REACTION	ACTION IMPULSE
SURPRISE • Shock • Astonishment • Startle • Bewilderment • Confusion	• **Shock**—Unexpected Negative Event. • **Confusion**—Unclear circumstances, statements, or situations.	• Eye-widening • Increased adrenaline	• Scream. • Step back. • Take in more information.
FEAR • Apprehension • Anxiety • Concern • Edginess • Nervousness • Terror • Consternation • Fright • Panic	• **Fear and/or Panic**—A Present Threat. • **Anxiety**—A Future Threat plus Uncertainty about ability to manage it.	• Spike in adrenaline and heart-rate • Blood to shunted to extremities	• Run, Hide, Attack. • Flight, Freeze, Fight
ANGER • Fury • Resentment • Hostility • Outrage • Frustration • Irritability • Wrath • Indignation • Animosity	• **Anger**—An Injustice or Violation plus Threat. • **Frustration**—Effort plus Lack of Success.	• Seeing red, tightening muscles, quickened breath. • Shut down of non-essential body functions.	• Do something. • Increase aggressiveness. • Physical or verbal outburst.
SADNESS • Grief • Melancholy • Dejection • Sorrow • Gloom • Despair • Loneliness • Depression	• **Grief**—A loss of something or someone valued. • **Loneliness**—Perception of disconnection with others or self.	• Slowing down. • Lethargy, apathy. • Reduced appetite	• Release. • Rest. • Reflect
DISGUST • Contempt • Abhorrence • Distaste • Disdain • Aversion • Revulsion • Scorn • Disappointment	• **Disgust**—Offense to taste or moral sense. • **Disappointment**—Unfulfilled expectations. • **Depression**—Dejection. Helplessness & Hopelessness.	• Gag reflex. • Closing off of senses.	• Limit exposure to stimulus. • Push away.
SHAME • Guilt • Embarrassment • Contrition • Chagrin • Humiliation • Remorse • Regret • Mortification	• **Embarrassment**—Social situation causing self-conscious distress. • **Shame**—Breaking norms of one's culture.	• Blushing. • Lowering of head and gaze.	• Hide/Become invisible. • Not be seen.
BOREDOM • Boredom • Ennui • Complacency	• Lack of Challenge. • Lack of Stimulation.	• Yawning. • Slowing down of system	• Sleep. • Seek stimuli.

TRIGGERS & REACTIONS
THRIVE EMOTIONS

EMOTION	TRIGGER	BODILY REACTION	ACTION IMPULSE
SURPRISE • Wonder • Amazement • Astonishment	• Unexpected Positive Event.	• Eye-widening. • Increased adrenaline	• Grin • Scream in delight
EAGERNESS • Eagerness • Anticipation • Excitement	• Anticipation of Positive experience. • Future opportunities. • Positive futures identified.	Increased adrenaline and dopamine	• Get started. Go after positive stimulus
HOPEFULNESS & OPTIMISM • Hopefulness • Optimism • Anticipation • Confidence • Pride	• Belief in Positive Future. • Belief in oneself. • Belief in one's influence over life events. • Potential for positive Future.	Increased serotonin	• Smile. • Proceed ahead.
CURIOSITY • Curiosity • Interest • Fascination	• Interesting and/or Complex Circumstances. • Interesting and/or Complex People • Interesting and/or Complex Problems	Increased sensitivity to stimuli	• Explore. • Investigate.
CONTENTMENT • Contentment • Satisfaction • Fulfillment	• Fulfilled expectations. • Appreciation for current state of things. • Satisfaction with the Present.	Slowing down of system	• Relax. • Take in surroundings.
ENJOYMENT & PLEASURE • Relief • Amusement • Happiness • Delight • Contentment • Joy • Thrill • Mania • Rapture • Ecstasy	• Doing things that you like. • Doing Pleasant activities. • Having Pleasant reflections. • Doing Relaxing things. • Doing Entertaining things. • Doing things with friends and/or family. • Doing Challenging things.	Increased dopamine	• Activate. • Approach and pursue.
HAPPINESS • Happiness • Elation • Joy • Gladness • Love • Affection • Gratitude • Compassion	• Satisfaction with *past* experience. • Pleasant *current* experience. • Anticipation of positive *future* experience. • Meaning and Fulfillment.	Increased norepinephrine	• Approach. • Get closer to positive stimulus.

SELF-AWARENESS

TRIGGERS & REACTIONS WORKSHEET

Emotions help us navigate a complex world. Describing an emotional state involves articulating its triggers, action impulses, and bodily reactions. A *trigger* is an aspect of experience such as an event or an interaction that elicits an emotional response. An emotion's *action impulse* is the urge to react in a certain way when that emotion is present. The *bodily reaction* serves the action impulse, readying the body for a particular action.

Use this worksheet in conjunction with the *Triggers and Reactions Chart* to identify causes and consequences of emotions.

1. EMOTION. What is the emotion?

"I am having the emotion of ___frustration___."

Intensity: Rate the intensity level of the emotion (1-10, with 10 being an intolerable level of the emotion):

1   2   3   **(4)**   5   6   7   8   9   10

Location: Identify the location in your body where you are feeling the emotion.

___head, arms, abdomen___

2. TRIGGER. What could be the trigger for this emotion?

Emotion Equation. What is the emotion equation (i.e., type of variables that trigger the emotion) for this emotion? (e.g., Loss, Anticipated pleasure, imminent threat, etc.).

___I've been putting in so much time, energy and effort in this project, yet I see no results___

My Specific Trigger. What is the *specific trigger* in this situation? (See the *Emotions & Triggers Checklist*).

___effort + lack of success___

3. ACTION IMPULSE. What action does the emotion tell me to do?

To Approach. Am I being moved to *approach pleasure*, to get more out of something? (Try Harder, Get closer, Connect). What is the action impulse?

_____
_____

To Avoid. Am I being moved to *avoid pain*, to get less out of something? (Fight, Flee, Give Up). What is the action impulse?

_____Give up_____
_____
_____

4. BODILY REACTIONS. What are the bodily reactions that I am having?

Feelings. How does the emotion make my body feel?

_____stressed_____
_____

Body State. What is my body state? (e.g., tense, heavy, lethargic, energized, light)?

_____tense_____
_____

Verbal & Non-Verbal Clues. What are my non-verbal and verbal expressions of the emotion? (Vocal tone, cadence, body language, facial expressions, emotionally-charged language or word choice, punctuation).

_____
_____
_____

5. DIRECTION. What does the emotion tell me about what I want or do not want in this situation?

Want. I want...

_____
_____

Don't Want. I don't want...

_____
_____

TRIGGERS & REACTIONS TRACKING LOG

DAY	**APPLICATION** Which emotion did I observe? What was the trigger for the emotion? What was the bodily reaction? What was the action impulse?	**IMPACT** What was the impact of identifying triggers & responses on me and my response to the situation?
Day 1		
Day 2		
Day 3		
Day 4		

TRIGGERS & REACTIONS TRACKING LOG

DAY	**APPLICATION** Which emotion did I observe? What was the trigger for the emotion? What was the bodily reaction? What was the action impulse?	**IMPACT** What was the impact of identifying triggers & responses on me and my response to the situation?
Day 5		
Day 6		
Day 7		

INSIGHTS - What patterns or benefits emerged?

_____
_____
_____
_____
_____
_____

COACHING GUIDELINES

Use the self-coaching process and coaching tools to create long-term change. For maximum effectiveness, focus on one skill at a time. For each skill, take an *assessment* if one is available, complete a *coaching worksheet*, practice high road and low road techniques, and track your application of the skill over a seven day period using a *Tracking Log*.

Select one skill. Consider which skill would make the greatest difference in your current life circumstances if you used it more frequently and effectively. It is easier to build new habits if you focus on one change at a time. Select the *one skill* in this chapter that is your highest priority:

- Monitor Thoughts & Beliefs
- Understand Emotions
- Observe Bodily Sensations
- Detect Emotions
- Identify Triggers and Reactions

STEP 1. ASSESS. Assess the need and benefits of practicing this particular skill. Assess your current mastery level of the skill. Use one of the on-line assessment tools if one is available for the skill. The Coaching Worksheet will also help you assess your need and benefits of using the skill.

Assessments—Questionnaires that assess your current skill level and provide data on your progress.

STEP 2. PLAN. To create an action plan, understand how a technique can help you build greater mastery of a skill. Next, consider how you can apply it to your own situations.

Coaching Worksheets—Tools for learning and creating an action plan for practicing the techniques.
- Identifying Interpretations Worksheet
- Journaling Worksheet
- Thought Labeling Worksheet
- The Effect of Emotions Worksheet
- Detect Emotions Worksheet
- Trigger & Reactions Worksheet

STEP 3. PRACTICE. During the following seven days, apply the skill daily. Use both the High Road techniques and the Low Road techniques to practice the skill.

Tracking Logs—Habit forming tools to guide your efforts as you practice the techniques for seven days.

- Identifying Interpretations Tracking Log
- Thought Labeling Tracking Log
- The Effect of Emotions Tracking Log
- Body Scan Meditation Tracking Log
- Trigger & Reactions Tracking Log

Meditation Guides—Low Road techniques to build the skill at the emotional or non-verbal level.

- Body Scan Meditation

STEP 4. TRACK RESULTS. In addition to systematically helping you to practice the techniques, *Tracking Logs* provide a place to note the impact of the skill on your experience. Tracking Logs help you become more aware of behaviors and patterns in yourself. They are a source of feedback so you can modify a technique to make it more effective.

SELF MANAGEMENT

"The ancestor of every action is a thought."

- Ralph Waldo Emerson

SELF-MANAGEMENT

Have the courage to change what you can, the serenity to accept what you can't, and the wisdom to know the difference. –Reinhold Niebuhr, "Serenity Prayer"

Self-Management is the ability to mindfully respond to circumstances with awareness, intention, and conscious choice. Individuals differ in their ability to manage their response. Like other skills, mastery of the skills involved in Self-Management can be learned and strengthened regardless of current mastery level.

OUTLINE

Introduction

SECTION ONE: MANAGE THOUGHTS

Skill 6: **CHALLENGE THOUGHTS**
Challenge Thoughts, Perceptions, and Beliefs
3 C's Technique
3 C's Worksheet & Tracking Log

Skill 7: **DISENGAGE FROM THOUGHTS**
How to Disengage from Thoughts
When to Disengage from Thoughts
Techniques for Disengaging from Thoughts
Disengage from Thoughts Worksheet & Tracking Log
Leaves in a Stream Meditation & Tracking Log

SECTION TWO: MANAGE EMOTIONS

Skill 8: **NEUTRALIZE EMOTIONS**
How to Neutralize Emotions
Feel into the Emotion
Feel into Your Emotions Meditation & Tracking Log

Skill 9: **PROCESS EMOTIONS**
How to Process Emotions—Take a S.E.A.T.
Take a S.E.A.T. Worksheet
Take a S.E.A.T. Meditation
Take a S.E.A.T. Tracking Log

Skill 10: **SELF COMPASSION**
Four Steps to Self Compassion
Self-Compassion Worksheet & Tracking Log
Self-Compassion Meditation & Tracking Log

Skill 11: **REDIRECT EFFORT**
Techniques for Redirecting Effort
Redirect Effort Worksheet & Tracking Log

Coaching Guidelines

INTRODUCTION

"Between a stimulus and a response is a space. In that space is our power to choose our response. In our response, lies our growth and our freedom." –Viktor Frankl

The objective of Self-Management skills is to regain clarity of mind and access to your internal wisdom so that you can redirect efforts effectively and efficiently toward your goals, values, or whatever is meaningful to you in a moment. The focus is on diminishing the interference of pains and problems so that you are free to re-engage with what's important to you and live life to your fullest.

HOW TO BUILD SELF-MANAGEMENT—Cultivate Mindfulness

The essential ability in Self-Management is the capacity to consciously choose a wise response. In other words, Self-Management requires moving from automatic, unconscious reaction to thoughtful, intentional response. The problem is that often we go on automatic pilot reacting without thinking about the causes and consequences of our actions. While this is common, it is highly ineffective. Wisdom is best accessed from a mindful state. When mindful, we expand that space between the stimulus and response that Frankl points to. When in a mindful state, we are centered and have clarity of mind, thereby promoting a conscious, intentional choice. Mindfulness is an essential factor in Self-Management and emotional intelligence in general. The techniques are designed to increase mindful thinking so that you can choose a wise response no matter what you face.

MODERN ENVIRONMENT, PRIMITIVE CIRCUITRY

Survival is essential—Thriving is optional.

The greatest challenge to effective Self-Management is our millions of years of evolution that have shaped our brains to be overly negative, reactive, and mindless.

Primitive Neural Circuitry. In our evolutionary past, the demands on the emotional system were simpler—as a species we wanted to survive, to pass on our genes, and to not get killed. The drive to thrive was secondary to the drive to survive. Now we not only want to survive, but we also want to thrive in a vast number of ways. From our primitive neural circuitry's perspective, we were not designed to pursue a life filled with joy, happiness, and contentment. For a system designed primarily to meet the species' survival needs, this is a lot to ask for. This is why need to put so much effort toward managing our emotional and mental systems.

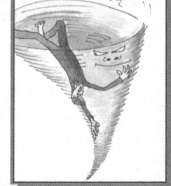

Amygdala Hijack—Act First, Think Later. When a threat is perceived, brain mobilizes to fight or flee. To do this, slow, higher order thinking shuts down in favor of quick, impulsive reactivity, which is far more useful when facing sudden life threats. This is what we refer to as "amygdala hijacking". In this state, the mind and body go into emotional reactivity, often characterized by impulsivity, highly focused and narrow thinking, and hyperawareness to change. The arousal in the mind and body during an emotional hijack is useful when one must fight off a threat to survival. This primitive reaction limits rational evaluation and response.

Think First, Act Later—The More Effective, Measured Response. Cooling down the amygdala and its emotional circuitry re-engages the higher brain systems like the prefrontal cortex, which is associated with problem-solving, analytical reasoning, perspective taking, and planning. Thus, when emotions spike and overwhelm or distort logical thinking, most of us would benefit from pausing, stepping back from the situation, and managing internal states. This fosters a more thoughtful and intentional response rather than impulsive reaction.

Success in Modern Environments. In the typically safer, more abundant environment that most of us have the privilege of enjoying today in many developed nations, that precautionary system is overly sensitive and overly reactive. In states of heightened negative emotion, creative problem-solving ability actually shuts down. Positive emotions promote moderate risk taking in contrast to negative emotions that promote seeking the shelter of extreme safety. According to Rick Hanson, author of *Buddha's Brain*, our primitive neural circuitry is highly adaptive at keeping us alive long enough to pass on genes, but it is a lousy system for happiness and contentment. The negativity bias is less well-suited for goals such as success, peace, and prosperity. Success, prosperity, and sustainable happiness require cooperation and collaboration rather than independence and zero-sum competition. Thriving is in the domain of positive emotions.

Positivity Provides Balance. The powerful pull of problems and pains explains why we need to bring intentional positivity to life circumstances. Typically, this will result in a more balanced perspective.

WHEN TO USE THESE SKILLS—The Presence of Both Distress and Interference

Distress and interference when present together, signal the need for Self-Management. If only one of these factors is present, it may not be necessary. Sometimes distress, while uncomfortable, is inevitable and even necessary. For example, in times of difficulty such as grieving the loss of a loved one, distress is an integral part of the experience. Sometimes there can be interference without distress. Thoughts and emotions may interfere with goals, but there may not be distress about it. We can imagine times when this is appropriate. For example, you may consciously choose to serve one value while compromising another competing and opposing value. If both distress and interference are present, then unnecessary problems likely could be mitigated with skillful attention and effort.

SECTION I. MANAGE THOUGHTS

In Ellen Langer's terms, we easily slip into mindlessness, which is characterized by a lack of awareness, limited perspective, judgment, and rigid thinking. Even for the most conscientious, we can easily fail to realize other ways of thinking about a situation, or become limited by our own perspective of a situation or others. Many stress management and resilience approaches hinge on this ability to reframe a situation.

When you feel distress and internal interference, an essential skill is managing thoughts. Perhaps you feel stressed, feel challenged by adversity, want to be more effective, innovate, or simply relate more objectively to reality. A measured, thoughtful response rather than automatic reactivity becomes more accessible as a result of managing thoughts.

There are two crucial and complimentary strategies for managing thoughts. The first is to challenge the accuracy of the thoughts or beliefs. This involves analyzing the content of the thought and evaluating the degree to which reality supports this thought. The second, which is an opposite strategy, is to disengage from the content of the thought. In this approach, it does not matter what the content is. If the thought is deemed unhelpful, thoughts are treated simply as mind chatter. There is an indifference to the content of the thought. It is simply a meaningless mind event. Both take into account the usefulness of the thought or belief.

THREE SIGNS OF PROBLEMATIC THINKING—Bias, Certainty, & Rumination

Unconscious Bias. The mind has the exquisite ability to make snap judgments. These unconscious determinations provide survival data on what's good or bad, what's safe or unsafe, who is a friend or a threat. Essentially, monitoring the environment for threats, the mind serves its primary evolutionary imperative, "Don't get killed...don't get killed...don't get killed..." These interpretations favor survival function over accuracy. Therefore, perceptions and interpretations are biased toward the threat detection and management. Most of our biases are skewed negative. Psychologists refer to this as the Negativity Bias.

Negativity Bias—Wired to Look for Threats to Well-Being. The emotional circuitry in the brain developed early in human evolution, when ancient ancestors faced predators and other life-or-death threats. It is more advantageous when, as a species that is prey rather than a predator, living in hostile, uncertain environments to have a threat detection system that is more prone to make false positive rather than false negative errors. This is what defines the Negativity Bias.

Numerous laboratory and naturalistic studies show that we detect threat signals much more quickly and accurately than safety signals. Ancestors who assumed the noise in the bush was just the wind did not survive; ancestors who assumed the noise was a saber-tooth tiger fled to safety. Better to be safe than sorry.

No matter how evolved we see ourselves, studies show that we are prone to three errors, referred to as the Negativity Bias:
- Overestimate threats
- Underestimate resources
- Underestimate opportunities

Naturally, this negativity bias continues even in safer environments where collaboration, cooperation, and slower, measured responses are more advantageous. Like a magnet pulling metal filings, problems capture our attention and imagination. Biases are like filters through which we interpret and develop understanding of situations. Information gets filtered through our mindsets, beliefs, expectations, and assumptions

MENTAL BIAS

The problem is that biased, narrow, rigid thinking and having unconscious biases typically lead to errors in understanding, because they arbitrarily filter details of a situation, magnifying portions and discounting others, independent of objective importance. For example, when looking through a biased mindset or assumption, misinterpreting another's intentions, words, or actions is likely. Becoming aware of common biases can diminish this effect. It is like taking off a lens that distorts reality.

MENTAL BIASES

1. CATASTROPHIZING
- Making a problem much bigger than it actually is.
- Exaggerating the importance of an occurrence.

Example: A mistake is blown out of proportion, thinking that it has ruined all hopes of success in life.

2. "ALL OR NOTHING" THINKING
- Seeing things in black and white categories.
- **Example:** If performance falls short of perfect, you see yourself as a total failure.

3. SHOULD STATEMENTS
- Thinking that there is a right and a wrong way of doing things, not paying attention to fact that we select certain criteria and disregard others when evaluating a situation.
- "Musts," "should's" and "oughts" signal the presence of this rigid mindset. The problem is that this bias fails to take into account all the relevant facts, causes, and complexity of situations.

Example: "I should have been able to perform better in that meeting." (i.e., perhaps he wished to have performed better, but it was not realistic given his lack of preparation. Therefore, more accurate would be to state that he *should not* have performed better, although he *wanted* to perform well).

4. "PSYCHIC" CONCLUSIONS

Making negative interpretations and conclusion even though there is an absence of evidence.
- **Mind Reading:** Assuming you know what another is thinking without inquiry or considering direct evidence.
- **Fortune Teller Error**: Assuming you know how the future will unfold, as if it were inevitable, a forgone conclusion. Treating the future as *fait accompli*.

5. OVERGENERALIZATION
- Seeing a single negative event as representative of universal patterns.

Example: One failure is evidence of a never-ending pattern of defeat.

6. SELF-FULFILLING PROPHECY
- Expecting the future to be a certain way. The problem is that expectations direct attention, distort interpretations, and shape behavior. In that way, expectations become self-fulfilling and limit possibilities.

The Problem with Certainty. The problem is that we often fail to realize our perception and interpretation may be skewed. We fail to recognize that there could be multiple interpretations for any given fact or event. As illustrated with the Information Processing Chain, the interpretation influences the other downstream steps, namely which emotion is triggered, which influences the plan and/or action. If the interpretation is negative, then a negative emotion ensues. If positive, then a positive emotion is triggered. We tend to latch onto one or two interpretations without appreciating that these represent a small sample among the population of logical interpretations. Moreover, once we attach to an interpretation we rarely stop to challenge that interpretation. We tend to relate to thoughts as facts rather than as interpretations.

Certainty leads to mindlessness. When we feel certain about something, we stop being interested and inquiring. We lose motivation to notice new developments, changes, or potential. Being certain can be useful in some instances, for example feeling certain about your personal values. More often, however, certainty is problematic and even dangerous. For example, when the stoplight turns green, should you be absolutely certain that it is safe to proceed into the intersection? Clearly, it is wiser to glance both ways to make sure there is no car or pedestrian running the light.

"The more we know, the more blind we become." –Ellen Langer

In complex situations or changing circumstances, the value of maintaining some uncertainty becomes particularly apparent. While you may feel certain that you want to stay married to your spouse for the rest of your life, is it wise to feel certain that it will *just happen*? Clearly, bringing a healthy amount of uncertainty to relationships is wise, because, it motivates us to invest and remain aware that relationships evolve and require effort, intention, and commitment to growth. Research on marriages suggests, for example, that partners who stop being curious about their spouse often become less emotionally connected. Understanding that we naturally fall into inattention, mental passivity, and mindlessness can help us intentionally maintain a more active quality to our attention.

Rumination—Problems stuck in the spin cycle of the mind. *Rumination* is characterized by a person's repetitive thought focus on a negative event, feeling, or belief. It is like a negative line of thinking stuck in a spin cycle of the mind, just like a washing machine spinning clothes.

When ruminating we remain fixated on the problems and on feelings about them without taking action. Rumination is being stuck in a rut. It is associated with poor coping and problems such as pessimism, neediness, hopelessness, self-criticism, and depression. Moreover, other people tend to respond negatively to people when they are ruminating, which often makes the ruminating person feel even worse about themselves and their situation.

The good news is that mindfulness techniques and challenging one's mind can be effective ways to break out of the rumination rut. Mindfulness meditation and thought disengaging techniques provide an experiential realization that thoughts are separate from self, that they are something the mind "does" but they need not define us or our experience. Thought challenging techniques also assist in separating an individual from their thoughts, challenge the validity of those thoughts, and lead to change in focus.

RESEARCH—RUMINATION

Poor problem solving. Rumination does not lead to active problem solving to change circumstances surrounding these symptoms. Instead, people who are ruminating remain fixated on the problems and on their feelings about them without taking action, according to Nolen-Hoeksema, Wisco, and Lyubomirsky (2008). Rumination is correlated with a variety of maladaptive cognitive styles, including negative inferential or attributional styles, dysfunctional attitudes, hopelessness, pessimism, self-criticism, low mastery, dependency, sociotropy, neediness, and neuroticism, as shown by Lyubomirsky and Nolen-Hoeksema, (1995).

SKILL 6. CHALLENGE THOUGHTS

"The only thing I know is to question every thought I believe until every thought ends in a question mark." –Byron Katie

THE OBJECTIVE OF CHALLENGING THOUGHTS

Challenging thoughts is necessary mainly because we all are prone to mindlessness. We fall into rigid mindsets and fail to question or notice changes and subtleties in our environment. A common way this manifests is through unconscious biases. Biases hamper the accuracy and distort reality. They cause us to lose touch with reality and live in a "virtual reality" that we've created in our minds. The problem is that we fail to notice biases and carry on believing we are accurate, logical, and objective.

BENEFITS OF THOUGHT CHALLENGING

Challenging thoughts and beliefs before acting can increase the ability to navigate a situation well. Challenging perspective and beliefs before acting is important, because we all are prone to narrow thinking or biased perspectives. Challenging thoughts is one way to get more accurate and objective in a situation. It results in clarity of mind, better problem solving, and the ability to self-correct problematic reactions.

These benefits emerge, because challenging thoughts lessens unconscious biases, improves objectivity, diminishes assumptions, and inaccurate forgone conclusions. Implicit biases and mindsets lead to inaccurate understanding and limit possibility for effective action. One step in challenging thoughts is to become aware of common biases. Biases signal the presence of distorted thinking, alerting the need to challenge thoughts.

THREE C'S TECHNIQUE

The Three C's Technique is a systematic way to challenge thoughts and widen perspective. This approach can help improve accurate understanding of situations and ability to respond effectively to difficult situations. This technique is adapted from the book *Peaceful Mind* by McQuaid and Carmona.

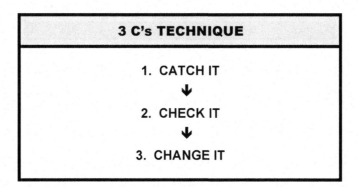

1. CATCH IT: Catch the distressing thought or belief.

• Notice the presence of distressing emotions and list them. These emotions can provide cues for the presence of negative thoughts and clues about interpretations of situations.

• Identify the thought or belief. If this belief is an example of a mental bias, identify which type.

2. CHECK IT: Check how true and useful the thought or belief is.

Look for direct evidence contrary to your thought or indirect evidence like prior history and other similar situations. You also might consider alternative interpretations. Considering completely different interpretations is particularly important in situations for which there is little evidence and much uncertainty. This step pulls on logical thinking and analysis.

Absolute Truth. Objectively, how true is this belief? How do you know this belief is absolutely true?

- What evidence do you have in support of this belief?
- What is the evidence that you have against this belief?
- If accuracy is difficult to determine, what are possible alternative explanations?

Usefulness.

- How useful is this belief?
- What would you do if you didn't have this belief?

3. CHANGE IT: Change the thought or belief to be more consistent with the evidence you gathered.

This is not simply changing it to be more positive. It is changing it to be *more logical* and likely to be more accurate, even if you do not *feel* like it is true or cannot conclude absolute truth.

- Combine the evidence and the possibility of alternative explanations. What is a more balanced belief?
- What can you do right now to take a step in a positive direction?

3C'S WORKSHEET

Catch It, Check It, Change It—Unlock mindsets of possibility.

Challenging negative thoughts in a systematic way can significantly reduce stress in the short term as well as long-term. It is important in the ability to overcome emotional challenges. The purpose of this exercise is to challenge your thoughts relating to an emotional situation. This situation could involve problems with coworkers, disagreements with your children, conflict in your relationships, difficulty dealing with your extended family, worry over your finances, problems with your health, etc.

SITUATION

YOUR SITUATION: Identify the "Who, What, and Where's" of the situation.

_____

_____

_____

_____

1. CATCH IT

Emotions. Notice the presence of distressing emotions. List the emotions:

_____

_____

Belief. What is the belief that triggered these emotions?

_____

_____

_____

_____

_____

2. CHECK IT

ABSOLUTE TRUTH. Objectively, how true is this belief? How do I know this belief is absolutely, positively true?

_____

_____

_____

_____

Evidence in Support. What evidence do I have in support of this belief?

_____

_____

_____

Evidence Against. What is the evidence that I have against this belief?

_____
_____
_____

Alternatives. What are possible alternative explanations?

_____
_____
_____

USEFULNESS. How useful is this belief? How would I act differently if I didn't have this belief?

_____
_____
_____
_____

3. CHANGE IT

More Balanced Belief. Given the evidence and/or the possibility of alternative explanations, what is a more balanced belief? If it doesn't check out, change the belief to be truer and more useful.

_____
_____
_____
_____

Small Step. What can I do today to take one small step in a positive direction?

_____
_____
_____
_____
_____

THREE C'S TRACKING LOG

SITUATION ONE (When, Where, Who, What?)

1. CATCH IT

DISTRESSING THOUGHT OR BELIEF	EMOTIONS & INTENSITY (scale 1-10)

2. CHECK IT

HOW TRUE IS IT?	
Evidence For	**Evidence Against**

HOW USEFUL IS IT? HOW WOULD I ACT DIFFERENTLY WITHOUT THIS BELIEF?

3. CHANGE IT

BALANCED AND/OR ALTERNATIVE BELIEF

THREE C'S TRACKING LOG

SITUATION TWO (When, Where, Who, What?)

1. CATCH IT

DISTRESSING THOUGHT OR BELIEF	EMOTIONS & INTENSITY (scale 1-10)

2. CHECK IT

HOW TRUE IS IT?	
Evidence For	Evidence Against

HOW USEFUL IS IT? HOW WOULD I ACT DIFFERENTLY WITHOUT THIS BELIEF?

3. CHANGE IT

BALANCED AND/OR ALTERNATIVE BELIEF

SKILL 7. DISENGAGE FROM THOUGHTS

The thought manifests as the word. The word manifests as the deed. Deeds develop into habits. And habits harden into character. So watch the thoughts and its way with care. And let it spring from love, born out of concern for all beings. –The XVI Dalai Lama

Disengaging from Thoughts refers to taking a step back from thoughts and observing them from a third party perspective. This approach is useful, because sometimes challenging thoughts is not enough. At times, thoughts that are not believed still persist. In this case, skillful Self-Management might be stepping away from thinking rather than diving into the tangle of thinking. This counterintuitive approach focuses on relating to thoughts differently. Usually we get caught in thoughts and don't pause to realize that we can watch thoughts rather than be caught in a flow of thinking. The mind constantly generates words, making predictions, drawing conclusions, and creating assumptions. No matter how hard we try, we cannot will thoughts to stop. In this approach, we don't try. Instead, we just step away from the content of thoughts and simply watch the mind do its thinking.

Have you ever considered the possibility that thoughts could be considered mind events? Just like a bird flying by is an event, so is a thought passing through the mind. In this approach, the content of the message is disregarded, because it is deemed habitual, conditioned, and not useful or important. This strategy is not intuitive for most people, yet it can be helpful to relate simply to the fact that there is a thought rather than analyzing or getting caught in the message of the thought.

For example, a negative, unhelpful thought appears:

"Although I prepared thoroughly, I will fail at this presentation. I'm not good enough for this job."

You skillfully disengage from the thought:

"This is just a thought, a mental event. This thought is getting in my way and will just make things worse."

Thoughts can be like pesky flies buzzing around your head that won't leave you alone. Or, they might feel like old messages stuck on replay looping over and again. For others it might feel like the mind is stuck on a "bad news" radio station, constantly hailing worse case scenarios and other catastrophes throughout the day. Some thoughts or implicit core beliefs replay overtime, even throughout life.

OBJECTIVE OF DISENGAGING

The objective is to disengage from thought content so that you can re-engage with more constructive aspects of experience. If you are problem solving well or if your thoughts are enjoyable or constructive, then this approach is not necessary. If you are ruminating, distress, and experiencing confusion, then skillfully disengaging can free yourself from their tyranny and increase clarity and calmness of mind. The intention is to diminish the distressing and damaging effect of believing false and unhelpful content so that you can take constructive action.

BENEFITS OF DISENGAGING

Skillfully disengaging from the content of thoughts has the surprising effect of improving clarity, widening perspective, and diminishing the effect of negative self-talk. It helps us not take the content so seriously. This results in decreased emotional reasoning and rumination, while perspective is improved. Ultimately, this leads to improved problem-solving and/or can make a situation feel more bearable even if unchangeable.

HOW TO DISENGAGE FROM THOUGHTS

Free yourself from the tyranny of thought.

This counterintuitive method is characterized by simply observing thoughts without believing the content of the thoughts or reacting to them. It is allowing them to just be, not to control them, and not feel threatened as a result of them, regardless of the message. Instead, it is regarding them as simply mind chatter. This enables one to cultivate an indifference to counterproductive thought content. This internal action is simply observing them as insignificant mind events and gently turning attention away from counterproductive thoughts. This frees you to turn toward constructive thoughts and action. This approach allows the stream of thinking without believing the content of the thoughts. This is not suppressing thoughts but instead being nonreactive to whatever content the mind generates.

Disengaging from thoughts requires an attitude of indifference, acceptance, and understanding the nature of the thinking mind. In this approach, thoughts do not need to be changed or go away. Simply, they are not reacted to no matter what the mind comes up with. Thoughts are related to simply as neutral mind chatter, mental events that are of no significance. No matter how dire the mind tells you something is, because you've already deemed it unhelpful, you bring an attitude of indifference and non-reactivity to the content of the mind.

BEWARE OF SUPPRESSION

That which you resist persists.

There is a subtle but important distinction between disengaging from thoughts and suppressing thoughts. This distinction is essential to understand, because disengaging from thoughts allows them to pass, but suppressing thoughts causes them to rebound. Suppression is trying not to have a thought. Research clearly demonstrates that the more a thought is suppressed, the more resistant that thought is to change.

David Schneider, professor of psychology, first demonstrated this paradoxical effect of thought suppression in a study in the 1980's at the University of Texas. Researchers instructed participants to "not think of a white bear" and then assessed how frequently they had the thought of a white bear. They found that the more participants tried to not think of a white bear the more they did. Studies of self-control strategies such as the "white bear study" show that trying not to think about something causes a rebound effect.

Try the experiment yourself. See if you can follow these instructions. If an image comes to mind you have experienced the difficulty in suppressing thoughts:

Don't think of a white bear.

Don't think of a yellow jeep.

Don't think of chocolate cake.

Examples of Attempts to Suppress Thoughts:

- "I need to think positively."
- "I shouldn't be so pessimistic."
- "I just need to get over it."

Affirmations. Affirmations can be helpful when used as reminders, but in practice, they are often thought suppression strategies and therefore cause rebound effects.

WHEN TO DISENGAGE FROM THOUGHTS

Stepping away from your thoughts is particularly useful in highly charged situations or after you have challenged your thoughts but they still have a hold on you. When you feel stuck, your mind has a frenetic quality, you are overwhelmed, or lack clear thinking, it is probably time to step back from your thoughts.

First, it may be useful to do some fact checking to determine the importance of thoughts. If thoughts emerge from new observations, add to understanding, or inform you of something you need to pay attention, you should probably spend time with your thoughts. In contrast, if they are not adding new information and are just getting in your way, turn away from them.

Consider disregarding thoughts when:

- You are ruminating.
- You are not problem-solving.
- Thoughts feel old, familiar, and lifeless.
- You are lost in unproductive and distressing thoughts and the external world disappears.
- Your mind is filled with criticism or "doom and gloom" thoughts.
- Your mind is foggy and confused.
- You have racing thoughts or a frenetic, busy mind.
- Your self-talk is judgmental or critical.

Self-Judgment. Self-judgment and self-criticism are often veiled attempts at suppressing negative thinking. They escalate and cause a rebound of negative thinking. It is common to become critical when we realize that we are having negative thoughts or falling into a rumination cycle. This attempt to diminish the negative thoughts simply adds to the negative thoughts. We become critical of ourselves that we are being critical of ourselves. This creates a "dog piling" effect of self-judgment.

For example:

"I can't believe I am still worrying about this. Come on, just get over it!"

"Here I go again, caught in negative thinking. Why can't I just clear my mind."

"I shouldn't be so self-critical."

TECHNIQUES FOR DISENGAGING FROM THOUGHTS

TECHNIQUES FOR DISENGAGING FROM THOUGHTS
1. EXPECT THOUGHTS
2. THANK YOUR MIND FOR THE THOUGHT
3. WORRY AS HARD AS YOU CAN
4. WATCH THOUGHTS

Technique #1. EXPECT THOUGHTS—List Reoccurring Thoughts and Evaluate Usefulness.

Because the mind is a "word chatter machine", you can relate to negative thoughts not as "threats" or facts but as mere habits of mind. Expect negative, reoccurring thoughts to arise. When they are predictable, they do not surprise and you can preemptively develop a plan to relate to them differently.

First, identify which negative thoughts tend to reoccur. Make a list of these negative thoughts.

Second, evaluate their usefulness. Are they workable? Ask yourself what effect they have. Do they help you deal more effectively with situations? Do they undermine your effectiveness? Do they bring you down, make you feel defeated, pessimistic, or disempowered? If their impact negative, they are not useful.

For example:

Identify: *"I am having the thought that I will fail at this presentation."*

Usefulness: *"This thought just makes me more anxious. This thought is getting in my way. It will just make things worse. This is not useful to me."*

Third, welcome them and even count the number of times they have shown up that day. Invite them to come in and take a seat as if they were old, familiar friends you were expecting.

Fourth, turn your attention to what will bring you in a productive or positive direction.

For example:

"Hello, Fear of Failure thought #62, come on in! I've been expecting you! You are one of my 50,000 thoughts and I see you almost daily. You are a regular visitor. I don't need you any more. But, I know you are here and that's okay, so come in and take a seat. You and your grimy little friends are welcome. I know you well. I am not afraid of you."

Technique #2. THANK YOUR MIND FOR THE THOUGHT

When a negative, expected thought arises, thank your mind for the thought. Acknowledge that the mind has a job to do, which is to determine cause and effect and warn of danger. The mind is designed with a negativity bias, which evolved as a highly adaptive survival mechanism to keep you safe, to not get killed. This is an important job and negative thoughts are a result of a highly refined ability to be vigilant and focused on threat. After you thank your mind, turn your attention to what will bring you in a productive or positive direction.

For example:

"Thank you, mind, for that thought. You are just doing your job, keeping me safe. Now I'm going to get back to the task at hand."

Technique #3. WORRY AS HARD AS YOU CAN

This counterintuitive technique involves exaggerating and amplifying the mind's tendency to worry. For a few minutes or less, intentionally imagine worse case scenario, intensify the worry, and scroll through unwanted outcomes. It is like playing "reverse psychology" on the mind. By exaggerating this tendency, often the worry loses strength. In a sense, wears out the power of the thoughts. There can be a tendency to avoid or try to get away from them, but like the adage says, "If you can't have it, you've got it." This technique counters that tendency. Insights or realizations sometimes arise especially related to the usefulness of negative thinking.

Technique #4. WATCH THOUGHTS

In your mind's eye, imagine sitting on the bank of a stream. In great detail see the stream and imagine leaves floating downstream. Next, place any thought that comes to mind on a leaf. Continue watching your thoughts as leaves passing by on a stream. Simply watch whatever comes into the mind. See the words and phrases, put them on a leaf, and watch the thoughts float downstream. The next thought that comes to mind, put that thought on a leaf. No matter what the content is (e.g., self judgment, judgment of this exercise, or anything else), put the thoughts on a leaf. If you find yourself in the flow of thinking, as if you have jumped into the stream, come back to shore and observe thoughts.

You can also do this as clouds in the sky or other moving scene. Modify to suit yourself. For example, I introduced this technique to client who was born and raised in New York City. Her homework was to practice this technique on her own. At our next meeting, she said it wasn't working for her. She said, "I'm a city girl. I don't like nature. It makes me nervous. Its quietness is unsettling. I decided to not use a stream for imagery. Instead, I imagined standing on a busy street with yellow NYC taxis driving by. I put each thought on the advertisement board on top of each taxi. That worked much better."

Recommended Additional Reading

Get Out of Your Mind & Into Your Life Steven Hayes & Spencer Smith

Enhancing Emotional Intelligence

DISENGAGE FROM THOUGHTS WORKSHEET

The purpose of this exercise is to practice techniques for disengaging from thoughts. Consider a current situation that is causing emotional distress. Perhaps it relates to problems with coworkers, disagreements with your children, conflict in your relationships, difficulty dealing with your extended family, worry over finances, problems with your health, etc.

YOUR SITUATION

SITUATION: Identify the "Who, What, and Where's" of the situation. *What are some of the thoughts that I am having about this situation?*

_____
_____
_____

TECHNIQUES TO DISENGAGE FROM THOUGHTS

TECHNIQUE #1 EXPECT NEGATIVE, REOCCURING THOUGHTS.

Step 1. List negative, reoccurring thoughts.

_____
_____
_____
_____

Step 2. Evaluate the usefulness of each thought. Identify the thoughts that are not workable, where there is nothing to do as a result of them. Consider the impact on effectiveness and wellbeing. *How useful is it?*

_____
_____
_____
_____
_____
_____

Step 3. Welcome the negative thoughts. Hold an indifferent, welcoming attitude towards them. If you wish, count the number of times they show up in a day. In the space below, describe self-talk that would express a welcoming, indifferent attitude toward negative thoughts, regardless of the content.

_____
_____
_____
_____

Step 4. Redirect attention. *What could I turn my attention to that would bring me in a productive or positive direction?*

TECHNIQUE #2. THANK YOUR MIND FOR THE THOUGHT. *What would be my self-talk be if I thanked my mind for this thought?*

TECHNIQUE #3. WORRY AS HARD AS YOU CAN. *What was the impact on my thinking when I tried this technique?*

TECHNIQUE #4. WATCH THOUGHTS—Leaves in a Stream or other manner of observing flow of thinking. In your mind's eye, watch your thoughts by placing them on leaves floating down a stream or on clouds passing through the sky of your mind. *What happens to my state of mind as I did this? Any insights?*

LEAVES IN A STREAM MEDITATION

The *Leaves in a Stream Meditation* practice is a technique for getting distance from thoughts. In this practice, look at your thoughts rather than from your thoughts. Although this practice may sound tedious or overly simplistic, habitually observing thoughts commonly weakens their power. It can be particularly helpful when in an emotional hijack or when chronic thought patterns have a negative effect or undermine presence. The objective is not to think more deeply about the thought, nor to suppress thoughts. The content is inconsequential.

INSTRUCTIONS
(5 to 8 minutes)

1. FOCUS INWARD: Breathe and Center

- **Close Your Eyes**—Close your eyes to better focus your attention inward.

- **Feel Your Breath**—Focus attention by feeling your breath enter and exit your body. Breathe deep into your abdomen. Place your hand on your abdomen to feel your diaphragm rise and fall. Slowly exhale and naturally inhale.

- **Set Your Intention**—To direct your attention in this time, place, and to the objective of this meditation.

2. DIRECT ATTENTION: LEAVES IN A STREAM

- **Visualize**—*Visualize a stream with leaves floating by.* Imagine a slow-moving stream. The water flows over rocks and once in a while a big leaf floats away down the river. Imagine you are sitting beside that stream on a warm sunny day, watching the leaves float by.

- **Observe**—*Observe the leaves as thoughts passing.* Now become conscious of your thoughts. Each time a thought or image pops into your head, place it on a leaf and let it float on by. If you think in words, put them on the leaf as words. If you think in images, put the image on the leaf.

Stay beside the stream and allow the leaves on the stream to keep floating by. No need to try to make the stream go faster or slower, no need to make your thoughts go faster or slower. Just notice the thoughts or images as they arise. As soon as you notice one, just place it on a leaf and watch it float on past you down the river. Watch the leaf float down the stream and out of sight.

If the leaves disappear, if you mentally go somewhere else, or if you find that you are in the stream or on a leaf, just stop and notice that this happened. Gently return your attention to the stream once again, watch a thought come into your mind, place it on a leaf, and let the leaf float away down the stream. Keep doing this for the next few minutes.

3. REFLECT ON INSIGHTS: Breathe and Reflect
- Come back to your breath.
- Reflect on the insights or benefits you gained during this meditation.

4. MAINTAIN YOUR INNER AWARENESS: Soft Gaze and Stay with It
- Slowly open your eyes and keep your gaze soft, directed downward, and settling on a neutral object.
- Stay with the awareness you gained during the meditation.

LEAVES IN A STREAM MEDITATION WORKSHEET

After you have completed the meditation, jot down observations about what came up during your meditation. Make note of thoughts you had, feelings you experienced, bodily sensations you felt, and/or detours that you took.

1. FOCUS INWARD: To what extent could I direct attention and turn my mind when it wandered?

_____
_____

2. DIRECT ATTENTION: Leaves in a Stream. What happened as I watched the leaves on a stream?

_____
_____
_____
_____
_____
_____
_____

3. REFLECT ON INSIGHTS: Breathe and Reflect. What insights or benefits did I gain in the meditation?

_____
_____
_____
_____
_____
_____

4. Personal Application. How and when could I use this practice to manage my internal state?

_____
_____
_____
_____
_____
_____
_____
_____

LEAVES IN A STREAM MEDITATION TRACKING LOG

DAY	APPLICATION What thoughts did I encounter? How did I observe these thoughts?	IMPACT What was the impact on me, others, and/or the situation?
Day 1		
Day 2		
Day 3		
Day 4		

LEAVES IN A STREAM MEDITATION TRACKING LOG

DAY	APPLICATION What thoughts did I encounter? How did I observe these thoughts?	IMPACT What was the impact on me, others, and/or the situation?
Day 5		
Day 6		
Day 7		

INSIGHTS - What patterns or benefits emerged?

_____
_____
_____
_____
_____

SECTION II. MANAGE EMOTIONS

The Guest House

This being human is a guest house. Every morning a new arrival.
A joy, a depression, a meanness, some momentary awareness comes
as an unexpected visitor.

Welcome and entertain them all!
Even if they're a crowd of sorrows,
who violently sweep your house
empty of its furniture,
still, treat each guest honorably.
He may be clearing you out
for some new delight.

The dark thought, the shame, the malice,
meet them at the door laughing,
and invite them in.

Be grateful for whoever comes,
because each has been sent
as a guide from beyond.

-Rumi, translated by Coleman Barks

Self-Management involves forging a healthy relationship with negative emotions. Negative emotions are designed to aid happiness and well-being. To manage negative emotions, we need to process, not fight or force them to go away. Not fighting emotions does not imply being passive, wallowing, or analyzing emotions. The key to influencing emotions is to work with them, not against them.

Expect distress—fear and loss, heartache and sadness, birth and death. They are all part of the deal.

PRIMAL INSTINCTS

Emotions are essentially primal instincts, just like the physical instincts of hunger, sleep, sex, or thirst. An important area of the brain for emotional experience is the limbic system, associated with survival processes in a region some refer to as the "Lizard Brain." This area is highly involved in primitive processes such as hunger and thirst. The "lizard brain" evolved at the time of the reptile stage of evolution. There is no conscious control over these primitive processes. Trying to turn emotions off would be like trying to not experience any other primal instinct like hunger or sleepiness. This would be the equivalent of hoping not to impulsively retract when you accidentally touch something surprisingly disgusting.

In the evolutionary past, members of the species who disregarded emotional messages did not survive. Imagine a prehistoric ancestor who after hearing a rustling behind the bush dismissed the fear, saying, "Don't worry. You are so paranoid about saber-toothed tigers! It's probably just the wind." Those ancestors did not survive.

Consider the modern disease called, "congenital analgesia" in which an individual cannot and has never felt physical pain. This is an extremely dangerous condition. The individuals have no warning system to keep them safe and often fall prey to accidents and bodily injury. This lack of pain awareness often leads to an accumulation of wounds, bruises, broken bones, and other health issues that may go undetected. Life expectancy is tragically reduced.

Emotional pain sensors as well as physical pain sensors are designed to keep us safe. From this perspective, it is unsurprising that this emotional alert system cannot be willfully turned off. Appreciating this crucial function and power behind emotions is the first step to managing them.

EMOTIONAL RESISTANCE

An obstacle to effectively managing emotions is emotional resistance, which is trying not to feel an emotion. Negative emotions, like sadness, frustration, disappointment, anxiety and regret, can feel like enemies to well-being. By design, they are aversive, physically painful, and cause psychological suffering. Pain is the greatest motivator, and emotions are responsible for motivating the actions that keep us alive.

Because they are inherently painful, it may seem life would be better without them. Many people spend their lives desperately trying to avoid negative emotions. Overworking, emotional eating, alcohol use, smoking, and even busyness are common emotional avoidance tactics.

Identifying Emotional Resistance. Emotional resistance can be subtle. The defining characteristic is judgment. Judgment, in this case, is any posture or self-talk that tries to avoid, suppress, or in any way make it bad to have an emotion. Although we may prefer to not have an emotion, refusing to accept the presence of an emotion, making it bad or wrong to feel an emotion, or suppressing an emotion is resistance.

Have you ever been frustrated with the intensity of your emotional reaction and asked yourself, "Why am I reacting so strongly to this? I should be calmer…If only I could be more level headed." This is an example of emotional avoidance, as are statements such as, "Just get over it," "Don't be angry," "Don't worry, be happy," or "Calm down." Judging yourself as bad, weak, or some other critical label are also resistance tactics. These mental tactics are no match for a system that evolved to survive and thrive in a dangerous predator-filled landscape.

Research shows emotional resistance is an ineffective coping strategy. Depression and anxiety worsen with the presence of emotional resistance. Because the evolutionary function of emotions is to keep us safe, until we actually believe we are safe or well, emotions will try to capture attention and ignite action. The more we fight to suppress them, the louder their cries. This is known as the rebound effect.

Resisting emotions makes them stronger—emotions demand to be heard.

There is one exception. Avoiding emotions can work as a short-term strategy to tolerate circumstantial, momentary pain. For example, it is very effective to use distraction to deal with anxiety as a nurse prepares his needle to give a shot or to diminish annoyance while waiting in a long check-out line.

What you resist persists.

Emotional Rebound. Any type of emotional resistance causes emotions to rebound. Just like in a tug-of-war, fighting emotions intensifies the struggle. Many people's approach to dieting is a common example of rebound. How effective is it to focus on *not wanting* to eat that chocolate cake? Generally, the more we tell ourselves that chocolate cake it is a forbidden food, that it is bad to want it, that we shouldn't want it, the more the cake craving grows. Then, when tired, overwhelmed, or other causes of depleted self-discipline, an impulsive binge becomes more likely. Dieting is unsuccessful largely because of this rebound phenomenon.

You can run but you cannot hide.

Like with the cake, trying to alleviate distress by fighting an emotion is a losing battle. To serve their evolutionary imperative, emotions must be heard. Even if it seems you are winning the battle for a while, the emotion will rebound when mental guard is down. It might happen in the quiet of night at 3am, when you are worn out, or when you take a moment to get still.

EMOTIONAL MANAGEMENT

Although resisting emotions is ineffective, this does not imply that one must remain passive allowing emotions to control actions and emotional state. In contrast, active, intentional relating, processing, and conscious turning attention away from emotions are crucial. The distinction between emotional resistance and emotional management can be subtle. Effective emotion management involves working with emotions rather than suppressing, avoiding, or other emotional resistance tactics. In this chapter, several techniques for actively managing emotions are presented.

SKILL 8. NEUTRALIZE EMOTIONS

What is the knocking? What is the knocking at the door in the night?

It is somebody wants to do us harm.

No, no, it is the three strange angels.
Admit them, admit them.
-DH Lawrence

While we can't eliminate or avoid emotions, we can change the quality of an emotional experience. They can become more tolerable, lighter, and less gripping. In a sense, we can neutralize the feeling of an emotion. The purpose of neutralizing emotions is not to make them go away—that is impossible. Instead, the purpose is to make them slightly more tolerable, to allow them to pass naturally and, at times, to receive the wisdom of the emotions. After neutralizing an emotion, you may wish to return to the situation, having the clarity of mind to process it more effectively.

HOW TO NEUTRALIZE EMOTIONS

Because emotions are bodily experiences, we can deal with emotional pain the same way we deal with physical pain. Many research studies have shown that a powerful way to cope with chronic physical pain is to experience the sensations as neutral, ever-changing sensations. When we do this with the sensations associated with emotional pain, we are neutralizing the emotions. This enables greater learning and measured response without impulsively reacting.

There are three steps to neutralizing powerful, negative emotions:

---

3 STEPS TO NEUTRALIZE EMOTIONS

1. Recognize the Changing Nature of Emotions.
2. Feel It as a Neutral Physical Sensation.
3. Experience Without Reacting.

STEP 1. Recognize the Changing Nature of Emotions. Recognize the changing nature of emotions. At a basic level, emotions are mental and body events. Like waves rolling onto shore, emotions come and go. They are events that begin and end in a matter of seconds. They are like energy currents that run through your body. Sometimes they are just ripples and other times mighty waves, and at times like a tsunami. Regardless of their intensity, they pass and another is right behind it. Sometimes the best we can do is ride it out until we get to shallower water. This is especially important to realize during times of overwhelm or emotional fatigue.

Change alone is unchanging. –Heraclitus

This too will pass.
No feeling is final. –Tara Brach

STEP 2. Feel It as a Neutral Physical Sensation. According to researcher Critchley (2009), an emotion is a basic physiological state characterized by predictable bodily changes. There are emotion-specific autonomic response patterns. Feel the physical manifestations of the emotion without judging them as bad or even painful. Experiment with feeling the effects the emotion on your body as neutral sensations. Feel into your emotions by closing your eyes and feeling their effect in your body. Feel the emotion and its flowing through your body, experiencing it with full presence and attention. It is crucial that you do not think or analyze during this step, but instead, to simply feel and observe without describing or analyzing it.

STEP 3. Experience Without Reacting. "E-motions" do just that—they put us in motion. Their job is to alert, motivate, and move us to grab the carrot or duck from the stick—in other words to seek desired experiences or situations and avoid undesirable ones. It goes against our evolutionary instincts to not react to our emotions. While we cannot choose to have or not have an emotion, we can choose to act on it or not. Emotions are informants not dictators. Use emotions as "interesting information" rather than as commands for action.

Psychologists refer to feeling emotions without reacting to them as "emotional nonreactivity." This ability is one of the strongest predictors of who will successfully quit smoking or other addictions. This does not imply that you will not choose to respond in some way, only that you will not impulsively, unconsciously react.

Feel the fear and do it anyway.

MEDITATION: FEEL INTO YOUR EMOTION

This technique is beneficial when emotions are strong and overwhelming or distorting perceptions. It can also be helpful when you want to pause, step back from a situation, and connect with your emotional experience. This enables a formulated, thoughtful, and intentional response rather than an automatic reaction.

Feel into emotions when:

- You determine the emotions are not useful or getting in your way.
- Optimal performance or well-being necessitates a lower level of emotional arousal.
- Distressing emotions are persistent and driving prolonged negative moods.
- You want to connect with your emotional experience.

FEEL INTO EMOTIONS MEDITATION

Often resistance to an emotion maintains it. You may have heard the phrase, "If you can't have it, you've got it." By allowing the sadness or anxiety to just be there, you are not adding secondary emotional reactions to it. Then the emotion can naturally fade away.

Experiment with feeling the effects an emotion has on your body as neutral sensations, noticing only the intensity and characteristics of the sensations. The aim is to feel the emotion flowing throughout your body and experiencing it with full presence, acceptance, and attention.

Choose an emotion that is of moderate distress but not extreme distress. For traumatic or overwhelming emotions this process is not advised without the guidance of a trained therapist. As Rick Hanson says about choosing distressing emotions for meditation, "Make sure that you will be able to swim back from the deep end of the pool." Do not go out so far that you cannot get back on your own. Use your own inner wisdom to decide what to make contact with and how far to feel into a negative experience.

INSTRUCTIONS
(5 to 10 minutes)

1. FOCUS INWARD: Breathe and Center
- **Close your eyes**— Close your eyes to let your attention turn inward.
- **Feel Your Breath**—Focus attention by feeling your breath enter and exit your body. Breathe deeply with a slower exhale and natural inhale. Place your hand on your abdomen to feel your diaphragm rise and fall.
- **Set your Intention**---To direct your attention in this time, place, and to the objective of this meditation.

2. DIRECT ATTENTION: Feel into your emotion.
- **Make contact** with an emotion you currently feel or recently felt. Words or phrases describing a difficult aspect of a situation might help you generate the emotion. Making a facial expression revealing how you feel can help make greater contact with the emotion.

- **Feel bodily sensations**—observe the emotion's effect in your body. Feel where it is located in your body. Notice the nature of this particular emotion's sensations and observe neutrally, objectively. Perhaps the sensation is prickly, warm, pinching; sensations of pressure or contraction.

- **Breathe into the emotion**—inviting it to expand throughout your body, filling every cell in your body, from finger tips to toes. Even if uncomfortable, keep going. Expand it even more. Have courageous presence with the emotion.

- **Experience without judgment**—Experience the emotion like an energy current that run through your body. Feel the physical manifestations of the emotion in your body. Release the judgment of the emotion as bad or good, pleasant or painful. There is no need to ask yourself whether you like or don't like them.

- **Acknowledge the changing nature of emotion**—no feeling is final. This emotion is a body event. Like waves rolling onto shore, emotions come and go. This feeling will pass.

3. REFLECT ON INSIGHTS: Breathe and Reflect
- Come back to your breath.
- Reflect on the insights or benefits you gained during this meditation.

4. MAINTAIN YOUR INNER AWARENESS: Soft Gaze and Stay with It
- Slowly open your eyes and keep your gaze soft, directed downward, and settling on a neutral object.
- Stay with the awareness you gained during the meditation.

FEEL INTO EMOTIONS MEDITATION WORKSHEET

After you have completed the meditation, jot down observations that emerged during your meditation. Make note of thoughts you had, feelings you experienced, bodily sensations you felt, and/or detours that you took.

1. FOCUS INWARD: Breathe and Center. Were you able to concentrate inward and turn your attention back to your intention for this exercise?

_____

_____

2. DIRECT ATTENTION: Feel into Emotions. What did you experience when you felt into your emotion?

Make contact. How did you conjure the emotion?

_____

_____

Feel bodily sensations as neutral and concrete. What sensations did you feel (e.g., prickly, warm, pinching; sensations of pressure or contraction)

_____

_____

Breathe into the emotion. What was it like to have courageous presence with the emotion? To expand the feeling?

_____

_____

Experience without judgment. To what extent did you release your judgment of pleasant or unpleasant? What was the effect?

_____

_____

3. REFLECT ON INSIGHTS: Breathe and Reflect. What insights or benefits did you gain in the meditation?

_____

_____

_____

_____

_____

_____

FEEL INTO EMOTIONS TRACKING LOG

DAY	APPLICATION Which emotions did I identify? How did I feel into emotions? What were some of the sensations I observed?	IMPACT What was the impact of Feeling Into Emotions on me and my response to the situation?
Day 1		
Day 2		
Day 3		
Day 4		

FEEL INTO EMOTIONS TRACKING LOG

DAY	APPLICATION Which emotions did I identify? How did I feel into emotions? What were some of the sensations I observed?	IMPACT What was the impact of Feeling Into Emotions on me and my response to the situation?
Day 5		
Day 6		
Day 7		

INSIGHTS - What patterns or benefits emerged?

_____
_____
_____
_____
_____

SKILL 9. PROCESS EMOTIONS

It is easy to be angry. What's difficult is to be angry at the right person, for the right reason, to the right degree, and for the right amount of time. –Aristotle

To what extent can you diminish an emotion's intensity? Do you learn from your emotions and gain valuable insights?

The path to happiness and success requires forging a healthy relationship with negative emotions. This healthy relationship with negative emotions does not mean dwelling on them, being passive, or wallowing in emotion. Instead, processing emotions is an active approach to managing them so that the value in them is captured, the underlying cause is addressed, and they are skillfully moved through. As discussed previously, fighting emotions with tactics such as suppression or avoidance backfires. This is a high level yet crucial skill in emotional intelligence. This approach takes the view that emotions have the potential to be aides or hindrances to happiness depending on how well they are managed.

Are your negative emotions friends or foes?

Negative emotions are like gentle—or fierce—warriors whose job is to keep us safe from harm. Honor the role of negative emotions in your well-being. Seeing them as friends not enemies positions you to move through them and skillfully use them.

HOW TO PROCESS EMOTIONS—TAKE A S.E.A.T.

Work with your emotions, not from your emotions.

This advanced technique draws upon all the emotional awareness and emotional management skills covered thus far. In order to do this, you will need the information you gathered, including feeling sensations, identifying emotions, and understanding the triggers and effects of each emotion. You will also need the skills you developed in neutralizing emotions. You can do this emotion processing technique as a high road or a low road exercise with slight modifications depending on which modality.

FOUR STEPS TO PROCESSING EMOTIONS
1. **S**top
2. **E**xpand
3. **A**sk
4. **T**ake care

FOUR STEPS TO PROCESSING EMOTIONS

STEP 1. Stop. When you notice that you have an emotion welling, stop and take a few deep breaths. This counters the physiological activation and gives space to center—or at least not make things worse. A common technique for women in labor and childbirth is to breathe through the pain. By breathing deeply and slowly, the neuromodulators at the base of the diaphragm, in your lower abdomen, get activated. This ignites the parasympathetic nervous system, which is the relaxation response.

STEP 2. Expand or Experience. Experience emotions as neutral bodily sensations. Fundamentally, that is what emotions are, but we tend not to think of them that way. Just like physical pain, emotional pain can be worsened by the way we attend to it. Mindfully experience them as temporary and feel the effects the emotion has on your body as neutral albeit intense sensations. Feel the physical manifestations of the emotion without judging the sensations as bad or even painful. Try experiencing them like energy currents running through the body. Feel the emotion flowing throughout your body, experiencing it with full presence and attention. Be still with the emotions without resisting them or demanding that they go away.

Next, bravely approach and counter the impulse to get away from pain by going closer to it. Amplify the sensations, breathing into the sensations associated with the emotion so that it expands, getting as large as it "wants" to be. Another way to do this is to imagine the emotion has a location and breath through the emotion to the other side of it. Often emotions feel like constriction, so this can create an opening feeling.

STEP 3. Ask. Like gentle (or fierce) warriors, emotions help us. They use pain to wake us up and ensure we pay attention to their message. Honor and thank these emotions, appreciating that they are coming from a survival instinct. Like other instincts, emotions communicate through the language of sensation. Nuanced sensations such as hollowness in the pit of the stomach, flushness and warmth, chills down the spine communicate that there is something that we like or don't like, that makes us feel secure or threatened. *Thank your "inner warrior."*

Your emotions are trying to tell you something. Are you listening?

Listen to the message. It is our job to inquire more deeply what the message is. First, identify which emotion is present. For example, identify if there anxiety, embarrassment, or fear. Second, consider what that emotion is telling you. Consider the emotional equation for that emotion. Get curious and discover what that emotion is "trying" to tell you or why it got triggered. This nonjudgmental understanding of emotions sees them as natural instincts and as making sense in the context of circumstances. This is an example of emotional acceptance rather than emotional resistance of unwanted emotions.

Listen for the message of the emotion:

"I am having the emotion of _____."

"This emotion is telling me something. What is the message of this emotion?"

Examples of listening to the message of the emotion:

- *"I am having the emotion of depression."*

"Of course, I am depressed about losing my job. I loved my job and it was part of my identity. I feel sad about losing it. I also feel anxious. This is arising because I'm uncertain I can find another before I run out of savings. Together, anxiety and sadness create depression, which is a natural response to losing something of value and feeling uncertain about my ability to overcome challenge."

- *"I am having the emotion of sadness."*

"Of course, I would feel sadness and devastation after my break-up. My system is hardwired to connect with a partner and to mate. Losing a mate is experienced by my evolutionary wired being as a major threat to my survival and ability to successfully procreate. Without physical affection, I am also experiencing Oxytocin withdrawal. The absence of that neuromodulator feels physically uncomfortable, just like an addict experiences withdrawal from their drug."

- *"I am having the emotion of anxiety."*

"It makes sense that I would be anxious about making a toast at the party. I don't want to make a fool of myself and be judged negatively by my friends and colleagues. I care about how others perceive me. After all, I am a social animal!"

Explore more deeply. If you wish to engage in deeper inquiry, explore the core desire, issue, or threat. There is usually some wisdom, a legitimate human need under the emotions, especially recurring strong emotions.

Ask yourself:

- What it is that I really wish for in this situation?
- What do I deeply desire?
- What feels threatened in this situation?
- What is the deeper longing?

STEP 4. Take care. After listening to the message of strong distressing emotions, use the information to make decisions and take appropriate action. Ignoring this information may result in making poor decisions. This does not mean you will always use the information communicated by your emotions. On the contrary, you may decide that the emotion is communicating useless information or is interfering with your ability to be effective. The message may be exaggerated, blown out of proportion, old, repetitive, or obsessive. In either case, a necessary step is to let the emotion be heard.

Determine if it is necessary to take some type of action. It might be heeding wise action to change a situation, make a direct request, or protect or advocate for yourself. Alternatively, taking action might mean offering yourself compassion simply because of the emotional pain. You might imagine calming raw nerves, breathing into your heart, self-soothing, offering tenderness, or resting your weary body.

You might ask yourself:

- What is needing my attention right now?
- Is there anything I could do or say to help my situation?
- How could I be tender and gentle with myself right now?
- If I were giving someone else advice, what would I tell them to do?

WHEN TO TAKE A SEAT

Take a SEAT with your emotions when you recognize that the emotions are:

- *Not useful.* You determine the emotions are not useful or actually getting in your way.

- *Obstructing performance.* You determine that optimal performance or well-being would occur at a lower level of emotional arousal.

- *Creating prolonged negative moods.* You determine that distressing emotions are persistent and driving prolonged negative moods.

- *Persistent.* You have challenged your thoughts or used other coping and yet your emotional state persists. There might be a deeper message that is unaddressed or simply that the emotions are a conditioned response and need to be processed through.

Amygdala Hijack. When you are in an emotional hijack or wish to reflect on the cause of a recent hijack, this technique can help provide release, insights, and deeper understanding.

TAKE A S.E.A.T. WORKSHEET

This worksheet guides you through the High Road approach to the Take a SEAT technique. It can be useful to do this prior to practicing the Low Road approach. Consider an emotionally challenging situation and explore your answers to the questions in each of the four steps. This technique can help you skillfully process difficult and persistent emotions.

STEP 1. <u>S</u>top: First, stop and take a few deep breaths. This counters the physiological activation and allows the opportunity to center or at least not make things worse. What is the benefit of stopping?

_____

_____

STEP 2. <u>E</u>xpand or <u>E</u>xperience. Experience your emotions as neutral bodily sensations. Fundamentally, that is what emotions are. What sensations do you experience? Try to describe in neutral language. Allow them to be as big as they "want" to be. How big are they when you allow them to just be?

_____

_____

_____

STEP 3. <u>A</u>sk

Listen to the message.

First, identify which emotions are present. There may be several.

"I am having the emotion of _____."

"I am having the emotion of _____."

"I am having the emotion of _____."

Second, choose one or two of the strongest emotions and consider what its message is. You might consider the emotional equation for each emotion. Discover what that emotion is "trying" to tell you or why it got triggered.

What is the message of this emotion?

_____

_____

_____

_____

_____

Explore deeper. Explore the core desire, issue, or threat. There is usually some wisdom, a legitimate human need under the emotions, especially with repetitive, old emotions.

Ask yourself:

- What it is that I really wish for in this situation?
- What do I deeply desire?
- What feels threatened in this situation?
- What is the deeper longing?

_____
_____
_____
_____
_____
_____
_____
_____
_____
_____

STEP 4. Take care. After listening to the message of strong distressing emotions, use the information to make decisions and take appropriate action. Action might be changing a situation, making a direct request, or protecting or advocating for yourself. Or, taking action might mean offering yourself compassion simply because of the emotional pain. You might imagine calming raw nerves, breathing into your heart, self-soothing, offering tenderness, or resting your weary body. Ask yourself:

- What needs my attention right now?
- Is there anything I could do or say to help my situation?
- How could I be tender and gentle with myself right now?
- If I were giving someone else advice, what would I tell them to do?

_____
_____
_____
_____
_____
_____
_____
_____
_____
_____
_____

TAKE A S.E.A.T. MEDITATION

When distressing emotions show up we usually want to make them go away as soon as possible. They are by their very nature painful. An important step in processing emotions is allowing them space to exist and listening to their message.

Work with a current situation, one that has emotional charge. This is probably not the time to process traumatic or overwhelming situations, however. As Rick Hanson says, "Make sure that you will be able to swim back from the deep end of the pool." Do not go out so far that you cannot get back on your own. Use your own inner wisdom to decide what to make contact with and how far to go.

INSTRUCTIONS
(5 to 10 minutes)

1. FOCUS INWARD: Breathe and Center
- **Close your eyes**— Close your eyes to let your attention turn inward.
- **Feel Your Breath**—Focus attention by feeling your breath enter and exit your body. Breathe deeply with a slower exhale and natural inhale. Place your hand on your abdomen to feel your diaphragm rise and fall.
- **Set your Intention**---To direct your attention in this time, place, and to the objective of this meditation.

2. DIRECT ATTENTION: Make Contact and Take a SEAT with Your Emotion.

Make contact with an emotion you currently feel or recently felt. Words or phrases describing a difficult aspect of a situation might help you generate the emotion. Making a facial expression revealing how you feel can help make greater contact with the emotion.

<u>S</u>TOP—**Breathe into the emotion.** Come into your body. Feel the physical manifestations of the emotion in your body.

<u>E</u>XPAND—**Experience and expand without judgment**—Experience the emotion like an energy current that run through your body. Release the judgment of the emotion as bad or good, pleasant or painful. Take a break from asking yourself whether you like or don't like them. Expand the sensations by breathing into or through them, inviting it to expand throughout your body, filling every cell in your body, from finger tips to toes. Even if uncomfortable, keep going. Expand it even more. Have courageous presence with the emotion.

<u>A</u>SK—**What is the deeper longing?** What is your underlying need or wish?

<u>T</u>AKE CARE: Like gentle (or fierce) warriors, emotions are there to help us. Heed their command and take action. This might mean directing compassion, imagining warm or protection, or figuring out what wise action to take.

3. REFLECT ON INSIGHTS: Breathe and Reflect
- Come back to your breath.
- Reflect on the insights or benefits you gained during this meditation.

4. MAINTAIN YOUR INNER AWARENESS: Soft Gaze and Stay with It
- Slowly open your eyes and keep your gaze soft, directed downward, and settling on a neutral object.
- Stay with the awareness you gained during the meditation.

TAKE A SEAT MEDITATION WORKSHEET

After you have completed the meditation, jot down any observations about what came up.

1. FOCUS INWARD: Breathe and Center. Were you able to concentrate inward and turn your attention back to your intention for this exercise?

_____

_____

2. DIRECT ATTENTION: Take a SEAT.

STOP—Breathe into the emotion. Come into your body. What did impact did stopping and breathing have?

_____

_____

EXPAND—Experience and expand without judgment—What was it like to experience the emotion like an energy current that run through your body? How did you attempt to expand it?

_____

_____

Experience without judgment. To what extent did you release your judgment of pleasant or unpleasant? What was the effect?

_____

_____

ASK—What is the message and the deeper longing? What is your underlying need or wish?

_____

_____

_____

_____

TAKE ACTION—How could you take action? What was it like when you directed compassion or other self-care method? Is there an action to take?

_____

_____

_____

_____

3. REFLECT ON INSIGHTS: Breathe and Reflect. What did you gain in the meditation?

_____

_____

_____

_____

TAKE A S.E.A.T. TRACKING LOG

DAY	APPLICATION Which situation did I Take a SEAT in? How did I do this?	IMPACT What was the impact of Taking a SEAT?
Day 1		
Day 2		
Day 3		
Day 4		

TAKE A S.E.A.T. TRACKING LOG

DAY	APPLICATION Which situation did I Take a SEAT in? How did I do this?	IMPACT What was the impact of Taking a SEAT?
Day 5		
Day 6		
Day 7		

INSIGHTS - What patterns or benefits emerged?

_____
_____
_____
_____
_____

SKILL 10. SELF-COMPASSION

If your compassion does not include yourself, it is incomplete.
-Jack Kornfield

The curious paradox is that when I accept myself just as I am, then I can change.
-Carl Rogers

Self-Compassion is extending compassion to one's self in instances of perceived inadequacy, failure, or general suffering. When in the throws of negative emotion, direct some gentle compassion toward yourself like you would to a child, an animal, friend or loved one if they were in pain. Simply the experiencing of emotional distress warrants compassion—by definition they are difficult to experience and disruptive to our sense of well-being. By having compassion rather than judgment or criticism, the intensity and quality of the negative emotion changes. Many describe a feeling of negativity melting away. Directing compassion towards oneself can be helpful when dealing with intense emotions and situations that cannot be sufficiently managed with other Self-Management tools.

The pioneer and leading expert on self-compassion, Dr. Kristen Neff, has defined self-compassion as the ability to hold one's feelings of suffering with a sense of warmth, connection, and concern. Neff proposes three main components of self-compassion:

Self-kindness. Being kind and understanding toward oneself in instances of pain or failure rather than being harshly self-critical.

Common humanity. Perceiving one's experiences of suffering and personal failure as part of the larger human experience rather than seeing them as isolating.

Mindfulness. Holding one's present-moment experience in balanced perspective, or "mindful awareness," rather than exaggerating the dramatic story line of one's suffering.

> "You will encounter frustrations. Losses will occur, you will make mistakes, bump up against your limitations, fall short of your ideals. This is the human condition, a reality shared by all of us."
>
> —Dr. Kristin Neff

Self-compassion versus Self-esteem. Self-esteem refers to a sense of self-worth, perceived value, or liking oneself. Although psychologists once praised the benefits of self-esteem, recent research has exposed costs associated with the pursuit of high self-esteem, such as narcissism, ego-defensive anger, inaccurate self-perceptions, self-worth contingency, or social comparison. In contrast to self-esteem, self-compassion is not based on self-evaluations. People feel compassion for themselves because all human beings deserve compassion and understanding, not because they possess some particular set of traits.

Unlike self-esteem, self-compassion isn't dependent on external circumstances. It's always available. Research suggests that in comparison to self-esteem, self-compassion is associated with greater emotional resilience, more accurate self-concepts, more caring relationship behavior, as well as less narcissism and reactive anger.

RESEARCH—SELF-COMPASSION

Below are abstracts from a selection of scientific studies published in major peer reviewed journals.

Compassion is Trainable. Geshe Thupten Jinpa and colleagues set out to determine if compassion is trainable. They studied a sample of 100 adults that were randomly assigned to a 9-week compassion cultivation training (CCT) program and found significant improvements in participants' compassion for others, ability to receive compassion from others, and self-compassion. Their findings suggest that compassion is trainable and is positively correlated to the amount of time one practices formal compassion (metta) meditation.

Jazaieri, H., Jinpa, G. T., McGonigal, K., Rosenberg, E. L., Finkelstein, J., Simon-Thomas, E., ... & Goldin, P. R. (2013). Enhancing compassion: A randomized controlled trial of a compassion cultivation training program. *Journal of Happiness Studies*, 14(4), 1113-1126.

Meditation Relieves Negative Emotions. Fred Luthans and colleagues examined randomized clinical trials to determine the effectiveness of mindfulness meditation in improving psychological stress. They found that mindfulness meditation had a moderate positive impact on anxiety, depression, and pain and underscore the importance of further studies to explore how meditation may improve the positive aspects of mental health.

Luthans, F., Avolio, B. J., Avey, J. B., & Norman, S. M. (2007). Positive psychological capital: Measurement and relationship with performance and satisfaction. Personnel Psychology, 60(3), 541-572.

Self-Compassion Is Associated with Psychological Health and Wellbeing. Most of the research on self-compassion so far has used the *Self-Compassion Scale*, which measures the degree to which individuals display the three elements of self-compassion. Results from the test indicate that self-compassion is significantly correlated with positive mental health outcomes, such as with measures of happiness, optimism, positive affect, wisdom, personal initiative, curiosity and exploration, agreeableness, extroversion, and conscientiousness. It also had a significant negative association with negative affect and neuroticism (Neff, Rude, & Kirkpatrick, 2007).

Self-Compassion Can Be Cultivated. There is a growing body of research that points to self-compassion interventions associated with improved aspects of psychological wellbeing. Baer (2010) asserts that self-compassion is closely related to mindfulness, and like mindfulness, it can be cultivated through meditation practices that originate in the Buddhist tradition and have been adapted for secular use in Western settings. Significant reductions in symptoms of stress and mood disturbance, as well as increases in mindfulness, spirituality and self- compassion were observed after participation in Mindfulness-based stress reduction (MBSR) programs (Birnie, Speca, & Carlson, 2010). Effective methods of teaching self-compassion that aren't based on Buddhist meditation also have been developed, such as Compassionate Mind Training, a form of therapy that emphasizes the development of self-compassion (Gilbert, 2000; Gilbert & Irons, 2004; 2005; Gilbert & Procter, 2006).

Compassion Lowers Stress. A research study suggests that having compassion for others may actually protect us from stress. Fifty-nine study participants took an online questionnaire that measured their levels of compassion. Then these people had to complete a series of stressful tasks while someone else evaluated them; that evaluator either offered supportive, positive feedback or didn't say anything. Participants who showed more compassion on the questionnaire interacted more with the supportive figures than the less compassionate people did, and they reaped the benefits of this support, showing lower blood pressure, heart rate, and levels of cortisol (a hormone released during stress) than their less compassionate counterparts. They also seemed less stressed than the compassionate participants who didn't receive the supportive feedback. The authors suggest compassion for others may open us up to receiving social support, which may lead to more resilience to stress.

Cosley, B.J., McCoy, S.K., Saslow, L. R., Epel, E.S. Is Compassion for Others Stress Buffering? Consequences of Compassion and Social Support for Physiological Reactivity to Stress. *Journal of Experimental Social Psychology*, Vol. 46, Issue 5, September 2010, 816-823.

Compassion is Trainable. Geshe Thupten Jinpa and colleagues set out to determine if compassion is trainable. They studied a sample of 100 adults that were randomly assigned to a 9-week compassion cultivation training (CCT) program and found significant improvements in participants' compassion for others, ability to receive compassion from others, and self-compassion. Their findings suggest that compassion is trainable and is positively correlated to the amount of time one practices formal compassion (metta) meditation.

Jazaieri, H., Jinpa, G. T., McGonigal, K., Rosenberg, E. L., Finkelstein, J., Simon-Thomas, E., ... & Goldin, P. R. (2013). Enhancing compassion: A randomized controlled trial of a compassion cultivation training program. *Journal of Happiness Studies*, *14*(4), 1113-1126.

Prejudice and Dehumanization. A research study suggests that having prejudice towards out groups that are stereotypically labeled as hostile and incompetent (i.e. homeless people, addicts) can be particularly troublesome and may lead to dehumanizing these extreme out-groups. Functional MRI's were used to examine brain activation in study participants that were shown photographs of social groups and objects. The researchers found increased neural activation to all images of social groups except extreme out-groups, supporting the prediction that extreme out-groups may be seen as less than human.

Harris, L. T., & Fiske, S. T. (2006). Dehumanizing the lowest of the low neuroimaging responses to extreme out-groups. *Psychological Science*, *17*(10), 847-853.

Recognizing Individuality. Social groups that elicit disgust are differentially processed in mPFC Social neuroscience suggests a decreased activation in the medial pre-frontal cortex (mPFC) to members of extreme outgroups that elicit disgust. Study participants were instructed to either make superficial categorical age estimations (e.g. broad generalizations) or individuating food-preference judgments (i.e. whether the social group member likes carrots) about people as fMRI recorded neural activity.

This study demonstrates that being instructed to see extreme out-groups through an individualistic lens as opposed to making superficial categorical judgments may lead to increased social cognition (demonstrated by increased activation in the mPFC) and help one see extreme out-group members as more similar to oneself - thereby increasing a sense of common humanity.

Harris, L. T., & Fiske, S. T. (2007). Social groups that elicit disgust are differentially processed in mPFC. *Social cognitive and affective neuroscience*, *2*(1), 45-51.

Consider Others. The danger in adopting dehumanizing perceptions, research suggests, is a failure to consider the mind of another person, which, in turn, may facilitate inhumane acts like torture.

Harris, L. T., & Fiske, S. T. (2011). Dehumanized perception: A psychological means to facilitate atrocities, torture, and genocide?. *Zeitschrift für Psychologie/Journal of Psychology*, *219*(3), 175.

GUIDED SELF-COMPASSION MEDITATIONS

Follow this link to Dr. Kristen Neff's website for a series of guided self- compassion meditations: www.self-compassion.org/guided-self-compassion-meditations-mp3

Follow this link to Dr. Kristen Neff's website to test how self-compassionate you are: www.self-compassion.org/test-your-self-compassion-level

FOUR STEPS TO SELF-COMPASSION

Self-Compassion is the ability to hold one's feelings of suffering with a sense of warmth, connection, and concern. It includes self-kindness, common humanity, and mindfulness directed at oneself. This method can be applied both when dealing with residual distress as well as excruciatingly painful states.

> **FOUR STEPS TO SELF-COMPASSION**
>
> 1. Feel into the Emotion.
> 2. Find the Positive Wish.
> 3. Replace Self-Critical Self-Talk with Kind Self-Talk.
> 4. Recognize the Universality of Difficulty.

STEP 1: FEEL INTO THE EMOTION

Bring increased awareness and presence to the physical sensations and emotional pain associated with the emotional experience. Acknowledge to yourself that you are experiencing discomfort or pain. Spend a moment feeling the physical sensations.

STEP 2: FIND YOUR POSITIVE WISH

Identify your unfulfilled desire or positive wish. Listen to what the emotion is telling you about what is important. Under most emotional reactions is an unfulfilled desire or a positive wish for something. Sometimes there is something deeply of value that is being protected or defended. The stronger the emotion the more coveted this underlying wish or desire tends to be. Uncovering the unfulfilled desire or positive wish can both change the intensity of the emotion as well as lead to effective solution finding or problem solving.

Ask yourself:
"What is my underlying positive wish or unfulfilled desire in this situation?"
"What is of deep value in this situation that my emotional self is desperately trying to protect?"

Dig deeper to find the source of distressful emotions and strong reactions. Look for a threat that has the power to elicit a significant charge for you. Ask one of the following questions:

- *What am I deeply needing here? Do I need connection, acceptance, reassurance, or respect?*
- *What is it that I deeply cherish and feels threatened?*
- *What part of me or my dreams am I trying to protect?*

For example:
In a minor annoyance like being in a long check-out line, the positive wish might be to get your errand done quickly so that you can get home to relax after a long work day. Your positive wish is to relax. The long line interferes with your ability to get home and relax.

In relationship challenges, negative emotions might signal an unfulfilled desire for love, acceptance or companionship.

Honor. The emotion is coming from your survival instinct. It has a role and is "trying to do its job." Honor these emotions. Understanding emotions as natural instincts can invite self-forgiveness for feeling unwanted emotions. This stance is less judgmental; therefore, there is less resistance to the emotions.

Thank your "inner warrior."

Your negative emotions are trying to keep you and your dreams safe. They are like "inner warriors" or "silent guardians" that are watching out for you. Negative emotions are trying to help you out. Their job is to alert and help you respond to trouble, imminent danger, and impending problems. They do their job with tough love. Just like a parent drawing a hard line with a wayward teenager, negative emotions remove the kid gloves and get serious. They use pain to wake us up and ensure we pay attention to their message. Paradoxically, this is an act of self-love.

Non-judgment. When you identify the positive wish, essentially you are validating the distressing emotion. In other words, it becomes understandable. This removes the judgment that it is "wrong" or "bad" to be feeling the way you do. It is this judgment that adds fuel to the fire of distressing emotions. There can be a tendency to judge distressing emotions as bad or unacceptable. Judging them as "bad," "wrong" or "weak" is a form of resisting emotions. Underlying judgment is an implicit demand that they go away. It is a variation on struggling with the emotion. This worsens the feeling of the emotion. Essentially it is dog-piling distressing emotions on top of distressing emotions.

STEP 3: REPLACE SELF-CRITICISM WITH KIND SELF-TALK

Catch negative self-talk and replace with less judgmental, more understanding self-talk. Oftentimes we go into harsh self-criticism when we have made mistakes or are in unwanted circumstances. You might imagine what you would say to a good friend or a child undergoing a difficult situation. Often people are more understanding with others than to themselves.

Self-criticism is sometimes a mechanism used in an attempt to motivate oneself to achieve a challenging outcome. Although self-criticism is often well-intended, it generally leads to negative rather than positive consequences, undermining confidence, self-care, and perspective. What's more effective—the carrot or the stick? Consider if critical self-talk is effective. If it's not, replace it with self-compassion.

Ways To Be Kind Rather Than Critical:

- When something painful happens, try to take a balanced view of the situation.

- When you fail at something important to you, try to keep things in perspective.

- Try to be understanding and patient toward those aspects of your personality that you don't like.

- Try to be less judgmental of your own perceived flaws and inadequacies.

- When going through difficult times, give yourself the caring, tenderness, and understanding.

- Do a self-compassion meditation.

STEP 4: RECOGNIZE THE UNIVERSALITY OF DIFFICULTY

Suffering such as disappointment, frustration, and other negative states are universal human experiences. Simply acknowledging that we are not alone can provide relief and normalize the experience.

For example:

- Try to see your failings as part of the human condition.

- When feeling down, bring to mind someone else who may be or has felt in a similar way.

- When feeling inadequate, lonely, or other negative emotions, remind yourself that these feelings are felt by most people.

SELF-COMPASSION WORKSHEET

Compassion powerfully transforms suffering and distress and often giving a moment of relief. When in the throws of negative emotion, direct some gentle compassion toward yourself like you would to a child, an animal, a friend or loved one if they were in pain. Often we are more compassionate to others than we are to ourselves.

DIFFICULT SITUATION

Describe a difficult situation when you felt painful emotions, and you'd like to direct compassion.

_____
_____
_____
_____

DIRECT COMPASSION TOWARDS YOURSELF

STEP 1: FEEL INTO THE EMOTION. What are the physical sensations of this difficulty?

_____
_____
_____
_____
_____

STEP 2: FIND POSITIVE WISH. Ask yourself, "What is my underlying positive wish or unfulfilled desire in this situation?" Or, "What is of deep value in this situation that my being is desperately trying to protect?" Look more deeply your positive wish or unfulfilled desire. Sometimes there is something deeply valuable that we are protecting.

Identify the unfulfilled desire or positive wish. What is my positive wish or unfulfilled desire?

_____
_____
_____
_____
_____

Honor Difficult Emotions. How are these emotions "trying" to protect me?

_____
_____
_____
_____
_____
_____
_____

STEP 3: REPLACE SELF-CRITICISM WITH KIND SELF-TALK. How can I use self-care when dealing with this difficulty? How can I replace self-criticism and negative judgments with gentle, understanding self-talk?

_____
_____
_____
_____
_____
_____
_____
_____

STEP 4: RECOGNIZE THE UNIVERSALITY OF DIFFICULTY. Disappointment, making mistakes, and suffering are universal human experiences. How do I observe others experiencing similar difficulties?

_____
_____
_____
_____
_____
_____
_____
_____

SELF-COMPASSION TRACKING LOG

DAY	APPLICATION What difficult situation did I encounter? How did I direct compassion to myself?	IMPACT What was the impact of directing self-compassion on my bodily state, emotional state, mental state, or actions?
Day 1		
Day 2		
Day 3		
Day 4		

SELF-COMPASSION TRACKING LOG

DAY	APPLICATION What difficult situation did I encounter? How did I direct compassion to myself?	IMPACT What was the impact of directing self-compassion on my bodily state, emotional state, mental state, or actions?
Day 5		
Day 6		
Day 7		

INSIGHTS - What patterns or benefits emerged?

_____
_____
_____
_____
_____

SELF-COMPASSION MEDITATION

Compassion happens at verbal and nonverbal levels. Both are important. Below is a Low Road technique for increasing self-compassion.

INSTRUCTIONS

(2 to 3 minutes)

1. FOCUS INWARD: Breathe and Center

- **Close your eyes**— Close your eyes to let your attention turn inward.

- **Feel Your Breath**—Focus attention by feeling your breath enter and exit your body. Breathe deeply with a slower exhale and natural inhale. Place your hand on your abdomen to feel your diaphragm rise and fall.

- **Set your Intention**---To direct your attention in this time, place, and to the objective of this meditation.

2. DIRECT ATTENTION: Direct compassion to yourself—Validate your pain: distressing emotions are designed to cause suffering.

- Imagine seeing yourself from above sitting here experiencing difficulty.

- Direct warmth and comfort to yourself.

- Say to yourself, *"May I have relief from suffering, be free from pain; may I have peace, contentment, joy."*

- With the in-breath, visualize filling your body with wellness, happiness, vitality, joy, health, and goodness.

3. REFLECT ON INSIGHTS: Breathe and Reflect

- Come back to your breath.
- Reflect on the insights or benefits you gained during this meditation.

4. MAINTAIN YOUR INNER AWARENESS: Soft Gaze and Stay with It

- Slowly open your eyes and keep your gaze soft, directed downward, and settling on a neutral object.
- Stay with the awareness you gained during the meditation.

SELF-COMPASSION MEDITATION WORKSHEET

After you have completed the meditation, jot down observations about what came up during your meditation. Make note of thoughts you had, feelings you experienced, bodily sensations you felt, and/or detours that you took.

1. FOCUS INWARD: Were you able to concentrate inward and turn your attention to the intention you set for this meditation?

_____
_____
_____
_____
_____
_____

2. DIRECT ATTENTION: Direct compassion. What was it like to direct compassion to yourself?

_____
_____
_____
_____
_____
_____

3. REFLECT ON INSIGHTS: What insights or benefits did you gain during the meditation?

_____
_____
_____
_____
_____

4. When to use this meditation. When do you think this meditation would be useful to use?

_____
_____
_____
_____
_____
_____

SELF-COMPASSION MEDITATION TRACKING LOG

DAY	APPLICATION What was the difficult situation or emotion? How did I direct compassion?	IMPACT What was the impact of the meditation on my bodily state, emotional state, mental state, or actions?
Day 1		
Day 2		
Day 3		
Day 4		

SELF-COMPASSION MEDITATION TRACKING LOG

DAY	APPLICATION What was the difficult situation or emotion? How did I direct compassion?	IMPACT What was the impact of the meditation on my bodily state, emotional state, mental state, or actions?
Day 5		
Day 6		
Day 7		

INSIGHTS - What patterns or benefits emerged?

_____
_____
_____
_____
_____
_____

SELF-MANAGEMENT

SKILL 11. REDIRECT EFFORT

While emotions signal important information and help us respond to circumstances, the degree to which we read that information, how we use it, and the way we respond is ultimately up to us.

Redirecting emotions does not force emotions to go away. By intentionally redirecting attention and actions, it exerts influence over them. This approach involves mindfully attending to aspects of experience that will trigger a different emotional state. These strategies provide guidance on how to work with emotions to transform them.

TECHNIQUES FOR REDIRECTING EFFORT

TECHNIQUES FOR REDIRECTING EFFORT
1. SIZE THE PROBLEM
2. USE ANTIDOTES TO THE EMOTION
3. ACT OPPOSITE TO THE EMOTION

TECHNIQUE #1. SIZE THE PROBLEM

How big of a deal is this problem? In the future, will it seem as big as it does now? Often when we are in the heat of a moment, we fight for things that are not as important as they seem. When the amygdala cools down, often the seemingly large threats shrink in significance. The mind often blows things out of proportion. It can be useful to consider this when triggered.

Ask yourself, objectively, "What is the true size of this problem?"

If you sense that this problem feels larger than it actually is, it might be useful to continue with the following technique to redirect your emotions before engaging in problem solving or taking action you might make things worse.

TECHNIQUE #2. USE ANTIDOTES TO THE EMOTION

An antidote is a remedy or other agent used to neutralize or counteract the effects of a poison or an agent that relieves or counteracts. This applies to emotions as well.

Examples of Using Antidotes to Emotions:

- Focus on the abundance in your life when you are in a scarcity mindset.
- Look for good intentions in another when you feel you have been treated badly.
- Look for ways that you are heroic when you feel disempowered.
- Consider positive aspects in the situation or person.

Example: Three Good Things Exercise. A powerful way to shift your mood and perspective is to attend to the positives in a negative situation. Ask yourself what three good things happened to you today or in a specific situation and then to identify your role in creating them.

TECHNIQUE #3. ACT OPPOSITE TO THE EMOTION

Act opposite to the emotion. Start by first conjuring the opposing emotion. It is impossible to have opposing emotions at the same time, so making contact with a distressing emotion's opposite can transform it.

Imagine you receive an email in your inbox from "that person." Alarm bells ring, anger and frustration emerge, and you feel the corresponding impulses for action. Although you don't like this person, you consciously choose to write a pleasant response as opposed to a critical, terse one. You turn away from the emotion and continue working

Determine the Opposite Emotion. The following questions can help you find and cultivate distressful emotions' opposites. Ask yourself: *"What is the opposite of what I am feeling?"*

WHAT IS THE OPPOSITE EMOTION?

Guilt/blame	versus	Forgiveness
Shame	versus	Compassion
Weakness	versus	Strength
Helpless	versus	Agency
Hopeless	versus	Hopeful

Determine the Action to Take. Look for the opposite of the emotion and focus you attention on the opposite and/or actually act opposite to what the negative emotion's action impulse, what it would have you do.

Examples of Acting Opposite:
- Intentionally be generous when you feel selfish.
- Do an act of kindness when you feel angry or withdrawn.
- When you feel down and lethargic, get out and do something.
- Push through anxiety when it tells you to avoid.
- Speak up when you feel like clamming up.
- Be gentle with someone when you feel aggressive.

SELF-MANAGEMENT

REDIRECT EFFORT WORKSHEET

The purpose of this worksheet is to give you an opportunity to practice techniques for redirecting effort when unhelpful emotions show up.

SITUATION

What was the situation?

_____
_____

Technique #1. SIZE THE PROBLEM

SIZE THE PROBLEM. What is the true size of this problem?

_____
_____
_____
_____
_____
_____

Technique #2. USE ANTIDOTES TO EMOTIONS

Unhelpful Emotion.

What was the unhelpful emotion?

_____
_____

USE AN ANTIDOTE TO THE EMOTION. How could I use antidotes to transform the emotion?
- Shift attention to the positives in this situation.
- Focus on the abundance in your life when you are in a scarcity mindset.
- Look for good intentions in another when you feel they have treated you badly.
- Look for ways that you are heroic when you feel disempowered.
- Three good things exercise.

_____
_____
_____
_____
_____
_____

Technique #3. ACT OPPOSITE TO THE EMOTION

ACT OPPOSITE. How could I Act Opposite to transform the emotion?
- Intentionally be generous when you feel selfish.
- Do an act of kindness when you feel angry or withdrawn.
- When you feel down and lethargic, get out and do something.
- Push through anxiety when it tells you to avoid.
- Do small acts of kindness.
- Act "as if" I am feeling the opposite emotion.

___

BRAINSTORM NEW TECHNIQUES TO REDIRECT

BRAINSTORM MORE TECHNIQUES. Consider new ways to redirect your attention and/or effort that suit you.

REDIRECT EFFORT TRACKING LOG

DAY	APPLICATION Which emotions did I work with? What is the SIZE of the problem? How did I use ANTIDOTES? How did I ACT OPPOSITE?	IMPACT What was the impact of Redirecting Effort on me and my response to the situation?
Day 1		
Day 2		
Day 3		
Day 4		

REDIRECT EFFORT TRACKING LOG

DAY	APPLICATION Which emotions did I work with? What is the SIZE of the problem? How did I use ANTIDOTES? How did I ACT OPPOSITE?	IMPACT What was the impact of Redirecting Effort on me and my response to the situation?
Day 5		
Day 6		
Day 7		

INSIGHTS - What patterns or benefits emerged?

_____
_____
_____
_____
_____

COACHING GUIDELINES

Use the self-coaching process and coaching tools to create long-term change. For maximum effectiveness, focus on one skill at a time. For each skill, take an *assessment* if one is available, complete a *coaching worksheet*, practice high road and low road techniques, and track your application of the skill over a seven day period using a *Tracking Log*.

Select one skill. Consider which skill would make the greatest difference in your current life circumstances if you used it more frequently and effectively. It is easier to build new habits if you focus on one change at a time. Select the *one skill* in this chapter that is your highest priority:

- Challenge Thoughts
- Disengage from Thoughts
- Neutralize Emotions
- Process Emotions
- Self-Compassion
- Redirect Effort

STEP 1. ASSESS. Assess the need and benefits of practicing this particular skill. Assess your current mastery level of the skill. Use one of the on-line assessment tools if one is available for the skill. The Coaching Worksheet will also help you assess your need and benefits of using the skill.

Assessments—Questionnaires that assess your current skill level and provide data on your progress.

STEP 2. PLAN. To create an action plan, understand how a technique can help you build greater mastery of a skill. Next, consider how you can apply it to your own situations.

Coaching Worksheets—Tools for learning and creating an action plan for practicing the techniques.
- 3 C's Worksheet
- Disengage from Thoughts Worksheet
- Take a S.E.A.T. Worksheet
- Self-Compassion Worksheet
- Redirect Effort Worksheet

STEP 3. PRACTICE. During the following seven days, apply the skill daily. Use both the High Road techniques and the Low Road techniques to practice the skill.

Tracking Logs—Habit forming tools to guide your efforts as you practice the techniques for seven days.
- 3 C's Tracking Log
- Disengage from Thoughts Tracking Log
- Leaves in a Stream Meditation Tracking Log
- Feel into Your Emotions Meditation Tracking Log
- Take a S.E.A.T. Tracking Log
- Self-Compassion Tracking Log
- Redirect Effort Tracking Log

Meditation Guides—Low Road techniques to build the skill at the emotional or non-verbal level.
- Leaves in a Stream Meditation
- Self-Compassion Meditation

STEP 4. TRACK RESULTS. In addition to systematically helping you to practice the techniques, *Tracking Logs* provide a place to note the impact of the skill on your experience. Tracking Logs help you become more aware of behaviors and patterns in yourself. They are a source of feedback so you can modify a technique to make it more effective.

SOCIAL AWARENESS

*What's important is to be able to see yourself, I think,
as having commonality with other people
and not determine, because of your good luck,
that everybody is less significant, less interesting,
less important than you are.*

~Harrison Ford

SOCIAL AWARENESS

Social Awareness refers to the ability to understand another's point of view as well as their behaviors, emotions, thoughts, and interpretations that result from their viewpoint and history. This ability to take another's perspective is the foundation of all the social intelligence skill sets.

Being socially aware requires both an understanding of the cognitive state as well as the emotional state of others. It also includes group dynamics and how groups' become entities in themselves. Socially aware people can recognize the subtle variations between emotions, describe emotional states, and articulate their own thoughts about situations. The skills in this chapter build upon those presented Self-Awareness.

OUTLINE

Introduction
- What is Social Awareness?
- Research—Interpersonal Neurobiology
- Mirror Neurons

Skill 12: **LISTEN MINDFULLY**
- Three Levels of Listening—Internal, Focused, Global
- Check Your Listening Style
- Signs of Mindless Listening
- How to Listen Mindfully
  - *Mindful Listening Worksheet & Tracking Log*

Skill 13: **READING OTHERS' EMOTIONS**
- Three Step Process for Reading Emotions
- Research—Detecting and Understanding Emotions
- Gender Differences
  - *Three Steps to Reading Emotions Worksheet & Tracking Log*
  - *Loving Kindness Meditation & Tracking Log*

Skill 14: **NOTICE SIMILARITIES**
- Look for Similarities
- Consider Vulnerabilities
- Research—Empathy
  - *Notice Similarities Worksheet & Tracking Log*
  - *Just Like Me Meditation & Tracking Log*

Coaching Guidelines

INTRODUCTION

"To love our enemy is impossible. The moment we understand our enemy, we feel compassion towards them, and they are no longer our enemy."
—Thich Nhat Hanh

WHAT IS SOCIAL AWARENESS?

Social Awareness is the ability to understand another's experience. This includes understanding their point-of-view, feelings, actions, intentions, values, motivations, and strengths.

The survival of the human species has depended upon the ability to understand others and group dynamics. This has tremendous survival benefit. Even in our modern era, this is crucial. I believe the continued survival of the human race, and certainly thriving as a species, depends upon understanding another's experience. As technology advances, the potential for massive destruction builds exponentially. Just as Thich Nhat Hanh stated, however, when we deeply understand another, no matter how hostile, egregious, or offensive they are, the relationship becomes transformed. Within deep understanding resides the potential for reconciliation, transformation, peace, and love.

Social Awareness Is Different from Caring. A common misconception about Social Awareness many people have is that it involves caring about the other. Social Awareness does not imply care. Social Awareness is independent from emotional valence. It is simply understanding another. Whether you care or not about the other's experience is a separate, independent process. We can know another is suffering but not feel for them or be moved to help. Research shows, for instance, that many psychopaths have a high level of Social Awareness. They can manipulate their victims because they understand.

Our Pledge—To Teach Social Awareness to Serve the Greater Good. Historically, we have witnessed many atrocities masterminded by individuals with high levels of Social Awareness. It is important to know this. For this reason, in our emotional intelligence program, we take a stand. We pledge to always teach Social Awareness coupled with a compassion component. We are a value-driven mission—our aim is to teach these skills in order to have a positive impact on society. Because we recognize their power, we offer these tools to be used in the service of the greater good.

BENEFITS

Social Awareness Is Empowering. Importantly, understanding another does not dictate action and it is not passive or capitulating. On the contrary, true Social Awareness empowers. It positions us for effective action. That action may be fierce or aggressive. It need not be nice, conciliatory, or foster connection.

For example, some years ago when I was a graduate student in Boston, I was walking home, books in hand, through the Boston Commons. This is a large park in the center of the city. It was about 10pm and I was walking alone across The Common on a dimly lit path. I turned around to see a large male figure walking purposefully toward me. By the aggressive stance and quick pace, I sensed he was following me. I walked faster and he did as well. Fear spiked. There was no one in sight and I was midway through the park. I turned around, squarely faced the figure pacing toward me, and yelled with the loudest, most commanding voice I could muster, "DO NOT FOLLOW ME. GO AWAY!" Surprised, he turned around and dashed into the shadows. In my mind, this confirmed my fears. I believe he was following me, intending to do harm. I could have been mistaken, but had I wrongly accused him, I believe his reaction would have been quite different rather than escaping anonymously into the darkness.

This experience reminds me of the power of Social Awareness. Social Awareness simply refers to *understanding another*. It does not mean agreeing, condoning, or allowing an action to occur. By reading his body language, I sensed malicious intention. This awareness positioned me to take fierce action and protect myself.

OBSTACLES

There are several obstacles to accurate and high level Social Awareness. First, Social Awareness is an aspiration—we can never truly know what another is experiencing. Further, our own experience and point of view distorts clear understanding. We tend to get caught in our own view and intentions—we look but we don't see others. An added challenge is that others may have difficulty communicating their experience, feelings, thoughts, and intentions. They may not even know for themselves, or they actively may attempt to conceal aspects of themselves by intentionally or unintentionally misrepresenting themselves. High-level Social Awareness requires imagination, guess work, Self-Awareness, and ability to communicate well in order to develop and clarify an understanding of another.

WIRED TO CONNECT

Humans are social animals. We can read and make snap judgments in milliseconds about others. In a sense, our brains evolved to detect whether another is a friend or a foe, trustworthy or dangerous. It also evolved to build social connection and deepen familial bonds. It as been said that humans are the winners of a bet that the weaker, clawless, social creatures with the capacity to collaborate and use tools would survive. Indeed, we have fundamental capacities and instincts to understand, connect, be altruistic, and build loving bonds with others.

In the past decade, understanding of the underpinnings of social connection has grown enormously. A field called *interpersonal neurobiology* illuminates the importance of relationships and social connections for surviving and thriving. Interpersonal neurobiology examines how brain structures and functioning are built to foster relationships and how these relationships shape its structures and functioning.

RESEARCH—Interpersonal Neurobiology

Below are abstracts from a selection of scientific studies published in major peer reviewed journals. Topics from the field of Interpersonal Neurobiology include Emotional Contagion, Mirror Neurons, and Empathy.

Stress Emotional Contagion. Female participants were exposed to high or low threat in the presence of another person believed to be facing either the same or a different situation. In Study 1, each dyad consisted of 2 actual participants, whereas in Study 2, each dyad consisted of 1 participant and 1 confederate, trained to convey either a calm or a nervous reaction to the situation. In both studies, a participant's felt affiliation towards their partner, defined in terms of the amount of time spent looking at the affiliate, were consistent with Schachter's (1959) "emotional similarity hypothesis;" threat increased affiliation and did so particularly with partners believed to be facing the same situation.

The authors also found evidence of behavioral mimicry, in terms of facial expressions, and emotional contagion, in terms of self-reported anxiety. The behavioral mimicry and emotional contagion results are considered from both primitive emotional contagion and social comparison theory perspectives.

Gump, B. and Kulik, J. (1997) Stress, affiliation, and emotional contagion. *Journal of Personality and Social Psychology,* 72(2): 305-319.

Mood Contagion. The current studies aimed to find out whether a non-intentional form of mood contagion exists and which mechanisms can account for it. In these experiments, participants who expected to be tested for text comprehension listened to an affectively neutral speech that was spoken in a slightly sad or happy voice. The authors found that:
- the emotional expression induced a congruent mood state in the listeners,
- inferential accounts to emotional sharing were not easily reconciled with the findings,
- different affective experiences emerged from intentional and non-intentional forms of emotional sharing, and

- findings suggest that a perception–behavior link (T. L. Chartrand & J. A. Bargh, 1999) can account for these findings, because participants who were required to repeat the philosophical speech spontaneously imitated the target person's vocal expression of emotion.

Neumann, R., Strack, F. (2000) Mood Contagion: The automatic transfer of mood between persons. *Journal of Personality and Social Psychology* 79(2): 211-223.

Stress Contagion. Previous research on multiple role stress has hypothesized the existence of two types of stress contagion: spillover, in which the stresses experienced in either the work or home domain lead to stresses in the other domain; and crossover, in which the stresses experienced by one's spouse at work lead to stresses for oneself at home. However, empirical evidence of these processes has been largely indirect and qualitative.

This study provides the first direct quantitative evidence on the causal dynamics of stress contagion across work and home domains in married couples. Contrary to previous thinking, results indicate that husbands are more likely than their wives to bring their home stresses into the workplace. Also, stress contagion from work to home was evident for both husbands and wives. Furthermore, the contagion of work stress into the home sets in motion a process of dyadic adjustment, whereby individuals, particularly wives, appear to modify their housework efforts to compensate for the work stresses of their spouses.

Such findings provide important insights into the dynamics of gender differences in role stress and confirm the value of studying chronic stress processes at the level of analysis where such stresses are inevitably manifest—in day-to-day events and activities.

Bolger, N., DeLongis, A., Kessler, R., Wethington, E. (1989). The Contagion of Stress Across Multiple Roles. *Journal of Marriage and Family*. 51(1): 175-183

Prewired Neural Basis for Emotional Contagion. Frequently, one individual becomes 'infected' with emotions displayed by his or her partner. Researchers tested the predictions that the automatic, mostly unconscious component of this process, called 'primitive emotional contagion', is repeatable and fast. Stronger facial expressions of the sender evoke stronger emotions in the viewer, and women are more susceptible to emotional contagion than men.

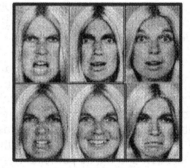

They presented photos on a computer varying the affective content (e.g., happy and sad), the expressive strength, and the duration of presentation. After each photo, subjects rated the strength of experienced happiness, sadness, anger, disgust, surprise, fear and pleasure (image from csupomona.edu). Feelings of happiness or sadness were significantly, specifically and repeatedly evoked in the viewer even with presentations lasting only 500 ms. Stronger expressions evoked more emotion. The gender of the viewer had weak effects.

Researchers posited that this fast and repeatable reaction is likely to have a 'prewired' neural basis. They propose the perception of emotionally expressive faces is related to the detection of emotional states in others and as the basis for one's own reactions.

Wild, B., Erbb, M., Bartelsa, M. (2001) Are emotions contagious? Evoked emotions while viewing emotionally expressive faces: quality, quantity, time course and gender differences. *Psychiatry Research*, 102(2): 109-124.

MIRROR NEURONS

Understanding the Actions of Others. "Mirror" neurons are neurons that discharge both when the monkey makes a particular action and when it observes another individual (monkey or human) making a similar action. Researchers attempted to give a neurophysiological account of the mechanisms underlying behaviors where an individual reproduces, overtly or internally, movements or actions made by another individual.

The basic concept of mirror neurons:

1. Person A performs a physical act.
2. Person B observes.
3. The brain activity in Person A and Person B are similar.

Two types of resonance behavior:

The first type is characterized by imitation, immediate or with delay, of movements made by other individuals. Examples of resonance behavior of this type are the "imitative" behaviors observed in birds, young infants and patients with frontal lesions.

The second type of resonance behavior is characterized by the occurrence, at the observation of an action, of a neural pattern, which, when internally generated, determines the making of the observed action. In this type of resonance behavior the observed action is, typically, not repeated (overtly). We argue that resonance behavior of the second type is at the basis of the understanding of actions made by others.

Rizzolatti, G., Fadiga, L., Fogassi, L., Gallese, V. Resonance Behaviors and Mirror Neurons. *Italiennes de Biologie*. 137(2/3).

Performed or Observed Causes Same Neural Response. Many object-related actions can be recognized both by their sound and by their vision. They describe a population of neurons in the ventral premotor cortex of the monkey that discharge both when the animal performs a specific action and when it hears or sees the same action performed by another individual. These 'audiovisual mirror neurons' therefore represent actions independently of whether these actions are performed, heard or seen. The magnitude of auditory and visual responses did not differ significantly in half the neurons. A neurometric analysis revealed that based on the response of these neurons, two actions could be discriminated with 97% accuracy.

Keysers, C., Kohler, E., Umilta, M., Nanetti, L., Foggasi, L., Gallese, V. (2003) Audiovisual mirror neurons and action recognition. *Experimental Brain Research*, 153 (4): 628-636.

Inferring Intention through Action. Is it possible to understand the intentions of other people by simply observing their actions? Many believe that this ability is made possible by the brain's mirror neuron system through its direct link between action and observation. However, precisely how intentions can be inferred through action observation has provoked much debate. Researchers suggested that the function of the mirror system can be understood within a predictive coding framework that appeals to the statistical approach known as empirical Bayes. Within this scheme the most likely cause of an observed action can be inferred by minimizing the prediction error at all levels of the cortical hierarchy that are engaged during action observation. This account identifies a precise role for the mirror system in our ability to infer intentions from actions and provides the outline of the underlying computational mechanisms.

Kilner, J., Friston, K., Frith, C. (2007) Predictive coding: an account of the mirror neuron system. *Cognitive Processing*, 8(3): 159-166

Brain Structures Involved with Understanding Emotions and Actions. Researchers examined the neural workings behind understanding others. They found that two separate but similar systems provide for the comprehension of the actions and emotions of others. The ability to experientially understand the emotions of others involves the viscero-motor centers. The mirror neuron system supports the ability to understand others' actions.

Gallese, V., Keysers, C., Rizzolatti, G. (2004) A unifying view of the basis of social cognition. *Trends in Cognitive Science*, 8(9): 396-403.

High-functioning autistic children and controls were monitored via fMRI as they imitated and observed emotional expression. Performance on the task was similar across both groups but autistic children did not show any mirror neuron activity in the inferior frontal gyrus (pars opercularis), which is tied to the severity of social deficiencies in autism. The research suggests that this area of the brain, in particular this mirror neuron system, plays a vital role in explaining the deficits in social ability in autistic children.

Dapretto, M. et al. (2006). Understanding emotions in others: mirror neuron dysfunction in children with autism spectrum disorders. *Nature Neuroscience, 9(1), 28-30.*

Participants completed a social cognition measure ("Visual Discrimination" and the "Static and Dynamic Emotion Recognition" task) while being administered transcranial magnetic stimulation to known mirror neuron areas. Greater neuron activity was observed in the premotor cortex that correlated with performance on the social cognition measure. More specifically, increased MEP amplitude was observed during emotion recognition of static faces; there were no significant correlations between mirror neuron activation and general facial processing, suggesting that mirror neurons do have a role in "variant" expressions (apart from neutral faces), as well as the importance of the mirror neuron system in the premotor cortex in social cognition.

Enticott, P.G. et al. (2008). Mirror neuron activation is associated with facial emotion processing. *Neuropsychologia, 46, 2851-2854.*

Participants completed tasks requiring them to observe, discriminate, and imitate facial expressions (i.e. neutral, happy, fearful, and disgust) as well as patterned bodily motion while monitored by fMRI. Passive observation of facial expressions was correlated with increases in the inferior frontal gyrus/insula and the posterior parietal cortex, which is associated with the execution of similar facial expressions. Some regions responded more to specific facial expression than patterned motion (bilateral ventral IFG, bilateral STS/MTG, bilateral amygdala, SMA). Emotional expressions elicited greater activity in the insula and frontal operculum while neutral faces elicited greater activity in the somatosensory cortices. The amygdala showed greater activity in the fear conditions, and the insula for disgust. In the discrimination and imitation tasks, the observed effects were heightened.

Van der Gaag, C., Minderaa, R.B., & Keysers, C. (2007). Facial expressions: What the mirror neuron system can and cannot tell us. *Social Neuroscience, 2(3-4), 179-222.*

SKILL 12. LISTEN MINDFULLY

Listening is such a simple act.
It requires us to be present, and that takes practice, but we don't have to do anything else.
We don't have to advise, or coach, or sound wise.
We just have to be willing to sit there and listen.
-Margaret J. Wheatley

Mindfulness is characterized by attending to the moment with awareness, openness, a spirit of receptivity, and non-judging. When we bring this quality of attention to listening, it is commonly referred to as mindful listening. Listening mindfully is being curious and working to understand another's message. The focus is on both the factual and emotional components of the message.

Our version of mindful listening is defined by Harvard Professor Ellen Langer's three elements of mindfulness:

(1) Being open to new information that arises in the present moment.
(2) Non-judgmentally taking multiple perspectives.
(3) Allowing mindsets to be revised based on new information.

When a composer listens to music, he or she hears far more than sound. The composer hears the underlying structure, the interplay of different instruments. The composer hears key changes, recognizes certain musical conventions, as well as unusual or creative additions to the normal patterns of the particular kind of music being played. In the same way, a mindful listener not only hears the words of the other person but also their significance in the context of the larger message. A mindful listener also notices what is not being said, which is often revealing.

Our technique for cultivating this type of attention is based on Lee Glickstein's method that he refers to as "Relational Presence." Relational Presence simply means being available for giving full attention without agenda. It is the pre-condition for connection. It involves being with others without judgment, demands, or expectations. This type of mindful presence improves the capacity to be comfortable with whatever situation arises and to respond in the moment, whether in conflict or sharing joy with another. Lee teaches this way of listening and speaking in a format he refers to as "Speaking Circles."

Sometimes this type of listening is referred to as "active listening," Generally, they refer to the similar practice. Mindful listening techniques generally emphasize the importance of presence, clear mindedness, and non-judgment. Sometimes this includes asking clarifying questions, summarizing the message, and checking for understanding.

Other programs that use mindful listening techniques to build empathy and social skills include but are not limited to: Robert Weissberg's Center for Academic and Social and Emotional Learning, The MindUp Curriculum created by the actor Goldie Hawn's The Hawn Foundation, Search Inside Yourself, and Martin Seligman's positivity-enhancing mindful listening technique he calls Active-Constructive Listening.

BENEFITS

Mindful listening is emphasized in many social intelligence programs, because it is crucial for understanding and managing interactions, relationships, and connection. Lee Glickstein describes a benefit of this method as increasing attunement between the speaker and the listener. Effective leaders do this regularly. Much more information is gained when mindfully listening. Perhaps the greatest benefit, however, is that the feeling of connection between the speaker and the listener improves. Barbara Fredrickson, a leading researcher in positive emotions, emphasizes the importance of this type of attention to create "micro-moments of connection."

MINDLESS LISTENING

Its opposite, mindless listening, is characterized by a quality of attention that is absent, rigid, and governed by mindsets, according to Ellen Langer. In this type of attention as she says, " the lights are on but nobody's home." In an era when attention is under siege, mindless listening seems to become the norm.

In our 21st Century era of distraction, mindful listening is more difficult than ever. Attention is pulled, stretched, and taxed by the constant bombardment of electronic messages. It is common in conversation for the mind to wander, and internal narratives and distracted thoughts to fragment attention. We tend to get caught in our own thoughts, missing emotional signs, verbal cues, and other vital information. Our attention is on our own experience, judging the other, assuming we already know what they will say, or planning a response. This is especially true in a conflict situation.

THREE LEVELS OF LISTENING—INTERNAL, FOCUSED, AND GLOBAL

In her book, *Co-Active Coaching*, Laura Whitworth describes three levels of listening. Mindful listening takes place when listening at Level 2 and Level 3. Mindless listening is characterized by Level 1. In a mindless listener, the focus is on something other than the speaker.

Level 1: Internal Listening. Internal listening is sometimes called "on and off" listening or "distracted" listening. When a person listens at level 1, her attention is on her own experience. She may hear the words of the other person, but she tends to be more aware of her own ideas, feelings, opinions, stories, judgments, and internal chatter. Level 1 listening is characterized by:
- Hearing sounds and words rather than listening.
- Getting only the gist of the conversation.
- Being more interested in talking than listening.
- Nodding and/or saying uh-huh as a cover for disengagement.
- Lack of eye contact.
- Being distracted by things such as mobile phone, email, television, surrounding events, etc.

Level 2: Focused Listening. Focused listening is sometimes called "attentive" listening. When a person listens at level 2, she pays attention to each individual word and phrase and how the other person expresses them. Level 2 listening is characterized by:
- Hearing the words and looking for the meaning.
- Listening for factual content.
- Listening for emotional content.
- Responding by restating, paraphrasing, questioning, and summarizing.

Level 3: Global Listening. Global listening is sometimes called "generous" listening. When a person listens at level 3, he hears the words, tunes into the emotions, and reads the body language, gestures, and tones being used by the other person. Level 3 listening is characterized by:
- Listening without judging.
- Focusing on the present moment.
- Fully processing what is said including factual and emotional content.
- Paying attention to words, tone of voice, and body language.
- Responding by restating, paraphrasing, questioning, and summarizing.

SOCIAL AWARENESS

CHECK YOUR LISTENING STYLE

Use the *Listening Style Self-Assessment* to become more aware of your listening style.

MINDFUL LISTENING SURVEY

Instructions: How true are the following statements about you? Please read each statement carefully, and circle the number that corresponds with your level of agreement. Go with your gut response without over-thinking the statements.

Very Strongly Disagree	Strongly Disagree	Mildly Disagree	Neutral	Mildly Agree	Strongly Agree	Very Strongly Agree
1	**2**	**3**	**4**	**5**	**6**	**7**

#	STATEMENT	YOUR RATING						
1.	When someone else is talking, I often am preparing my response rather than concentrating on what they are saying.	1	2	3	4	5	6	7
2.	I sometimes finish other people's sentences for them.	1	2	3	4	5	6	7
3.	I get impatient or distracted and start doing other things when I'm bored or annoyed with what another is saying.	1	2	3	4	5	6	7
4.	I interrupt others when they are speaking.	1	2	3	4	5	6	7
5.	I have a hard time looking people in the eye when I am speaking.	1	2	3	4	5	6	7
6.	It is difficult for me to listen without offering my opinion or point-of-view.	1	2	3	4	5	6	7
7.	I find myself changing topics before the person I am talking to is finished with their point.	1	2	3	4	5	6	7

TOTAL SCORE: _____

INTERPRETING YOUR SCORE. If your score was on the higher end, you may especially benefit from practicing mindful listening.

Higher scores *(scores over 35)* indicate that you may be distracted and not really listening well to others. You may find that your attention is on your own experience rather than on the other's experience or message. The words of the other person may be heard, but you may be more aware of your own ideas, feelings, opinions, stories, judgments, and internal chatter.

Midrange scores *(scores 15-34)* indicate that you sometimes engage in mindful listening, but could still improve your ability to listen well.

Low scores *(scores under 14)* indicate that you tend to listen well and focus on the message, speaker, and their spoken and unspoken experience. You are likely to not only hear the content but also tune into the emotions, read the body language, and notice gestures and tones.

SIGNS OF MINDLESS LISTENING

It has been said that communication is a joint game in which the talker and the listener play against the forces of confusion. Mindful listening is important, because communication is difficult even under the best circumstances. When obstacles to mindful listening arise, *mindless* listening is likely to arise. This is characterized by not paying attention to new information, taking narrow or rigid perspectives, judging, and staying in biases or mindsets. Mindless listening compounds difficulty, increasing the probability of mistakes, misunderstanding, hurt feelings, miscommunication, and wasted time and effort.

To reduce impediments to effective communication, watch for signs that you may be more mindless rather than mindful in your listening. The following obstacles or bad habits impede mindful listening and give rise to a mindless listening mode.

Internal Focus. Focusing attention on one's own thoughts, opinions, experiences, or emotions. Often people mean well by listening in this way, especially when they are thinking about how they have had a similar experience or can relate. This prevents mindful listening, however, because the listener is focusing on their own experience, perhaps judging the other from the lens of the listener's experience, assuming they already know what will be said, or planning a response. In conflict, this tends to show up as preparing a reply or thinking some version of "what about me…"

Interruptions. Interrupting the speaker before they finish. The speaker is not allowed to finish thoughts. Interruptions are often interpreted as a lack of respect or interest. Further, the listener who interrupts runs the risk of misinterpreting the message since the speaker was cut short from fully articulating his or her thoughts. People speak at different speeds. A slower speaker may pause frequently to gather thoughts. If another jumps in during their pause, it may feel like interruption to a slower speaker.

Bias. Preconceived ideas or judgments the listener has about the speaker or the message. Biases can distort understanding, acting like a filter that catches some aspects of their message but not others.

Expectations or assumptions about what the other thinks typically result in mindless listening. When holding a belief, we tend to find evidence to confirm it and become blind to contrary evidence. Psychologists refer to this as the Confirmation Bias. This is especially true in a conflict situation. For example, if you believe the other person does not respect you, you are more likely to miss words that express respect and interpret a side-glance or yawn as evidence they are bored with you.

Lack of Focus. Tuning-out, daydreaming, or multi-tasking while a speaker is speaking is a very common poor listening habit. Because the listener is not focused on the speaker, elements of the message will be missed and all of the above habits are likely to strengthen. This is common in our busy, distracted modern culture.

Giving full attention is even more difficult during conflict, because the other's message is inherently hard to hear and distressing. For many, conflict triggers the fight, flight, or freeze reaction. Tuning out is a common attempt to calm the body but this puts us in mindless listening mode.

HOW TO LISTEN MINDFULLY

Listening mindfully generally requires stopping all activity, looking into the speaker's eyes if in person, and allowing the speaker the space to express themselves without interruption. This helps create the conditions through which mindful listening can occur. This is an active process. The conversation can feel quite animated, lively, and balanced. Don't judge what you hear or add meaning to the message initially. Simply observe and experience the speaker and their message. If you become restless or impatient, notice these feelings and allow them, but do not react to them.

> **HOW TO LISTEN MINDFULLY**
>
> **1. Focus.** Give full attention, eye contact, and stop multi-tasking.
>
> **2. Listen without Interrupting.** Speak only when the speaker is finished.
>
> **3. Curiosity.** Notice something new in the message.
>
> **4. Listen Deeply.** Listen for feeling, tone, and intention.

1. Focus. Stop multi-tasking and give full attention. The listener simply offers the speaker undivided attention. This is simple yet challenging and surprisingly, uncommon. When one focuses and gets still in mind and body, then mindful listening happens quite effortlessly. This is similar to sleep. If the body is sufficiently tired, the body will naturally fall into sleep without us doing a thing. What tends to get in the way of this process is the mind. When the mind gets busy thinking, worrying, figuring out, regretting, etc., it disrupts the natural sleep process and insomnia ensues. This is the same with listening. When we get still in our mind and direct focus to the speaker, mindful listening simply happens. However, giving full attention is harder than it seems. Often we think we are giving full attention, but actually we are judging, anticipating our response, thinking about other things, multi-tasking, not looking at the person, and so on.

2. Listen without Interrupting. Speak only when the speaker is finished. When listening mindfully, the listener does not interrupt to provide an opinion, agreement, or a counter viewpoint. Instead, the listener waits until the speaker pauses and then the listener speaks. Oftentimes, interrupting stems from trying to help the speaker understand better, to offer help, out of excitement, or other well-intended reasons; however, the impact is often the same regardless of the intention. It can send the message that what you have to say is more important than what the speaker is saying. Typically, no one likes to be interrupted.

3. Curiosity. Notice something new in the message. This is the crux of mindful listening. Bring curiosity to the conversation. Rather than assume you know "how it will go," bring a curious, open mind. Allow yourself to be surprised or learn something about the person or situation. When curious, we naturally become more mindful, which is characterized by being open to new information, taking different perspectives, and revising old mindsets. Every conversation can teach us something and impact us in some small way when we bring curiosity to it.

I once met Michael Wallace, one of the original correspondents on the famous American TV show *60 Minutes*. We chatted for a while in a casual, small bookstore on Martha's Vineyard. I asked him what his secret is to interviewing people and his exceptional ability to reveal personal stories. He said, "Everyone has an interesting story—you just have to ask the right questions to pull it out of them." This is a classic demonstration of bringing curiosity to a conversation and, more generally, a high level of mindful listening.

4. Listen Deeply. Consider feelings, intention, or underlying significance (in addition to content). In mindful listening, the listener attends to a deeper level of experience. Slowing down and paying attention enables access to subtle clues about what the speaker is communicating about their emotional and deeper experience. It can be helpful to intentionally direct attention and take note of the feeling tone of the message, rather than simply the content. It gets really interesting when the speaker's words point to one experience, but the feeling tone conveys an opposite experience. Paying attention at a deeper level also gives access to clues about what matters most to the speaker, what is really important, or significant. This subtle yet critical information often gets lost when not mindfully listening.

MINDFUL LISTENING WORKSHEET

Mindful listening involves getting still in the mind and attention so that we truly hear what the other is saying, what's under their words, what's significant for them, and information about their deeper level of emotional experience. This application gives you an opportunity to practice mindful listening.

SITUATION

Who, Where & When Did I Attempt to Listen Mindfully?

_____
_____
_____

What were some OBSTACLES to mindful listening or SIGNS OF MINDLESS LISTENING that came up? (Interruptions, Criticism, Judgment, Multi-tasking, Preoccupation, Tuning Out)

_____
_____
_____
_____

MINDFUL LISTENING

1. FOCUS. How did I give full attention, stop mullti-tasking, and focus?
Consider intentions, instructions, or reminders you gave yourself. Notice what it looked like, for example, did you give eye contact, stop doing other things, refrain from judgment or rehearsing your response, etc.? What was the impact of listening with full attention?

_____
_____
_____
_____

2. LISTEN WITHOUT INTERRUPTING. To what extent was I able to listen without interrupting? What was the impact of doing this?

_____
_____
_____
_____

3. CUROSITY. What were some new things that I noticed about the message or speaker? What was the impact of listening with curiosity?

_____
_____
_____
_____

4. LISTEN DEEPLY. Which emotions did I pick up on? What was the speaker's intention? What was most significant or important in the speaker's message? What was the impact of listening for feelings, intention, and underlying significance?

_____
_____
_____
_____

5. DEEPER UNDERSTANDING. To what extent did I develop a deeper understanding by listening mindfully? What did I pick up that I might not have otherwise noticed?

_____
_____
_____
_____

6. EMPATHY. What impact did this level of listening have on my level of empathy and sense of connection with the speaker?

_____
_____
_____
_____
_____

7. BENEFIT. How did I benefit from listening mindfully?

_____
_____
_____
_____

8. APPLICATION. How might I improve your ability to listen mindfully during natural conversations to improve understanding and avoid misunderstanding and/or de-escalate conflict situations?

_____
_____
_____
_____
_____

MINDFUL LISTENING TRACKING LOG

DAY	APPLICATION Whom did I mindfully listen to today? How did I do this (i.e., Where was your focus? What was the self-talk or reminders you gave yourself?)	IMPACT What was the impact of mindful listening on me, others, and/or the situation?
Day 1		
Day 2		
Day 3		
Day 4		

SOCIAL AWARENESS

MINDFUL LISTENING TRACKING LOG

DAY	**APPLICATION** Whom did I mindfully listen to today? How did I do this (i.e., Where was your focus? What was the self-talk or reminders you gave yourself?)	**IMPACT** What was the impact of mindful listening on me, others, and/or the situation?
Day 5		
Day 6		
Day 7		

INSIGHTS—What patterns or benefits emerged?

_____
_____
_____
_____
_____
_____

SKILL 13. READING OTHERS' EMOTIONS

The ability to read another's emotions requires being able to detect and interpret emotional signals, label emotions, and identify likely triggers.

THREE STEP PROCESS FOR READING EMOTIONS

1. **EXAMINE EMOTIONAL SIGNALS.** Notice Verbal & Nonverbal Signals.
2. **IDENTIFY THE EMOTIONS.** Be Specific
3. **CONSIDER THE EMOTIONAL TRIGGERS.** Consider Possible Triggers

---

STEP 1. EXAMINE EMOTIONAL SIGNALS

Verbal and nonverbal signals reveal much about another's experience. Often we miss verbal and nonverbal cues because we are so caught up in our own perspective that we don't really "see" the other person. Making a practice of truly observing another's vocal tone, eye contact, body language, and facial expressions can be a highly effective but simple practice that can greatly increase ability to read another's emotional state. Their body state and likely action impulses can inform how to deal with them. Gauging the "temperature" and "flavor" of their emotional state might tell you how close they are to losing their temper or acting rashly, for example.

VERBAL AND NONVERBAL SIGNALS

Verbal and nonverbal signals can be used to understand what bodily reactions are associated with their emotions. The verbal and nonverbal signals of emotions reveal a lot about what their bodily reactions and action impulses are.

Verbal Signals. What are the verbal expressions of the emotion?

- Vocal tone
- Cadence
- Emotionally-charged language or word choice
- Punctuation (in written messages)

Nonverbal Signals. Nonverbal signals reveal clues about what another is feeling. These are often involuntary physical manifestations of an emotion. In poker games, a "tell" is a subtle, unconscious physical manifestation of an underlying emotion. A tell reveals what a player is trying to hide from opponents. For example, if a player has drawn a bad hand, anxiety is likely to ensue. Tells of anxiety might be fidgeting, foot tapping, sighs, or darting eyes. Tells for a good hand might be eyebrow raising or a smirk. Just like poker players use tells to inform strategy, we can watch for nonverbal signals, or tells, to decode another's emotional experience.

There are three categories of nonverbal signals that can reveal clues about emotions: *Body State, Body Language,* and *Facial Expressions.*

Body State. The body state refers to the general way that one is holding their body. Consider, for example, if they look and sound tense, slow, lethargic, energized, agitated, or calm. Recall that all emotions have a physiological effect—they have a distinctive stamp on the body. Watch for body reactions associated with emotional states such as:
- Speed and depth of breath
- Flushed face
- Sweaty palms
- Tense muscles
- Posture
- Speed of movements
- Hand and foot movements
- Eye movements and placement (e.g., direct stare or darting eyes)

For example, the "Fight or Flight" response accompanies fear or anxiety, which elicits:
- Increased heart rate, respiration, and blood flow prepare the muscles for action.
- Spikes in adrenaline, which rushes through the body to mobilize for immediate action.
- Narrowed attention, heightened vigilance, muscle tensing and increased perspiration.

Body Language. Body language refers to the actions or cues that one performs. They communicate what type of emotion is being experienced. Dacher Keltner, PhD, a researcher at UC Berkeley, has identified several realms in the language of emotions. The following list is adapted in part from his research.

Sign Language. Nonverbal gestures that are culturally translated as a word. For example, the peace sign or A-OK sign.

Conscious Cues. Nonverbal behaviors that individuals use during speech to signal emphasis or drama. For example, eye brow raise, waive of the hand, making a fist.

Unconscious Cues. Automatic behaviors that are associated with emotions, often appearing as expressions of anxiety. For example, face touches, leg shaking, ear touching, eyebrow raising.

Facial Expressions. There are innumerable configurations of the approximately 30 sets of facial muscles that accompany an emotion. This is considered the most complex and important of the nonverbal displays of emotions. Two types of facial expressions are micro-expressions and longer duration facial expressions, which are more easily identifiable.

Research shows that facial expressions of emotions have identifiable properties:

- Duration of 1 to 5 seconds (micro-expressions last only milliseconds)
- Symmetrical muscle movements
- Reliable muscle action

Dozens of research studies demonstrate that certain facial displays are universal. Specifically, displays of anger, disgust, fear, sadness, surprise, and happiness are observed across all cultures using the same facial expressions. On the other hand, there are cultural differences in specific displays of emotion, too. For example, the tongue bite to express embarrassment in many Southeast Asian cultures.

Facial Micro-Expressions. Micro expressions are the fleeting emotional signals lasting only milliseconds that communicate emotion. They can be extremely difficult to detect and people differ widely in their detection accuracy. Getting better at detecting micro expressions can greatly enhance one's ability to identify another's emotional state.

Paul Ekman, PhD at UCSF is considered the top researcher in emotion expression identification. He is known for his famous cross-cultural facial expression studies and more recently for his collaborative work with The Dalai Lama and consultation to governmental agencies particularly in homeland security and law enforcement. You may have seen a popular TV show drama based on his ideas called "Lie to Me."

A Micro-Expressions Detection Training program can be found at PaulEkman.com. This highly regarded, scientifically developed and validated online training program increases accuracy in identifying fleeting micro expressions of emotions. The training takes about one hour to complete.

STEP 2. IDENTIFY EMOTIONS

Labeling an emotion involves detecting, categorizing, and articulating the specific emotional state. This seemingly simple process requires accurate emotional perception and a nuanced understanding of the distinctions between emotions. The ability to label an emotion is a fundamental skill in social intelligence. It makes it possible to understand another's experience and work with their emotions.

Individuals differ in their ability to detect, categorize, and articulate another's emotions, but like other skills, reading emotional states can be learned and strengthened regardless of current mastery level. We often have a general sense of what others are feeling. In this practice, however, we focus on developing a more sophisticated understanding and ability to read emotional states.

Primary Emotions. While there are hundreds of emotions, and even more blends of emotions, research shows that there are six basic types of emotions that all humans experience: surprise, fear, anger, disgust, sadness, and joy. Cross-cultural research by Paul Ekman, a leading authority on emotional expression, and other emotion researchers show that these are biologically universal emotions. In *Emotional Intelligence,* Daniel Goleman expands Ekman's list to eight families of emotions:

BASIC FAMILIES OF EMOTIONS

Surprise:	shock, astonishment, amazement, and wonder.
Fear:	anxiety, apprehension, nervousness, concern, consternation, misgiving, wariness, qualm, edginess, dread, fright, terror and in the extreme cases phobia and panic.
Anger:	fury, outrage, resentment, wrath, exasperation, indignation, vexation, acrimony, animosity, annoyance, irritability, hostility, and perhaps these are manifest in the extreme as hatred and violence.
Sadness:	grief, sorrow, cheerlessness, gloom, melancholy, self-pity, loneliness, dejection, despair, and depression in the extreme case.
Disgust:	contempt, distain, scorn, abhorrence, aversion, distaste, and revulsion.
Shame:	guilt, embarrassment, chagrin, remorse, humiliation, regret, mortification, and contrition.
Enjoyment:	happiness, joy, relief, contentment, bliss, delight, amusement, pride, sensual pleasure, thrill, rapture, gratification, satisfaction, euphoria, whimsy, ecstasy, and at the far edge, mania.
Love:	acceptance, friendliness, trust, kindness, affinity, devotion, adoration, infatuation, and agape.

Be Specific. As stated in Self-Awareness, often we do not get specific about which emotion the person is experiencing. For example, when attempting to label emotions commonly people identify feeling "stressed." "Stressed" however, is not an emotion. It is a state that refers to a combination of distressing emotions such as anxiety, frustration, annoyance, and surprise. Likewise, feeling "upset" is a general state but not an emotion. "Upset" may be comprised of as anger, frustration, disappointment, or sadness. This level of precision in emotional perception improves the ability to work with another's emotional state.

Which emotion do I detect?   *"She/he is having the emotion _____."*

Intensity: Rate the intensity level of the emotion (1-10, with 10 being an intolerable level of the emotion):

1   2   3   4   5   6   7   8   9   10

STEP 3. CONSIDER EMOTIONAL TRIGGERS

As described in Self-Awareness, a trigger is the event or stimulus that elicits an emotional response. Emotions have predictable origins, which is tied to the interpretation of an event or stimulus. For example, a perception of some form of threat and an injustice results in anger. The intensity of the trigger typically parallels the intensity of the emotion. The perceived problem is significantly large, and correspondingly, the emotion's intensity will be significantly distressing.

EMOTIONAL EQUATIONS	
DISTRESSING EMOTIONS	
EMOTIONS	**TRIGGERS**
Anger →	Injustice/Violation + Threat
Fear / Panic →	Present Threat
Anxiety →	Challenge + Doubt
Frustration →	Effort + Lack of Success
Disappointment →	Unfulfilled Positive Expectation
PLEASANT EMOTIONS	
EMOTIONS	**TRIGGERS**
Joy →	Pleasant Experience
Excitement →	Anticipation of Positive Experience
Love →	Intimacy + Respect
Contentment →	Satisfaction with Present
Hopefulness →	Positive Future Potential

RESEARCH—Detecting and Understanding Emotions

Below are abstracts from a selection of scientific studies published in major peer reviewed journals.

Facial Expressions as Involuntary Cues. Facial expressions such as anger, fear, sadness, and happiness are universally recognized. Ekman explored what information can be assessed from these signals. Typically, facial expressions are thought to express emotions but whether or not there other meanings to be gleaned from these involuntary movements is not established. Along with displaying emotions, Ekman describes facial expressions as also communicating hidden internal states. Ekman's research shows there are many messages to uncover in the secret cues of facial expressions.

Ekman, P. (1997) Expression or Communication about Emotion. *Uniting Psychology and Biology: Integrative Perspectives on Human Development.*

The Neurology Behind Empathy and Theory of Mind. New research in the field of social neuroscience is uncovering the neuronal differences in understanding others' mental and emotional states. Although the two terms are often used interchangeably, the terms theory of mind and empathy are differentiated by the authors. Expounding on the separate neuronal circuitry of each ability researchers illustrate the neuronal differences in these two forms of understanding.

The ability to attribute mental states such as intentions and beliefs to others as well as understand these mental processes as affecting behavior is termed theory of mind or mentalizing. Empathy is the ability to understand the emotions of others at an experiential level. The neuronal structures behind Theory of Mind are the temporal lobe and the pre-frontal cortex.

Empathy relies on sensorimotor cortices as well as limbic and para-limbic structures. The authors also point to the spectrum of cognitive processes implied in the everyday use of the term empathy, which extends from simpler forms of emotional contagion to complex cognitive perspective taking.

Additionally the authors show that the differing ontogenetic trajectories of these two abilities point to the differences in developmental maturation of their underlying neural structures. Empathy, relying heavily on limbic structures, develops earlier than theory of mind which relies primarily on the slower maturing lateral temporal lobe and pre-frontal structures.

Singer, T. (2006) The neuronal basis and ontogency of empathy and mind reading. *Neuroscience and Biobehavioral Reviews,* 30(6): 855-863.

Misinterpreting Emotions. Bipolar disorder, with its episodes of depression and mania, can severely disturb the social and academic life of youth suffering from this disorder. A recent study may have uncovered clues to the disruptive nature behind these episodes.

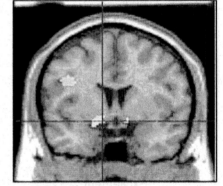

Researchers at the National Institute of Mental Health (NIMH) conducted a study on the neural reactions of youths suffering from bipolar disorder. When the youth were exposed to neutral faces they often misinterpreted the facial expressions to be hostile.

The left amygdala, a known fear center, along with other related structures became more activated in youth suffering from bipolar disorder than in other youth in the study when exposed to a neutral facial expression. The more hostile the expression was interpreted, the greater the reaction in the amygdala. This research suggests that the inability to correctly identify expressions may underlie the social and interpersonal difficulties faced by youth suffering from this disorder.

The left amygdala and related structures (yellow area where lines intersect) are part of an emotion-regulating brain circuit where children with bipolar disorder showed greater activation than controls when rating the neutral faces. The image illustrates the structural MRI image with functional MRI data superimposed.

NIH/National Institute of Mental Health (2006, May 30). Fear Circuit Flares As Bipolar Youth Misread Faces. *ScienceDaily.*

GENDER DIFFERENCES

Gender Differences In Decoding Emotions. A study of 77 female and 60 male undergraduate students focused on differences between the two sexes involved in accurate recognition of emotional expressions. Subjects were exposed to 120 pairs of facial expressions covering a range of six emotions. Half of the subjects were asked to empathize with the expression while the other half were asked to simply label it. All subjects were momentarily shown the second expression in either the left or right visual field and then asked to decide if the two expressions represented the same emotion.

The study found that when the second image was exposed to the right-visual field, women were more accurate at comparing the two emotional expressions. Men were more accurate in identify the same emotion when the second expression was shown to their left-visual field. When asked to empathize with the first facial expression both men and women displayed higher accuracy when the second image was shown in the left-visual field.

In accurately identifying and decoding emotions, the difference between men and women's hemisphere and perceptual-strategies when recognizing emotion points to differences in access to verbal and imagery codes.

Safer, M. (1981) Sex and hemisphere differences in access to codes for processing emotional expressions and faces. *Journal of Experimental Psychology,* 110(1): 86-100.

Gender Specific Neuronal Activation in Emotional Processing. A study on the neural correlates of emotion recognition illustrates the difference between the way men and women process happy and sad faces. This study examined the fMRI results of 12 men and 12 women subjected to various facial expressions. The subjects were shown twelve photographs depicting sad, happy, or neutral faces. The results showed distinct sets of neural correlates for processing happy and sad faces. Additionally, the study found that men and women use different sets of neural correlates when processing these varying emotional expressions.

This study supports the speculation that the different sexes respond differently on a neurological level to sad and happy expressions. It is suggested that the gender of the subjects must be taken into account when assessing for neural correlates in relation to emotion recognition.

Lee, T., Liu, H., Hoosain, R., Liao, W., Wu, C., Yuen, K., Chan, C., Fox, P., Goa, H. (2002) Gender differences in neural correlates of recognition of happy and sad faces in humans assessed by functional magnetic resonance imaging. *Neuroscience Letters,* 333(1): 13-16

Loving-Kindness Meditation Helps Build Personal Resources. This study found that adults who practiced loving-kindness meditation increased their daily experience of positive emotions; this further led to an increase in personal resources. These personal resources included aspects such as "increased mindfulness, purpose in life, social support, decreased illness symptoms." Many of the personal resources could be grouped into one of two categories: having a loving attitude towards oneself and others or feeling a competence about one's own life. Adults who had access to larger personal resources had higher life satisfaction and fewer depressive symptoms.

Fredrickson, B.L., Cohn, M.A., Coffey, K.A., Pek, J., & Finkel, S.M. (2008). Open hearts build lives: Positive emotions, induced through loving-kindness meditation, build consequential personal resources. *J Pers Soc Psychol, 95(5),* 1045-1062.

READING EMOTIONS WORKSHEET

The purpose of this application is to give you an opportunity to practice examining verbal and non-verbal emotional signals.

Identify a Situation. Briefly describe an emotionally charged situation (i.e., Who, What, Where, When).

_____
_____
_____
_____

STEP 1. EXAMINE EMOTIONAL SIGNALS

Verbal and nonverbal signals can tell a lot about what people are experiencing. Making a practice of truly observing another's vocal tone, eye contact, body language, and facial expressions can be a highly effective but simple practice that can greatly increase the ability to read another's emotional state. They act as tells, revealing hints about their emotional experience. In the following step of this worksheet, either recall an emotional situation of your own or observe people interact and watch for emotional signals.

VERBAL SIGNALS

What were some verbal signals of emotions and which emotions did these signals indicate?
(Identify signals like vocal tone, cadence, emotionally-charged language, word choice, or punctuation if written communication.)

VERBAL SIGNAL	POSSIBLE INDICATOR OF WHICH EMOTION?

SOCIAL AWARENESS

NONVERBAL SIGNALS

Nonverbal signals reveal clues about what another is feeling. Noticing the occurrence and timing of fidgeting, foot tapping, sighs, eyebrow raising, darting eyes, etc., might help you discriminate between similar emotions. There are two categories of nonverbal signals that can reveal clues about emotions: Body State and Body Language.

BODY STATE & FACIAL EXPRESSIONS. Which physical signs appeared and which emotion might they have indicated? (Consider speed and depth of breath, flushed face, sweaty palms, tense muscles, posture, speed of movements, hand and foot movements, eye movements and placement.)

BODY STATE & FACIAL EXPRESSIONS	POSSIBLE INDICATOR OF WHICH EMOTION?

BODY LANGUAGE. What body language was apparent, and what emotion might they have indicated?

_____

_____

_____

Sign Language—What nonverbal gestures were used that are culturally translated as a word? (For example, the peace sign or A-OK sign).

_____

_____

Conscious Cues—What nonverbal behaviors were used to signal emphasis or drama.? (For example, eye brow raise, wave of the hand, making a fist.)

_____

_____

_____

Unconscious Cues—What automatic behaviors that are associated with emotions did you notice? (For example, face touches, leg shaking, ear touching, eyebrow raising.)

_____

_____

_____

STEP 2. IDENTIFY EMOTIONS

LABEL EMOTIONS. Which Emotions Were Present?

Surprise: shock, astonishment, amazement, and wonder.
Fear: anxiety, apprehension, nervousness, concern, consternation, misgiving, wariness, qualm, edginess, dread, fright, terror and in the extreme cases phobia and panic.
Anger: fury, outrage, resentment, wrath, exasperation, indignation, vexation, acrimony, animosity, annoyance, irritability, hostility, and perhaps these are manifest in the extreme as hatred and violence.
Sadness: grief, sorrow, cheerlessness, gloom, melancholy, self-pity, loneliness, dejection, despair, and depression.
Disgust: contempt, distain, scorn, abhorrence, aversion, distaste, and revulsion.
Shame: guilt, embarrassment, chagrin, remorse, humiliation, regret, mortification, and contrition.
Enjoyment: happiness, joy, relief, contentment, bliss, delight, amusement, pride, sensual pleasure, thrill, rapture, gratification, satisfaction, euphoria, whimsy, ecstasy, and at the far edge, mania.
Love: acceptance, friendliness, trust, kindness, affinity, devotion, adoration, infatuation, and agape.

Identify ONE emotion that you detect in another (ex: anxiety, anger, sadness, embarrassment, etc.).

_____

Intensity. Rate the intensity level of the emotional state (1-10, with 10 being an intolerable level of the emotion).

    1   2   3   4   5   6   7   8   9   10

STEP 3. CONSIDER EMOTIONAL TRIGGERS

A trigger is the event or stimulus that elicits an emotional response. Emotions have predictable origins, which is tied to the interpretation of an event or stimulus. This worksheet provides an opportunity to better understand an emotional situation by analyzing the emotional experience of the other person. It may be useful to refer to the *Emotional Equations Table* and/or the *Emotions and Reactions Table* in the Self-Awareness chapter.

TRIGGER. What was the likely trigger for this emotion?

Emotional Equation. What is the Emotional Equation for this emotion? (Ex: Anger = Injustice + Threat) See the *Emotional Equations Table*.

_____

_____

Translate the Emotional Equation. Given the details of the situation, translate the emotional equation into the specific variables that represent the emotional trigger in this context. (Ex: *Injustice:* He seemed to interpret my comment in the meeting as unjustly blaming him for the failed project. *Threat:* He was probably concerned this called into question his competence in front of our boss)

_____

_____

_____

_____

INSIGHTS. What does the emotion reveal about what he/she wants or does not want?

_____

_____

_____

SOCIAL AWARENESS

READING EMOTIONS TRACKING LOG

DAY	**APPLICATION** Which emotional signals did I observe? Which emotions did I identify? What were the likely triggers for this emotion?	**IMPACT** What is the impact of reading their emotions on me, others, and/or the situation?
Day 1		
Day 2		
Day 3		
Day 4		

READING EMOTIONS TRACKING LOG

DAY	APPLICATION Which emotional signals did I observe? Which emotions did I identify? What were the likely triggers for this emotion?	IMPACT What is the impact of reading their emotions on me, others, and/or the situation?
Day 5		
Day 6		
Day 7		

INSIGHTS—What patterns or benefits emerged?

_____
_____
_____
_____
_____

LOVING-KINDNESS MEDITATION

This meditation explores the universal desire for an end to suffering and for contentment. It will guide you through bringing to mind these universal desires in different kinds of relationships in your life, including yourself. This meditation when practiced regularly has been shown to increase feelings of connection, happiness and lower feelings of loneliness and depression. It does not require that you neglect your own well-being; instead, it allows you to adjust your reaction to unavoidable suffering by assigning a new value to it.

During all the meditations, try to let go of expectations about how this practice is supposed to feel or what is supposed to happen. Your job is to experience what happens in a nonjudgmental, explorative manner, and each time your mind wanders into thought, turn your attention back. After the exercise please jot down observations about your experience.

INSTRUCTIONS
(8-12 minutes)

1. FOCUS INWARD: Breathe and Center

- **Center**—Close your eyes and turn your attention inward.

- **Anchor in your Breath**—Feel Your Breath fill and release your body. Breathe deeply with a slower exhale and natural inhale. Place your hand on your abdomen to feel your diaphragm rise and fall. Feel your feet as the rest on the floor. Notice the sensations on the bottom of your feet making contact with the earth. Feel your hands as they rest on your thighs. Open them and notice the sensations and invite them to relax.

- **Set your Intention**—To direct your attention in this time, place, and to the objective of this meditation.

2. DIRECT ATTENTION: *Send Loving and Kindness toward others and yourself.*

Step 1: Focus on a positive person and send vitality. Bring to your mind a positive person in your life. On an exhale, visualize sending them all your happiness vitality, good fortune, health, and goodness. If they are suffering, ill, or having difficulty, imagine they are well or full of joy.

Step 2: Focus on a neutral person and send vitality. Bring to your mind a neutral person in your life or someone you do not know well. On an exhale, visualize sending them all your happiness vitality, good fortune, health, and goodness. If they are suffering, ill, or having difficulty, imagine they are well or full of joy.

Step 3: Focus on a suffering person and send vitality. Bring to your mind a person in your life who is suffering. On an exhale, visualize sending them all your happiness vitality, good fortune, health, or goodness. If they are suffering, ill, or having difficulty, imagine they are well or full of joy.

Step 4: Focus on your desire to be well and receive vitality. Bring to your mind your desire to be well and happy in your life. On an exhale, visualize your distress, suffering and illness leaving your body. On an inhale, visualize filling your body with wellness, happiness vitality, good fortune, health, and goodness.

Step 6: Focus on the suffering in the universe and send vitality. Bring to your mind the fact that there is suffering in the universe. On an exhale, visualize sending happiness vitality, health, and goodness to all the suffering and disease. Imagine the universe being filled with goodness. When you inhale, visualize your heart as a bright, luminous sphere. There is no sense that you are burdened.

3. REFLECT ON INSIGHTS: Breathe and Reflect
- Come back to your breath.
- Reflect on the insights or benefits you gained during this meditation.

4. MAINTAIN INNER AWARENESS: Soft Gaze and Stay with Awareness.
- Slowly open your eyes and keep your gaze soft, directed downward, and settling on a neutral object.
- Stay with the awareness you gained during the meditation.

LOVING KINDNESS MEDITATION WORKSHEET

After you have completed the meditation, jot down observations about what came up during your meditation. Make note of thoughts you had, feelings you experienced, bodily sensations you felt, and/or detours that you took.

1. FOCUS INWARD: Breathe and Center. How well were you able to concentrate inward and turn your attention to your intention in this meditation?

_____

_____

2. DIRECT ATTENTION: *Send Loving and Kindness toward others and yourself.*

Step 1: Focus on a <u>positive person</u> and send vitality. Who did you bring to your mind? What did you experience when you visualized sending them all your happiness vitality, good fortune, health, and goodness?

_____

Step 2: Focus on a <u>neutral person</u> and send vitality. Who did you bring to your mind? What did you experience when you visualized sending them all your happiness vitality, good fortune, health, and goodness?

_____

Step 3: Focus on a <u>suffering person</u> and send vitality. Who did you bring to your mind? What did you experience when you visualized sending them all your happiness vitality, good fortune, health, and goodness?

_____

Step 4: Focus on <u>your desire</u> to be well and receive vitality. What happened when you brought to your mind your desire to be well and happy in your life? What did you experience when you visualized your distress, suffering and illness leaving your body? What did you experience when you visualized filling your body with wellness, happiness vitality, good fortune, health, and goodness?

_____

Step 6: Focus on the <u>suffering in the universe</u> and send vitality. What did you bring to your mind when you thought about the fact that there is suffering in the universe? What happened when you visualized sending happiness vitality, health, and goodness to all the suffering and disease? What happened when you imagined the universe being filled with goodness? What happened when you visualized your heart as a bright, luminous sphere?

_____

3. Personal Application. How can I use this Mindfulness Practice in developing my Social Awareness?

_____

_____

_____

LOVING-KINDNESS MEDITATION TRACKING LOG

DAY	APPLICATION When and what did I meditate on?	IMPACT What is the impact of doing a loving-kindness meditation on me, others, and/or the situation?
Day 1		
Day 2		
Day 3		
Day 4		

LOVING-KINDNESS MEDITATION TRACKING LOG

DAY	APPLICATION When and what did I meditate on?	IMPACT What is the impact of doing a loving-kindness meditation on me, others, and/or the situation?
Day 5		
Day 6		
Day 7		

INSIGHTS - What patterns or benefits emerged?

_____
_____
_____
_____
_____

SOCIAL AWARENESS

SKILL 14. NOTICE SIMILARITIES

"How far you go in life depends on your being tender with the young, compassionate with the aged, sympathetic with the striving and tolerant of the weak and strong. Because someday in your life you will have been all of these."
–George Washington Carver

Noticing similarities refers to intentionally considering others' intentions, needs, desires, dreams, fears, or other internal feeling states, perspectives, or objectives.

The Root of Empathy. Seeing similarities in others is at the root of empathy. When we notice the internal experiences of others including their motives, fears, hopes and dreams, we can't help but recognize similarities to ourselves. This leads to a natural bonding and care that manifests both in a feeling sense of connection and often action. People who see others as similar, as in the "in group" tend to engage in more altruistic acts and protective gestures. In contrast, the worst atrocities occur when another is out-casted, deemed different, vilified, and at worst dehumanized. Tragically, we have seen this phenomenon repeat itself countless times across human history.

Wired for detecting difference. Our brains are wired to see differences. Just like we are more adept at detecting danger signals than safety signals we more quickly can identify differences than similarities. From an evolutionary perspective this ability has a survival advantage. We might think of difference as a form of change. When things stay the same we know what to expect. We know that if we are safe we will continue to be safe. When things are different, an element of uncertainty is introduced. Through the lenses of the "caveman and cavewoman brain" differences should be attended to because they may indicate arrival of threat. People within the tribe were safe; people from outside the tribe are more likely to be dangerous.

CONSIDER ANOTHER'S INDIVIDUALITY

This Stranger

"This stranger has parents and people who love her, just like me.
This stranger has moments of joy, just like me
This stranger has moments of anguish and suffering, just like me.
This stranger will one day grow old, just like me.
This stranger will go through the cycles of illness and recovery, just like me.
This stranger will one day die, just like me."

–Deepak Chopra

Research suggests that the root of aggression resides in the failure to consider the individuality of another person. This provocative line of research shows that at extremes, this failure may facilitate inhumane acts like torture. Members of extreme outgroups that elicit disgust (e.g., homeless people and drug addicts) are differentially processed in the brain. This effect, however, can be undone very simply. It only requires considering a member of this group's individuality. In Harris and Fiske's study, they simply asked people if they thought this person (a homeless person) in the photograph would like carrots. This simple question was enough to create a sense of common humanity, and the brain regions associated with disgust became deactivated. These findings have profound implications for conflict not only between individuals but also for prejudice in society and violence between societies with clashing belief systems.

Try looking for similarities when resolving conflict or to deepen connection to enhance empathy and interpersonal problem solving.

Consider another's:
- Roles in life
- Goals
- Joys
- Challenges
- Insecurities and concerns

CONSIDER VULNERABILITIES

Considering vulnerabilities can be an especially effective way to transform power differentials and improve one's ability to manage conflict by building empathy. Vulnerabilities are often personal insecurities or areas where people have had difficulty previously. Typically, only close, trusted friends or family know of one's vulnerabilities, and sometimes not even they know. Vulnerabilities often remain hidden, and strong defenses can arise in an attempt to conceal them. Considering another's vulnerabilities can deepen understanding, help us to make sense of unexpected or confusing reactions, and help us feel compassionate during conflict. Awareness of another's vulnerabilities can greatly improve one's ability to deal with a difficult person in a sensitive and effective manner.

Common vulnerabilities are:
- Perfectionism
- Low self-worth
- Self-criticism
- Unrealistic expectations of self or others
- Need to be right
- Need to be liked
- Need for reassurance or approval, or to prove oneself
- Fear of failure
- Fear of not being good enough or feeling unlovable
- Need for predictability
- Excessive need for control
- Insecurity
- Social anxiety

Even in the workplace you might consider another's vulnerabilities or hidden insecurities. Although they may never admit to their insecurities, it can be useful to consider what they might be. This can both increase compassion, empathy, and understanding as well as make others in opposing positions or extreme power positions "more human." This skill can be invaluable when dealing with a difficult person who is strongly opinionated, stubborn, aggressive, or exhibiting other hard to understand behaviors. It is counterintuitive to see fierceness as a sign of vulnerability, but often fear and vulnerability underlie aggression. Unchecked fear can drive impulsive, strong, and extreme behaviors. Think of how fierce a grizzly bear can become when protecting her young. Aggression often emerges from the perception of threat or insecurity as a defensive or offensive attack to regain safety.

RESEARCH—EMPATHY

Below are abstracts from a selection of scientific studies published in major peer reviewed journals.

Considering Perspective Increases Empathy. In one study showing that empathy can be increased though a simple practice of considering another's perspective, 92 students were assigned to either a point-of-view writing or a clinical reasoning condition as part of a second year doctoring course. At the end of the year they completed a writing assignment about ER death from cardiac arrest. Results showed that students who were trained in point-of-view writing improved in certain affective dimensions.

Shapiro, J. (2006). Point-of-View Writing: A Method for Increasing Medical Students' Empathy, Identification and Expression of Emotion, and Insight. *Education for Health*, 19(1), 96-105.

Empathy through Mindfulness. A pilot project was assessed as a method to teach culturally sensitive, empathic communication skills. It attempted to integrate and communicate the theoretical, conceptual, and experiential understanding of cross-cultural empathy through the practice of mindful attitudes. Students were introduced to materials through a series of exercises, which included mirroring breathing observation, posture, and moving awareness. These exercises fostered a state of openness through the experience of emptying, contemplation, and being-present.

The preliminary findings indicated that the students were able to verbalize new learning experiences, which included: being more attuned with their bodily awareness, sensing the flow of energy with the other, letting go of power struggles, and pre-existing ideas, and experiencing a greater human connectedness with the other.

Lu, E., Dane., B., Gellman, A. (2005). The name assigned to the document by the author. This field may also contain sub-titles, series names, and report numbers. An Experiential Model: Teaching Empathy and Cultural Sensitivity. *The entity from which ERIC acquires the content, including journal, organization, and conference names, or by means of online submission from the author. Journal of Teaching in Social Work,* 25(3-4): 89-103

Prejudice and Dehumanization. This study suggests that having prejudice towards out groups that are stereotypically labeled as hostile and incompetent (i.e. homeless people, addicts) can be particularly troublesome and may lead to dehumanizing these extreme out-groups. Functional MRI's were used to examine brain activation in study participants that were shown photographs of social groups and objects. The researchers found increased neural activation to all images of social groups except extreme out-groups, supporting the prediction that extreme out-groups may be seen as less than human.

Harris, L. T., & Fiske, S. T. (2006). Dehumanizing the lowest of the low neuroimaging responses to extreme out-groups. *Psychological Science,* 17(10), 847-853.

Recognizing Individuality. Social groups that elicit disgust are differentially processed in mPFC Social neuroscience suggests a decreased activation in the medial pre-frontal cortex (mPFC) to members of extreme outgroups that elicit disgust. Study participants were instructed to either make superficial categorical age estimations (e.g. broad generalizations) or individuating food-preference judgments (i.e. whether the social group member likes carrots) about people as fMRI recorded neural activity. This study demonstrates that being instructed to see extreme out-groups through an individualistic lens as opposed to making superficial categorical judgments may lead to increased social cognition (demonstrated by increased activation in the mPFC) and help one see extreme out-group members as more similar to oneself - thereby increasing a sense of common humanity.

Harris, L. T., & Fiske, S. T. (2007). Social groups that elicit disgust are differentially processed in mPFC. *Social cognitive and affective neuroscience,* 2(1), 45-51.

Consider Others Undoes Dehumanizing Tendencies. The danger in adopting dehumanizing perceptions, research suggests, is a failure to consider the mind of another person, which, in turn, may facilitate inhumane acts like torture.

Harris, L. T., & Fiske, S. T. (2011). Dehumanized perception: A psychological means to facilitate atrocities, torture, and genocide?. *Zeitschrift für Psychologie/Journal of Psychology,* 219(3), 175.

Cultivating Compassion and Empathy. Research shows that even when confronted with distressing life events, we can train our compassion "muscle" and reshape our brain to respond with more empathy. Study participants that previously reacted with negative affect before compassion training were found to exhibit increased positive affective experiences, even in response to witnessing others in distress, after compassion training. This finding further suggests that deliberately cultivating compassion can increase positive affect, affiliation, and common humanity.

Klimecki, O. M., Leiberg, S., Lamm, C., & Singer, T. (2012). Functional neural plasticity and associated changes in positive affect after compassion training. *Cerebral Cortex,* bhs142.

Teaching Empathy—An Overview of Two Models. Whether empathy can be "taught" has long been debated. Can we teach an individual to feel for another person, to "walk in someone else's shoes?" Not only is an ability to empathize with others essential for counseling professionals, but empathic individuals fare better in a variety of interpersonal relationships, whether professional, familial, or friendship. The capacity for empathy serves as a foundation for relationships, has preventative potential in preserving emotional health, and also provides a basis for coping with stress and resolving conflict.

Hatcher, S., Nadeau, M., Walsh, L., Reynolds, M., Galea, J., Marz, K. (1994) The teaching of empathy for high school and college students: testing Rogerian methods with the interpersonal reactivity index. *Adolescence Magazine,* winter.

Empathy Prevents Aggression. Current research is establishing the importance of teaching empathy skills to youth in order to prevent aggression and to teach important interpersonal and work skills. The Center for Safe Schools and Communities has developed supplementary Aggression Replacement Training materials (the PEACE Curriculum) that emphasize empathy training with students.

Salmon, S. (2003) Teaching Empathy: The PEACE Curriculum. *Reclaiming Children and Youth: The Journal of Strength-based Interventions,* 12(3): 167-173.

Israeli-Palestinian Group Interventions. The workshops of Jewish-Israeli and Palestinian youth conducted in the post-Oslo era with the aim of promoting reconciliation and peace building between the sides. The workshops were organized by an Israeli-Palestinian organization, in the framework of a peace education project. In these workshops, youth from pairs of Israeli and Palestinian high schools met for two days to discuss social, cultural and political topics. Each workshop included approximately 20 youths from each side that were led jointly by a Jewish-Israeli and a Palestinian group facilitator.

The study examined four facets of these dialogue events, using both quantitative and qualitative research methods:

• structure of activities and practices of transformative dialogue used in the encounter events;
• attitudes and mutual stereotypes held by youth from both sides prior to the beginning of the workshops;
• mutual perceptions and attitudes expressed by participants during the encounter;
• effects of participation in the workshops on stereotypes held by the Jewish-Israeli and Palestinian youth (pre-post comparisons).

The study found that the youths initially came to the workshop with negative stereotypes and minimal interactions with each other. However, after participating in the workshops, the youths had more favorable perceptions of each other. They were more likely to view the other group as "tolerant" or "considerate of others."

Maoz, I. (2000) An Experiment in Peace: Reconciliation-Aimed Workshops of Jewish-Israeli and Palestinian Youth. *Journal of Peace Research,* 37(6):721-736.

SOCIAL AWARENESS

NOTICE SIMILARITIES WORKSHEET

Counter the tendency to form the in-group and out-group bias by intentionally looking for similarities in others. This practice is especially helpful when resolving conflict or deepening connection. A fundamental principle in Buddhist philosophy is that all humans share a core need: *All humans are suffering, and all humans seek an end to their suffering.* It can be helpful to keep this in mind when confronted with what may look like inappropriate or irrational behavior. Seeing similarities can be a basis for empathy and interpersonal problem solving.

This application guides you through exploring similarities in others, which can help to deepen connections and/or resolve conflicts.

SITUATION

Consider an individual with whom you have some difficulty and/or a recent situation in which you were in conflict with another. Briefly describe the difficulty you are having with the individual and/or the situation. (Who, What, Where?)

_____
_____
_____
_____

1. LOOK FOR SIMILARITIES

- Roles in life
- Goals
- Joys, Hopes, Dreams
- Challenges

Roles in life. What are his/her roles in life?

_____
_____

Goals. What are his/her possible goals?

_____
_____
_____

Joys, Hopes, & Dreams. What are his/her possible joys, hopes, and dreams?

_____
_____
_____

Challenges. What are his/her possible challenges?

_____
_____
_____

2. CONSIDER VULNERABILITIES

- Perfectionism
- Low self-worth
- Self-criticism
- Social Anxiety
- Fear of failure
- Need to succeed or prove oneself
- Need for reassurance or approval
- Need to be liked, right, or in control

Vulnerabilities. What are some possible vulnerabilities?

_____
_____
_____
_____
_____

Insecurities and Concerns. What are some possible Insecurities and concerns?

_____
_____
_____
_____
_____

3. USE INSIGHTS—To Strengthen Relationship/Resolve Conflict

Explore how you could use the insights from your answers above to:

Strengthen the Relationship.

_____
_____
_____
_____
_____
_____

Resolve Conflict.

_____
_____
_____
_____
_____
_____

NOTICE SIMILARITIES TRACKING LOG

DAY	APPLICATION What SIMILARITIES did I notice and with whom? What VULNERABILITIES did I sense and with whom?	IMPACT What was the impact of noticing similarities on me, others, the situation, and/or our relationship?
Day 1		
Day 2		
Day 3		
Day 4		

NOTICE SIMILARITIES TRACKING LOG

DAY	APPLICATION What SIMILARITIES did I notice and with whom? What VULNERABILITIES did I sense and with whom?	IMPACT What was the impact of noticing similarities on me, others, the situation, and/or our relationship?
Day 5		
Day 6		
Day 7		

INSIGHTS—What patterns or insights emerged?

_____
_____
_____
_____
_____
_____

JUST LIKE ME MEDITATION

Pausing to look deeper into another's experience often results in the realization that we all share universal human experiences. The purpose of this meditation is to practice taking another's perspective and imagine what it would feel like to be them. This meditation is designed to help you to notice similarities and build empathy.

This meditation guides you through different realms of common experience. It is adapted from Deepak Chopra's compilation of healing affirmations. During all the meditations, try to let go of expectations about how this practice is supposed to feel or what is supposed to happen. Your job is to experience what happens in a nonjudgmental, explorative manner, and each time your mind wanders into thought, turn your attention back.

INSTRUCTIONS
(3-8 MINUTES)

1. FOCUS INWARD: Breathe and Center

- **Center**—Close your eyes and turn your attention inward.
- **Anchor in your Breath**—Feel Your Breath fill and release your body. Breathe deeply with a slower exhale and natural inhale. Place your hand on your abdomen to feel your diaphragm rise and fall. Feel your feet as the rest on the floor. Notice the sensations on the bottom of your feet making contact with the earth. Feel your hands as they rest on your thighs. Open them and notice the sensations and invite them to relax.
- **Set your Intention**—To direct your attention in this time, place, and to the objective of this meditation.

2. DIRECT ATTENTION: *To the way a stranger is Just Like Me.*

- *Make Contact*—Bring to mind a stranger or acquaintance you know. Choose someone who's life story you know little about.

This person has parents and people who love her, just like me.

This person has moments of joy, just like me

This person has moments of anguish and suffering, just like me.

This person will one day grow old, just like me.

This person will go through the cycles of illness and recovery, just like me.

This person will one day die, just like me.

- *Soak in the feelings*—Feel into the experience and sense the energy that runs through your body as you focus on the way that this person is just like you.

3. REFLECT ON INSIGHTS: Breathe and Reflect
- Come back to your breath.
- Reflect on the insights or benefits you gained during this meditation.

4. MAINTAIN YOUR INNER AWARENESS: Soft Gaze and Stay with It
- Slowly open your eyes and keep your gaze soft, directed downward, and settling on a neutral object.
- Stay with the awareness you gained during the meditation.

JUST LIKE ME MEDITATION WORKSHEET

After you have completed the meditation, jot down any observations about what came up during your meditation. Make note of thoughts you had, feelings you experienced, bodily sensations you felt, and/or detours that you took.

1. FOCUS INWARD: Breathe and Center. How well were you able to concentrate inward and turn your attention to your intention in this meditation?

_____
_____
_____

2. DIRECT ATTENTION: *That a stranger is Just Like Me.*

Make Contact. Bring to mind a stranger or acquaintance you know. Choose someone who's life story you know little about.

> *This person has parents and people who love her, just like me.*
> *This person has moments of joy, just like me*
> *This person has moments of anguish and suffering, just like me.*
> *This person will one day grow old, just like me.*
> *This person will go through the cycles of illness and recovery, just like me.*
> *This person will one day die, just like me.*
> *This person wants to feel safe and relaxed, just like me.*
> *This person wants to feel loved, just like me.*

Person. What person came up for you?

_____
_____
_____

Images and Feelings. What images or feelings came up?

_____
_____
_____

Soak in the feelings—What was the experience and sense the energy that ran through your body as you focused on the way that this person is just like you?

_____
_____
_____

3. REFLECT ON INSIGHTS: What insights or benefits did you gain?

_____
_____
_____

JUST LIKE ME MEDITATION TRACKING LOG

DAY	APPLICATION Which people or person did I focus on? What internal or external factors helped me successfully complete this meditation?	IMPACT What was the impact of doing this meditation on me, my emotions, thoughts, and/or plan for action in a situation? What insights emerged?
Day 1		
Day 2		
Day 3		
Day 4		

JUST LIKE ME MEDITATION TRACKING LOG

DAY	**APPLICATION** Which people or person did I focus on? What internal or external factors helped me successfully complete this meditation?	**IMPACT** What was the impact of doing this meditation on me, my emotions, thoughts, and/or plan for action in a situation? What insights emerged?
Day 5		
Day 6		
Day 7		

INSIGHTS - What patterns or benefits emerged?

_____
_____
_____
_____
_____

COACHING GUIDELINES

Use the self-coaching process and coaching tools to create long-term change. For maximum effectiveness, focus on one skill at a time. For each skill, take an *assessment* if one is available, complete a *coaching worksheet*, practice high road and low road techniques, and track your application of the skill over a seven day period using a *Tracking Log*.

Select one skill. Consider which skill would make the greatest difference in your current life circumstances if you used it more frequently and effectively. It is easier to build new habits if you focus on one change at a time. Select the *one skill* in this chapter that is your highest priority:

- Listen Mindfully
- Reading Others' Emotions
- Notice Similarities

STEP 1. ASSESS. Assess the need and benefits of practicing this particular skill. Assess your current mastery level of the skill. Use one of the online assessment tools if one is available for the skill. The Coaching Worksheet will also help you assess your need and benefits of using the skill.

Assessments—Questionnaires that assess your current skill level and provide data on your progress.

STEP 2. PLAN. To create an action plan, understand how a technique can help you build greater mastery of a skill. Next, consider how you can apply it to your own situations.

Coaching Worksheets—Tools for learning and creating an action plan for practicing the techniques.
- Mindful Listening Worksheet
- Three Steps to Reading Emotions Worksheet
- Notice Similarities Worksheet

STEP 3. PRACTICE. During the following seven days, apply the skill daily. Use both the High Road techniques and the Low Road techniques to practice the skill.

Tracking Logs—Habit forming tools to guide your efforts as you practice the techniques for seven days.
- Mindful Listening Tracking Log
- Three Steps to Reading Emotions Tracking Log
- Loving Kindness Meditation Tracking Log
- Notice Similarities Tracking Log

Meditation Guides—Low Road techniques to build the skill at the emotional or non-verbal level.
- Loving Kindness Meditation

STEP 4. TRACK RESULTS. In addition to systematically helping you to practice the techniques, *Tracking Logs* provide a place to note the impact of the skill on your experience. Tracking Logs help you become more aware of behaviors and patterns in yourself. They are a source of feedback so you can modify a technique to make it more effective.

RELATIONSHIP MANAGEMENT

*Don't flatter yourself that friendship authorizes you to say disagreeable things to your intimates.
The nearer you come into relation with a person, the more necessary do tact and courtesy become.*

-Oliver Wendell Holmes

RELATIONSHIP MANAGEMENT

Connect, build trust, transform conflict, and deepen bonds.

As social animals, humans have a fundamental need to connect to others and be part of a community. Many people report that relationships are the number one source of happiness, yet many also identify relationships as the biggest source of difficulties, frustration, and emotional pain. The ability to manage relationships well is a crucial part of well-being success, and happiness. It enables deeper friendship, more effective collaboration, and bonding.

In this chapter, we present a number of skills for relationship management.

OUTLINE

Introduction: Relationship Positivity Ratio

***Skill 15:* BIDS FOR CONNECTION**
How to Respond to Bids for Connection
Examples of Responses to Bids for Connection
Bid for Connection Worksheet & Tracking Log

***Skill 16:* IDENTIFY CONFLICT ESCALATORS**
Conflict Escalators—The Four Horsemen
Identify Conflict Escalators Worksheet & Tracking Log

***Skill 17:* CRAFT CONSTRUCTIVE CONFLICT**
The Key to Crafting Constructive Conflict
First, Do Your Homework
How to Craft Constructive Conflict—Conflict De-escalators
Craft Constructive Conversation Worksheet & Tracking Log

***Skill 18:* DEEP DIVE CONVERSATIONS**
Craft Deep Dive Conversations
Craft Win-Win Solutions
Deep Dive Conversations Worksheet & Tracking Log

Gift of Relationship Meditation
Gift of Relationship Meditation Guide & Tracking Log

Coaching Guidelines

STANFORD SERIES: Positive Psychology & Keys to Sustainable Happiness

INTRODUCTION

*Find joy in everything you choose to do. Every job, relationship, home...
it's your responsibility to love it, or change it.*
-Chuck Palahniuk

The happiest 10% of people have just one thing in common. It's not that they are on the *Fortune 500* list, live in sunny California, or even that they have more objectively positive events—it's that they report having satisfying close relationships.

Feeling connected with others gives a tremendous happiness boost. Even those who tend to be introverted and enjoy solitary pursuits benefit by prioritizing relationships. Most people report relationships as the number one source of happiness and rate love as the most powerful positive emotion. Shame and loneliness are often said to be the most devastating emotions. Most also identify relationships as the biggest source of difficulties, frustration, and emotional pain.

Humans have a fundamental need to connect to others and be part of a community. Historically, our survival depended on interdependence. In modern society, much of our success depends upon our ability to effectively navigate relationships. Our survival as a species and as individuals has always and still does depend on our ability to connect with others.

Trust provides a foundation for managing relationships whether it is resolving conflict or deepening intimacy. Research shows that people with the strongest and most satisfying relationships have the ability to build and maintain trust with others across situations, even during conflict.

RELATIONSHIP POSITIVITY RATIO (5 to 1)

John Gottman is a world-renowned expert known for his work on marital stability and divorce prediction. He has authored 190 published academic articles and is the author or co-author of 40 books. In his work at the Relationship Research Institute at University of Washington, John Gottman and colleagues have demonstrated that strong, healthy intimate relationships have a 5:1 ratio of positive to negative emotions. In other words, we need to have five positive interactions for every equally negative interaction. He suggests the keys to creating positive resonance in relationships are frequent, small displays of kindness and responding well to bids for connection.

SKILL 15. BIDS FOR CONNECTION

We are afraid to care too much, for fear that the other person does not care at all.
-Eleanor Roosevelt

"Bids" are any verbal or nonverbal invitation for connection. John Gottman's research defines bids as the fundamental unit of emotional connection. A smile, eye contact, humor, a friendly tone, and reflective comments are examples of bids for connection. So are sending a friendly text or leaving a thank you note. How the bid is responded to is crucial to the quality of the relationship. Gottman and colleagues' research shows that how a bid is responded to predicts how long a couple will stay together. Even during conflict, skillful communicators demonstrate bids and positive responses to bids by verbally and nonverbally displaying that they are paying attention, understand, and respect the other person.

HOW TO RESPOND TO BIDS FOR CONNECTION

Body language, tone, word choice, and timing communicate a response to a bid for connection. Gottman has defined three categories of responses to a bid for connection:

THREE TYPES OF RESPONSES TO BIDS
1. TURN TOWARD
2. TURN AGAINST
3. TURN AWAY

1. Turning Toward. Turning Toward is a verbal or nonverbal invitation for connection or emotional "joining." A smile, humor, a friendly tone, and reflective comments are examples of Turning Toward responses. Eye contact is an especially simple, powerful turn toward response.

2. Turning Against. Turning Against is a verbal or nonverbal expression of negativity. Blaming is a common turn against response. Even when the words are positive, a negative tone can transform a Turn Toward into a Turn Against.

For example—Two friends meet for lunch. Mark arrives 15 minutes late.

Mark's Bid: *"Hey, great to see you."*

Zackary Turns Against: In a snarky tone, he says *"So glad you decided to show up..."*

Turning Against engages others but in a negative manner that often elicits defensive or aggressive counter responses. Turning Against responses beget more Turning Against responses. Gottman's research shows that couples that have a high proportion of Turning Against responses eventually break-up. The separation happens less quickly than those with a high proportion of Turning Away responses, however. The conclusion is that even fighting, while aversive, is better than no connection at all.

3. Turning Away. Turning Away is a verbal or nonverbal non-response that creates distance or expresses disinterest in connection. Consider how you feel when you are trying to talk to someone, but they are fiddling with their phone or when talking on the phone with someone and you can hear them typing on their computer. These are classic Turning Away responses. They are often unintentional, but research shows they extinguish connection. Studies show after approximately three consecutive instances of Turning Away, people tend to stop bidding for connection. Turning Away responses tend to leave the other feeling rejected or disregarded.

This is the most toxic of the three responses. Couples with a high proportion of Turning Away responses break-up faster than couples with frequent Turning Away or Turning Toward responses. Turning Away implicitly communicates that the other is not worth paying attention to. It's not even worth a fight.

Be Aware of How a Response Is Received. Often we overlook the subtle impact of our verbal and nonverbal messages. Just because we intend to send one type of response, does not mean it will be received as such. For example, we have all had times when we turned down an invitation to socialize because of other pressing demands but have unintentionally communicated a Turning Away or Turning Against response as the invitee perceives it personally as disinterest or dislike.

I have a friend who, while well-intentioned, has sometimes forgotten that we made plans or changed them without being clear and often does not respond to text messages. These Turning Away responses have created problems in our friendship, leaving me feeling that I valued time with her more than she valued time with me. While I knew she did value our friendship just as much as I, it made me less apt to make plans with her. Just as the research shows, it only takes a few turning away responses before the giver tires of extending unreciprocated bids. Seeing my reaction, I discussed this dynamic with her. She did not realize that I felt that way and attributed her actions to busyness, feeling overwhelmed by her schedule, and wanting to "do it all". Thankfully, she committed to be more conscientious around planning, which I received as a well-delivered and genuine Turning Toward. I committed to extending bids more clearly and to asking explicitly for her response. Together, we repaired the rupture in our relationship.

RELATIONSHIP MANAGEMENT

EXAMPLES OF RESPONSES TO BIDS FOR CONNECTION

The following chart shows three types of responses to bids for connection—Turning Toward, Away, and Against. For further examples refer to *The Relationship Cure* by John Gottman.

TURNING TOWARD, AGAINST, AWAY RESPONSES

BIDS FOR CONNECTION	TURNING TOWARD RESPONSES	TURNING AWAY RESPONSES	TURNING AGAINST RESPONSES
"I finally finished painting the kitchen."	"What a big job. I bet you're glad it's done."	"Have you seen my glasses?"	"It took you long enough."
"I haven't seen you in so long. Would you like to grab dinner after work?"	"That's a nice invitation. I'm booked up this week. Would lunch next week work instead?"	"Sorry, I already have plans tonight."	"Oh, I just don't have time for socializing right now."
"I'm having the worst computer problems again. I lost 3 hours of work. I want to throw it out the window!"	"Oh, computers can be so frustrating. Do you want me to get the IT number for you?"	"Yesterday my computer totally crashed. I was so mad- I lost so much work!"	"Well, didn't you back it up? You said you've been having problems with it."
"I don't want to go to school today."	"You don't? That's strange. Usually you do. It makes me wonder if you're worried about something."	"Get your lunch, let's go."	"You are going to school. I don't want to hear your complaining!"
"You never listen to me."	"I want you to feel like I listen because I do care about what you have to say. How can I help you feel listened to?"	"I was just reading an article about listening in my emotional intelligence class. Let me tell you about it."	"You are too sensitive."

BID FOR CONNECTION WORKSHEET

The leading researcher in intimate relationships, John Gottman, has identified the core units of interpersonal connection as "bids" and has shown that people who skillfully make bids for connection are more likely to have fulfilling relationships. A smile, eye contact, humor, a friendly tone, and reflective comments are examples of bids for connection. Even during conflict, skillful communicators demonstrate verbally and nonverbally that they are paying attention, understand, and respect the other person.

The purpose of this application is to become more aware of the impact of bids for connection in challenging moments in relationships or with difficult people. Practicing extending bids when it is most difficult can improve your ability to manage both positive and trying relationships.

MY BID FOR CONNECTION WITH A DIFFICULT PERSON

1. My Bid for Connection with a Difficult Person. In a difficult situation, when did I extend a bid for connection to someone with whom there was conflict, tension, or dislike? (It may be a small amount of tension or a longstanding major conflict.) What was my bid for connection and the impact on me and them? Importantly, the purpose is not to change their response but to practice giving bids.

To whom did I make the bid? _____

Describe components of my bid for connection, including tone, eye contact, word choice, and gestures.

_____
_____
_____

2. Their Response. What was their response to my bid (i.e., Turn Toward, Away, or Against)?

_____
_____

Words. What did they say that indicated the type of response (i.e., Turn Toward, Away, or Against)?

_____
_____
_____

Actions. What did they do that indicated the type of response (i.e., Turn Toward, Away, or Against)?

_____
_____
_____

Body Language. What body language or other nonverbal cues indicated the type of response?

_____
_____

3. Impact on Me. How did my bidding for connection and their response impact me?

_____
_____

RELATIONSHIP MANAGEMENT

ANOTHER'S BID FOR CONNECTION WITH ME

1. Another's Bid for Connection. Focus on an area of life where you feel need or desire for more connection. Perhaps you wish for more connection or ease with family members, romantic relationships, co-workers or boss, or with children. You may choose one person or a realm of life like family or work. Identify when someone extended a bid for connection to you. These need not be grand gestures. Look even for brief, subtle bids.

Who made the bid? _____

Describe components of their bid for connection, including tone, eye contact, word choice, and gestures.

_____
_____
_____
_____
_____

2. My Reaction. What was my response to the bid (i.e., did I Turn Toward, Away, or Against)?

_____
_____

Words. What did I say that indicated the type of response (i.e., Turn Toward, Away, or Against)?

_____
_____
_____

Actions. What did I do that indicated the type of response (i.e., Turn Toward, Away, or Against)?

_____
_____
_____

Body Language. What body language or other nonverbal cues indicated the type of response?

_____
_____
_____

3. Improve My Skill. How could I have more effectively delivered my bids for connection so that they have more impact? How could I improve my response to bids?

_____
_____
_____

BID FOR CONNECTION TRACKING LOG

DAY	APPLICATION (1) How did I make a bid for connection that impacted an important relationship or interaction? (2) What was my response to an important other's bid for connection (i.e., how did I Turn Toward, Away, or Against)?	IMPACT What was the impact of: (1) Extending bids for connection (2) Responding to bids on me, others, and/or our relationship?
Day 1		
Day 2		
Day 3		
Day 4		

BID FOR CONNECTION TRACKING LOG

DAY	APPLICATION (1) How did I make a bid for connection that impacted an important relationship or interaction? (2) What was my response to an important other's bid for connection (i.e., how did I Turn Toward, Away, or Against)?	IMPACT What was the impact of: (1) Extending bids for connection (2) Responding to bids on me, others, and/or our relationship?
Day 5		
Day 6		
Day 7		

INSIGHTS—What patterns or insights emerged?

_____
_____
_____
_____
_____

SKILL 16. IDENTIFY CONFLICT ESCALATORS

Truth is, I'll never know all there is to know about you just as you will never know all there is to know about me. Humans are by nature too complicated to be understood fully. So, we can choose either to approach our fellow human beings with suspicion or to approach them with an open mind, a dash of optimism and a great deal of candor.
-Tom Hanks

John Gottman has studied over 2,000 married couples over two decades and has identified communication characteristics that cause a breakdown in communication and damage relationships. Based on the degree to which these characteristics are present, Gottman and trained observers can predict with 94% accuracy, which marriages will succeed and which will fail. Gottman's work has been so impressive, that it has been very influential in academic circles as well as in popular media. It has been featured in numerous books, TV interviews, and magazines including the Harvard Business Review.

The four communication characteristics that Gottman posits escalate conflict are Criticism, Defensiveness, Contempt, and Stonewalling. These characteristics are so toxic that he refers to these escalators as the "*Four Horseman of the Apocalypse.*" Each behavior paves the way for the next one.

FOUR HORSEMEN OF THE APOCALYPSE

CONFLICT ESCALATORS—THE FOUR HORSEMEN

1. Criticism. Criticism is attacking another person's personality or character, usually with the intent of making someone right or someone wrong. A critical comment is often preceded by a generalization such as:

> *You always...*
> *You never...*
> *Why are you so...*
> *Why can't you just...*

2. Defensiveness. Defensiveness is trying to position oneself as innocent, not to blame, or as the victim. It is generally an ineffective effort to protect oneself from a perceived attack and is a common reaction to blame and criticism. Often defensiveness feels justified and necessary, so it is typically the most difficult to detect. Healthy alternatives to defensiveness are helping others to understand one's point-of-view, needs, and experience in a situation. Some typical examples of defensiveness are listed below:

- "Yes, but..."—Starting off agreeing but ending up disagreeing.
    I understand your perspective, but I just...

- Making excuses—Attributing external circumstances to being beyond one's control forcing them to act in a certain way.
    It's not my fault...
    I didn't...
    I was just trying to...

- Cross-Complaining. Meeting a partner's complaint or criticism with a different complaint.
    Well, you do that all the time, too...
    My habit is not as bad as your habit of...
    I wouldn't do that if you didn't always...
    That's not true, you're the one who...

- Whining.
    It's not fair...
    It never changes...

3. Stonewalling. Stonewalling is withdrawing from the relationship as a way to avoid conflict. Partners may think they are trying to be neutral, but stonewalling conveys disapproval, icy distance, separation, disconnections, a power play, or smugness. It is a potent Turning Away response that can be very damaging to connection and trust. Some typical expressions of stonewalling are listed below:

- Stony Silence.

- Monosyllabic mutterings.

- Changing the subject.

- Removing yourself physically.

- Ignoring what your partner said.

- Repeating yourself without paying attention to what the other person is saying.

4. Contempt. Contempt is attacking another person's sense of self with the intention to insult or psychologically abuse him or her. Gottman shows that once contempt takes hold in a relationship, it is pretty much doomed. Below are listed some typical expressions of contempt:

- Insults and name calling (ex: jerk, drama-queen, wimp, stupid, lazy, slob)

- Hostile humor, sarcasm, or mockery. (ex: "That extra 40 pounds really looks good on you.")

- Body language and/or tone of voice. (ex: Sneering, eye rolling, curling upper lip.)

IDENTIFY CONFLICT ESCALATORS WORKSHEET

Conflict is to be expected even in the best relationships. Conflict escalators can quickly turn a potential problem solving session into a destructive argument.

This application provides an opportunity to deconstruct a conflict situation that you experienced recently, analyze what may have led to the conflict, and what may have increased the intensity of the conflict. Choose a conflict situation you have had with someone, perhaps with a customer/client, a colleague, a family member, significant other, or a close friend.

CONFLICT SITUATION

Identify a recent situation in which a discussion or disagreement escalated beyond the productive stage. (Briefly describe who, what, where, when, how, and why)

WHO. Who was involved in the conflict? _____

WHERE & WHEN DID IT HAPPEN? Did the time, location, or context contribute to the conflict?

_____

_____

WHO DID OR SAID WHAT? What happened?

_____

_____

_____

_____

_____

WHAT WERE THE PRECEDING CIRCUMSTANCES? Were there preceding factors that made it more likely or made me/other more emotionally vulnerable or on edge?

_____

_____

IDENTIFY CONFLICT ESCALATORS

Identify conflict escalators that escalated the situation to the point where it became unproductive.

1. CRITICISM. How was criticism displayed? How might I have brought in criticism?

(Criticism is attacking another person's personality or character, usually with the intent of making someone right or someone wrong. A critical comment is often preceded by a generalization like: *You always…You never…Why are you so….*)

_____

_____

_____

_____

_____

2. DEFENSIVENESS. How was defensiveness displayed? How might I have brought in defensiveness?

Defensiveness is seeing one's self as the victim, and warding off a perceived attack. Often defensiveness feels justified and necessary so it is typically the most difficult to detect. Making excuses—External circumstances beyond my control forced me to act in a certain way. *It's not my fault...I didn't...I was just trying to...*Cross-Complaining. Meeting your partner's complaint or criticism with a complaint of your own. *Well, you do that all the time, too...My habit is not as bad as your habit of...*
*I wouldn't do that if you didn't always...*Disagreeing and then Cross-Complaining. *That's not true, you're the one who...*Yes-butting. Start off agreeing, but end up disagreeing. *I understand your perspective, but I just...* Whining...*It's not fair...It never changes...*)

_____
_____
_____
_____
_____
_____
_____

3. STONEWALLING. If any, how was stonewalling displayed? How might I have stonewalled?

(Stonewalling is withdrawing from the relationship as a way to avoid conflict. Partners may think they are trying to be neutral, but stonewalling conveys disapproval, icy distance, separation, disconnections, and/or smugness. It is a potent turning away response that can be very damaging to connection and trust. Some typical expressions of defensiveness are: Stony Silence; Monosyllabic mutterings; Changing the subject; Removing yourself physically ignoring what your partner said. Repeating yourself without paying attention to what the other person is saying.)

_____
_____
_____
_____
_____
_____
_____

CONTEMPT. Was any contempt displayed? How was it directly or indirectly communicated? How might I have shown contempt?

(Contempt is attacking another person's sense of self with the intention to insult or psychologically hurt them. It might include: insults and name calling (jerk, drama-queen, wimp, stupid, lazy, slob, etc.); hostile humor, sarcasm, or mockery (ex: "That extra 40 pounds really looks good on you."); or body language and/or tone of voice. (Sneering, eye rolling, curling upper lip.)

_____
_____
_____
_____
_____
_____
_____

IDENTIFY CONFLICT ESCALATORS TRACKING LOG

DAY	APPLICATION Which CONFLICT ESCALATOR did I use? (Criticism, Contempt, Defensiveness, Stonewalling) What were the words, tone, and body language that communicated this Conflict Escalator?	IMPACT What was the impact of the conflict escalator on me, others, the situation, and/or the relationship?
Day 1		
Day 2		
Day 3		
Day 4		

IDENTIFY CONFLICT ESCALATORS TRACKING LOG

DAY	APPLICATION Which CONFLICT ESCALATOR did I use? (Criticism, Contempt, Defensiveness, Stonewalling) What were the words, tone, and body language that communicated this Conflict Escalator?	IMPACT What was the impact of the conflict escalator on me, others, the situation, and/or the relationship?
Day 5		
Day 6		
Day 7		

INSIGHTS—What patterns or benefits emerged?

___
___
___
___
___

SKILL 17. CRAFT CONSTRUCTIVE CONFLICT

Courage means to keep working a relationship, to continue seeking solutions to difficult problems, and to stay focused during stressful periods.
-Denis Waitley

Skillful communication during conflict has one thing in common—the focus is on moving toward a desirable outcome. We posit that constructive conflict builds more positivity. It is not manipulative, malicious, or one-sidedly advantageous. Instead, it elevates both parties to a higher way of being and is fundamentally a mission to find and create seemingly unavailable possibility and opportunity. It serves the greater good. This process is difficult, sometimes painful, replete with compromise, and all too rare.

Crafting constructive conflict hinges on the ability to communicate clearly and to establish trust and respect no matter how aggressive the message. This requires a commitment to not introducing conflict escalators and attending to the process. These communications typically require a significant amount of effort, planning, and intention—more than most of us presume.

Although positive conflict can lead to innovation, destructive conflict is often extremely wasteful of time and emotional energy. Max Messmer, CEO of Robert Half International, the world's largest staffing firm, conducted a study to assess the percentage of management time spent on resolving personality conflicts. They found that on average 18% of management time is spent managing personality conflicts. Managers waste almost one-fifth of their time as referees.

THE KEY TO CRAFTING CONSTRUCTIVE CONFLICT

Deliver negative messages without activating "threat sensors"
It is not about "making nice"—it is about being effective.

Constructive conflict is guided by the knowledge that we easily feel attacked. Our primitive emotional circuitry evolved in life or death evolutionary contexts. Therefore, amygdala hijacks easily overwhelm our higher brain centers, and the negativity bias distorts messages.

Amygdala Hijacked Conflict. Most of us fail to realize just how easily the Fight or Flight system gets activated. John Gottman's research suggests that a heart rate of 100 beats per minute indicates an amygdala hijack, shutting down higher brain centers and therefore, effective communication. He suggests that if heart rate exceeds 100 beats per minute during conflict, pause and regain calm before continuing.

FIRST, DO YOUR HOMEWORK

Rewrite Your Victim Story. When we believe someone has wronged us, often we fall into a victim story. Before entering a conflict, challenge and rewrite your "victim story." Challenge thoughts and consider alternative interpretations.

- Consider ways of taking some degree of personal responsibility.
- Challenge thoughts of righteous indignation.
- Make contact with an attitude of emotional generosity and the possibility of forgiveness.
- Let go of your version of things for a moment and listen to the other point of views.
- Claim responsibility for your own well-being.
- Ask yourself what you learn from this conflict.

Digital Communication—Save not Send. Research shows that the emotional distance and lack of cues inherent to email and texts allows for impulsive, reactive actions, and lack of empathy. Without nonverbal indicators, digital communication becomes hard to interpret and requires filling in data points without direct evidence. It also is distancing, becoming impersonal in the absence of nonverbal feedback about the impact on the other person. Thus, proceed cautiously when communicating digitally. Instead of quickly hitting the "reply" button, it can be best to "Save not Send." Consider flagging a heated email correspondence for later response or composing a draft and only sending after calming down or even sleeping on it. All the challenges inherent to face-to-face communication are exponentially larger when communicating in the absence of nonverbal data.

Good Timing. Consider when to begin the conversation. We are much more likely to resolve the issue if we prevent the conflict from escalating in the first place. The best time to begin a difficult conversation is when all parties are well-rested, calm, centered, and have clarity of mind.

HOW TO CRAFT CONSTRUCTIVE CONFLICT—CONFLICT DE-ESCALATORS

Do you want to be right or do you want to be effective?

HOW TO CRAFT CONSTRUCTIVE CONFLICT
Stage 1. Begin With Connection
Stage 2. Deliver The Negative Message Skillfully
Stage 3. End With Connection

Disarm, Connect, and Orient Toward a Positive Outcome. Structure conflict conversations in a way that is likely to disarm and maintain connection while keeping an eye on reaching a mutually positive outcome. The primary objective in conflict is to be clear, direct, authentic, constructive, maintain trust, communicate respect for the person, and serve a positive outcome. This model provides the structure for incorporating the conflict de-escalators. Consider using the following structure as a guide.

STAGE 1. BEGIN WITH CONNECTION

How it starts is how it will end.

The purpose of beginning with connection is to set a constructive tone. A positive beginning might include a genuine compliment, an acknowledgement, or validation, for example. This approach can still be direct and have transparency, but it skillfully introduces the conflict without putting the other on defense. Setting a positive tone can communicate an intention not to fight but to co-create a solution and respect. John Gottman's research shows that how a conversation starts is generally how it ends: if it starts in conflict, it ends in conflict.

Start Slow. Slow starts refer to easing into the charged part of the conversation. Gottman's research suggests that if it gets of to a bad start, it is best to stop, take a break, and restart the conversation. A slow start:

- Begins with a spirit of kindness and collaboration toward a solution.
- Might include a statement that expresses commonality and understanding.
- Gently introduces the issue that concerns you.

Example of a Slow Start. Marcia is angry that Mike has harshly criticized her publicly at work. She begins the confrontation effectively by starting slowly. She said, "You know I've been really enjoying my first few months here. One thing I really like is that everyone really seems to work well together. It seems like people help each other out and support each other. Even though I am the newest one here, I want to make sure that I find ways to support you and the others on our team. I hope it has seems that way so far."

Mike didn't respond, so Marcia asked directly, "Does it seem that I've been supportive to you and the others?" She goes on to introduce the more charged part of her concern, explaining that she does not feel supported by Mike. Later, she gives examples of his criticism as times when she wonders if he intends to support her.

Harsh Starts. Harsh starts put people on the defensive. Note the implied criticism in the following examples. Although perhaps well-intended, these start-ups would probably cause escalation:

"I don't want to make this a big deal, but…"
"Don't get mad when I say this, but…"
"I'm not being critical, but…"
"You are very sensitive, so I'm going to try to say this very carefully…"

Example of a Harsh Start. Marcia could have started with a statement like: *"Mike, I would like to talk to you. What was going on with you in last week's meeting? I really didn't feel supported by you."*

While some might think this is an effective start because it is direct and to the point, it is likely to immediately put Mike on defense and feel like a criticism. According to research, this would introduce one of the Four Horsemen, escalating the conflict.

Invite an Exploration. Suggest that you work together to explore an issue and find a solution together. This phrasing directly introduces the topic but without introducing criticism, the first of the Four Horseman.

Marcia could say something like: *"Mike, I have sensed some tension between us. I'd like to explore with you what this is and understand it better. Would you be willing to chat with me about this?"*

Commit to a Constructive Process. Talk about how to talk about it. Quite often we know from experience that a conversation is likely to be challenging. It can be open helpful to acknowledge it and create "ground rules" or at least an intention to have a constructive, respectful conversation. This is especially helpful in longstanding issues that are common familial and romantic relationships.

"Many times when we discuss your family visiting, I notice we both get tense. It's something I would really like for us to have a constructive conversation about. I am committed to doing my best to keep it constructive. This time, I intend on really hearing your perspective."

Check-In on the Other's Current State. In an effort to gather information and seek understanding, simply ask how the other is doing in that moment. If someone changes his or her behavior for the worse—a daughter begins locking herself in her room, a romantic partner returns phone calls less frequently, or a co-worker's productivity declines dramatically—an initial reaction may be to confront the individual with an accusation or complaint. This will likely put them on defense.

Consider starting with an invitation to share about personal issues, feelings or conflicts that may be influencing their actions. There may be significant contributing factors of which you were unaware. If they are not asked directly with an attitude of support, you may not learn important contributing factors. For example, your teen may be having problems with their friends, a romantic partner may be more stressed than you realize about work, or the co-worker may be dealing with a serious health issue.

Simply, ask: *"Lately, you seem more stressed than usual. How have things been going for you?"*

Inquire about the Other's Perspective. Consider asking the other person to describe what happened. This neutral inquiry avoids the other feeling like you are on a fault-finding mission, and instead, engages them in a neutral fact-finding inquiry.

For example, ask: *"Can you describe what happened?"* or *"Will you walk me through what happened last night?"*

STAGE 2. DELIVER THE NEGATIVE MESSAGE SKILLFULLY

Separate the Person from the Problem. Stay focused on behaviors and actions you'd like to see rather than on abstract issues or personal attacks on character or personality. Communication breaks down when we feel personally insulted, attacks on character, or rejected.

This is sometimes referred to as *issue-focused* conflict rather than *person-focused* conflict. Issue focused conflict more easily fosters win-win negotiation. Person-focused conflict tends to escalate into heated emotional disputes and moral indignation. Issue-focused conflict is likely to stay with actions that are doable and changeable. This also avoids what social psychologists call the "Actor-Observer Error." This is the common tendency to overestimate the role of character traits in problematic situations while underestimating the role of the situational variables.

Make a Neutral Observation. Consider opening a conversation with an observable fact rather than with feelings. It is indisputable and can help direct issue-focused conflict resolution.

Example: "I notice that you left the meeting as soon as Nancy began delegating project roles."

Acknowledge. Acknowledgement does not mean agreeing or making concessions. Instead, it is demonstrating respect for the other and his or her needs and viewpoint. There are several ways show acknowledgement. One way to demonstrate respect is to acknowledge the other's point of view. It is possible to show that you understand another's position without sharing it.

For instance, imagine your employee asked for a raise and you refused. You might say, *"I appreciate that you have been working hard. We feel your contributions are very valuable. We will consider a raise when you hit the next benchmark."*

Or, with a teenager who asks to borrow the car, *"I know you are enjoying the freedom of being able to drive yourself around, and I know you really want to drive tonight. However, I do not feel comfortable with you driving tonight since there will be drinking at the party."*

Validate the Other's Point-of-View. Validating someone's feelings means showing you understand their perspective. If it is true, you might add that you believe their view makes sense given their history, objectives, or values. You do not need to agree or think it is reasonable to understand how they arrived at their point of view. This is simply validating the legitimacy of their viewpoint. This shows the other that you respect their point of view, even if you disagree with it.

For example, *"It makes a lot of sense to me that you are feeling angry that I said 'no'. I know you really wanted that."*

Or, to the employee who was upset about the review, *"It is natural to want your hard work to be recognized."* Or, *"Anyone putting in the number of hours you are is bound to feel overworked."*

Common phrases that express validation:
- *I understand that you are feeling...*
- *I can see your point of view.*
- *It makes sense that you _____, given that you are trying to _____.*
- *I can see that what I said made you feel _____.*
- *I hear you saying that_____.*

Be Specific. Be specific in what you want. Make your requests and/or complaints specific rather than general.

For example, if your positive outcome is for someone to be more responsible, requesting "increased accountability," may not be as clear as saying:

"Increased accountability might include doing things like calling me if you are running more than 10 minutes late to a meeting."

Focus on Positive Outcomes. Explicitly describe the positive outcome you want. Describe in actionable, specific behaviors that the person can do.

For example—Marcia redirects to a positive outcome that is actionable and specific.

"It is important to me that we collaborate in a timely manner. Could we agree that if a deadline becomes too difficult to meet, then we give at least 48-hour notice by email?"

STAGE 3. END WITH CONNECTION

Focus on a new beginning. Consider positive steps forward and express good will if genuinely felt.

Take Responsibility for Wrongdoings—The Four-Part Apology. Being willing to take responsibility for mistakes or wrongdoings engenders trust. Most people underestimate the power of a well-expressed apology. Referred to as the "Four Part Apology," the following guidelines can help transform an interaction and repair a rupture. The 4 R's are: Responsibility, Remorse, Repair, Recommit. The power of the Four-Part Apology is that it demonstrates responsibility for actions.

(1) Responsibility. Take responsibility for what you've done. Use "I statements" to show that you're the one behind the action.

Example: *"I know that I've canceled our plans at the last minute more than once. I can imagine this is frustrating."*

(2) Remorse. Explain your remorse: *"I apologize for hurting you by wasting your time and making you feel disrespected."*

(3) Repair. Repair the damage. Right the wrong by going above and beyond what was done.

Ask, *"How can I make it right?"*

Examples: Some examples of a repair:

- You show up late for a team meeting, so the next time bring a batch of cookies for everyone.
- Your child was upset that you missed one of his/her events, so you plan a special outing.
- You cancelled for a friend's party last minute, so take that friend out to a nice dinner.
- You lost a borrowed book, and you give a gift card to replace it and buy an additional one.

(4) Recommit: Show commitment to prevent further harm. Perhaps formulate a realistic plan to avoid harm in the future.

Shift To Appreciation. Before ending the conversation, shift to appreciation. Focus on ways to reconnect with the positive in the person and the relationship.

ADDITIONAL RESOURCES

Stone, D., Patton, B., & Heen, S. (1999). *Difficult Conversations: How to discuss what matters most.* New York, NY: Viking.

Gallagher, Richard (2009). *How to Tell Anyone Anything.*

Ury, William (2007). *The Power of a Positive No.*

CRAFT CONSTRUCTIVE CONFLICT WORKSHEET

Constructive conversations are a result of the words that are said, they way that they are said, and the conversation strategy that is used by both parties. Your strategy should include techniques that will make the conversation constructive, safe, and outcome oriented. You will also want to use conflict de-escalators to head off conflict before it starts, or to mitigate conflict when it happens. Using conflict de-escalators provides alternatives to the conflict escalators during conflict, and they can foster a sense of connection even when a negative message needs to be delivered. Skillful communication during conflict is having the ability to be firm, direct, have boundaries, and to say "Yes" or "No" without using the *Four Horsemen.* Conflict de-escalators can help to turn a potential problem situation into one in which the problem can be resolve din a reasonable way.

The purpose of this application is to give you an opportunity to practice using some of the techniques for crafting a constructive conversation. First, begin by thinking of a conflict situation that you have experienced recently, and analyze what may have led to the conflict, and what may have increased the intensity of the conflict. Situations might include an interaction with:

- A customer/client.
- A colleague.
- A family member.
- A close friend.

CONFLICT SITUATION

Identify a recent situation in which a discussion or disagreement escalated beyond the productive stage. (Briefly describe who, what, where, when, how, and why)

WHO. Who is/was involved in the conflict?

_____

_____

WHERE & WHEN DID IT HAPPEN? Did the time, location, or context contribute to the conflict?

_____

_____

WHO DID OR SAID WHAT? What happened?

_____

_____

_____

CONSTRUCTIVE CONVERSATION TECHNIQUES

How might constructive conversation techniques might have been used in this conflict situation?

1. CONFLICT DE-ESCALATORS. What conflict de-escalator might have been helpful?

1. Separate Person From Problem.
2. Rewrite Your Victim Story.
3. Validate Other's Viewpoint
4. Start Slow.
5. Be Specific.
6. Positive Outcome Focus.
7. Repair.
8. Shift To Appreciation.

_____

_____

2. CONNECT—DELIVER—CONNECT.

Stage 1. Connect. (Slow Start, Make a Neutral Observation, Acknowledge, or Validate).

_____
_____
_____
_____
_____
_____
_____
_____

Stage 2. Deliver Message Skillfully. (Positive Outcome Focus, Separate the Person from the Problem, Be Specific, Positive Outcome Focus)

_____
_____
_____
_____
_____
_____
_____
_____

Stage 3. Connect. (Take Responsibility for Wrongdoings, Shift to Appreciation.)

_____
_____
_____
_____
_____
_____

3. INSIGHTS. What insights or solutions emerged from doing this process of crafting constructive conflict?

_____
_____
_____
_____
_____

CRAFT CONSTRUCTIVE CONVERSATION TRACKING LOG

DAY	APPLICATION How and with whom did I craft constructive conflict? Which conflict de-escalators did I use? What worked about what I did?	IMPACT What was the impact on me, others, the situation, and/or our relationship?
Day 1		
Day 2		
Day 3		
Day 4		

CRAFT CONSTRUCTIVE CONVERSATION TRACKING LOG

DAY	APPLICATION How and with whom did I craft constructive conflict? Which conflict de-escalators did I use? What worked about what I did?	IMPACT What was the impact on me, others, the situation, and/or our relationship?
Day 5		
Day 6		
Day 7		

INSIGHTS—What patterns or benefits emerged?

_____
_____
_____
_____
_____

SKILL 18. DEEP DIVE CONVERSATIONS

The only real security is not in owning or possessing, not in demanding or expecting, not in hoping, even. Security in a relationship lies neither in looking back to what it was, nor forward to what it might be, but living in the present and accepting it as it is now.
-Anne Morrow Lindbergh

When things fall apart, people tend to focus on their short-term goals and how and why another person or variable in the situation is blocking their objective. Conversations tend to be about what is right or wrong, on what the other person should have done, what could have been different, etc. Typically, attempts to resolve conflict generally fail when they stay on the level of content. More often, conflict lives at deeper levels of experience. The problem, however, is that we tend to stay on the surface and do not dive deeper into the roots of what people are fighting for. In conflict, whether it is in the workplace or at home, take a step back and consider deeper levels of conflict from each person's perspective.

CRAFT DEEP DIVE CONVERSATIONS

HOW TO CRAFT DEEP DIVE CONVERSATIONS

1. **SURFACE.** Identify Target Behavior
    Positive Behavior
    Negative Behavior

2. **UNDER WATERLINE.** Identify the underlying:
    Goal, Intention, Objective
    Needs and Wants

3. **DEEPER NEED.** Identify the deeper needs:
    Trust
    Respect
    Other

1. Surface—Target Behavior (Both positive and negative behavior). The behavior that you want to see is the positive target behavior. Also identify the problem behavior, the behavior that is creating an obstacle, or the negative target, that which you want to avoid or get rid of. By focusing on the positive and negative target behavior, you are naturally separating the person from the problem—a crucial component to conflict resolution. Some minor conflicts can be resolved by staying at this surface level, especially if there is a foundation of trust. Oftentimes, however, conflicts live in deeper water, so we need to dive deeper in order to resolve the conflict.

2. Under The Waterline—Underlying Goal, Intention, Or Objective. The underlying goal, intention or objective is the more important or significant issue that underlies the problem behavior. When the underlying goal, intention, or objective is threatened, we tend to act in an extreme manner. Consider what you or the other really wants or needs in the situation, or why you or the other is bothered by the problem behavior. Often this has little to do with the other person; it has more to do with one's perception of their ability to achieve the underlying goal.

"People miss the 'buttons' all the time. I'll be on a conference call with a client and I'll hear a colleague hit a 'button,' something the client really cares about, but then they just pass it by—so often people don't even realize they just came upon a button. They lost an opportunity for an in."
–John Hammond, Sales Manager at a San Francisco SEO company

3. Deeper Need—Trust & Respect. At a deeper level of experience, conflicts with others typically make us feel threatened. Our bodies go into fight or flight mode by increasing attentional vigilance (putting us on high alert for a predator), heart rate, blood pressure, skin conductance (sweating) and other physiological reactions preparing us to fight the attacker. The primitive systems of the body and mind are in "don't get killed mode." Now, in the context of interpersonal conflicts, this primitive circuitry is reacting as if it were a life or death situation. For that reason, at a very primitive level, trust is the foundation of all good relationships.

When in conflict, trust and safety (which translates in modern interactions as respect) are in question. It is often this deeper level that people defend, fight for, and also where the damage occurs if the conflict is not dealt with well. Above all, during conflict, we need to preserve the sense of trust and respect. Otherwise, put simply, the other person will activate this primitive "don't get killed" circuitry and the relationship can slip into doubt, suspicion, self-interest, and defensiveness. Although it feels much more complicated than that in interpersonal dynamics, often the strength of trust and sense of safety (i.e., respect) predicts the potential of relationships.

Decades of research support this proposition. John Gottman, considered the foremost researcher in romantic relationships, identifies trust as the fundamental unit of relationship health. Positive conflict management addresses the problem without threatening the other's sense of trust and feelings of respect in the relationship. This plays out in unspoken, often unconscious assessments of whether the other person is trustworthy and respects you. At an emotional, unconscious level, we may be asking ourselves questions like, "Are you with me or against me?; Do you like me?; Are you on my team?; Can I depend on you?; Are you safe?"

At work these questions often translate into inquiries into issues around competition versus cooperation, deceit and manipulation versus transparency and honesty, criticism versus support, trust and betrayal, etc. Concerns for one's reputation, likeability, acceptance on teams, and other subtle, unspoken insecurities are often examples of one's deeper need for trust and respect. In conflict conversations, it can be useful to consider the degree to which each party feels threatened at a fundamental level and how to preserve or directly address threats to trust and respect.

CRAFT WIN-WIN SOLUTIONS

Creating win-win solutions requires focusing more on the positive alternatives than the obstacles. Of course it is useful to problem solve, but most of us tend to overly focus on the problems rather than the possibilities. Focusing on ways to serve both parties' underlying goals can lead to win-win solutions. The conflicts of interest may not be as large and insurmountable as it initially seemed when viewed from this larger perspective.

DEEP DIVE CONVERSATION WORKSHEET

Conflict is to be expected even in the best relationships. In conflict, rebuilding connection may require you to take a step back and consider the variables at play for each party involved. The purpose of this exercise is to give you an opportunity to analyze a recent conflict and gain a greater level of insight by applying the Deep Dive Conversation approach. Choose a conflict situation you have had with someone, perhaps with a customer/client, colleague, boss, supervisor, manager, or supervisee.

CONFLICT SITUATION

WHO, WHERE, WHEN, & WHAT. Who was involved in the conflict? What happened?

_____
_____
_____

3 LEVELS OF CONFLICT—YOUR PERSPECTIVE

1. SURFACE—Identify Target Behavior

Negative Target. What is the problem behavior, the behavior that is creating an obstacle (the negative target), that which I want to avoid or get rid of.

_____
_____
_____

Positive Target. What is the behavior do I want to see, the behavior I want them to do instead of the problem behavior (the positive target behavior).

_____
_____
_____

2. UNDER THE WATERLINE—Identify Underlying Goal, Objective, Or Intention (situation). What is MY underlying, more important objective that is threatened by the problem behavior. Consider what I want in this situation.

_____
_____
_____

3. DEEPER NEED—Identify the Deeper Needs: Trust & Respect (personal). What is my deepest level of need? Consider the degree of trust or respect I feel in the relationship and what I really want and need to feel in this relationship. (e.g., Do they like me as a person? Are they with me or against me?)

_____
_____
_____

3 LEVELS OF CONFLICT—THE OTHER'S PERSPECTIVE

1. SURFACE—Identify Target Behavior

   Negative Target. What is the problem behavior, the behavior that is creating an obstacle (the negative target), that which they want to avoid or get rid of.

   _____
   _____
   _____

   Positive Target. What is the positive behavior they want to see, the behavior they want me (or another) to do instead of the problem behavior.

   _____
   _____
   _____

2. UNDER THE WATERLINE—Identify Underlying Goal, Objective, Or Intention (situation). What is their underlying, more important objective that is threatened by the problem behavior. Consider what they want in this situation.

   _____
   _____
   _____
   _____

3. DEEPER NEED— Identify the Deeper Needs: Trust & Respect (personal). What is their deepest level of need? Consider the degree of trust or respect they feel in the relationship and what they really want and need to feel in this relationship. (e.g., Do they believe I like them as a person? Do they feel I am with them or against them?)

   _____
   _____
   _____
   _____

ACTION PLAN

WIN-WIN SOLUTIONS. What are potential win-win solutions or ways to reconnect that address these three levels of conflict?

   _____
   _____
   _____
   _____

DEEP DIVE CONVERSATION TRACKING LOG

DAY	**APPLICATION** Which Deep Dive Conversation did have today? What were my and their 3 levels of conflict? (Target Behaviors, Underlying Goal, Deeper Need for Trust/Respect)	**IMPACT** What was the impact of this technique on me, others, the situation, and/or the relationship?
Day 1		
Day 2		
Day 3		
Day 4		

DEEP DIVE CONVERSATION TRACKING LOG

DAY	APPLICATION Which Deep Dive Conversation did have today? What were my and their 3 levels of conflict? (Target Behaviors, Underlying Goal, Deeper Need for Trust/Respect)	IMPACT What was the impact of this technique on me, others, the situation, and/or the relationship?
Day 5		
Day 6		
Day 7		

INSIGHTS - What patterns or benefits emerged?

_____
_____
_____
_____

GIFT OF RELATIONSHIP MEDITATION

Relationships can be considered as gifts. This meditation explores the gifts that relationships bring to life. It will guide you through feeling the positive impact someone has in your life. You may choose to focus someone with whom your relationship is mostly positive and not too complicated or on someone with whom you are in conflict.

This meditation is a Low Road technique for feeling greater connection and positive feelings with others. It can help you feel more gratitude and abundance in relationships and can build the habit of appreciating other's role in your life. It can also be used to cultivate a balanced state of mind before initiating a constructive conflict conversation.

During all the meditations, try to let go of expectations about how this practice is supposed to feel or what is supposed to happen. Your job is to experience what happens in a nonjudgmental, explorative manner. Each time your mind wanders into thought, turn your attention back.

INSTRUCTIONS
(4 to 8 minutes)

1. FOCUS INWARD: Breathe and Center

- **Center**—Close your eyes and turn your attention inward.

- **Anchor in your Breath**—Feel Your Breath fill and release your body. Breathe deeply with a slower exhale and natural inhale.

- **Set your Intention**—To direct your attention in this time, place, and to the objective of this meditation.

2. DIRECT ATTENTION: *To the ways that a relationship is a gift.*

- *Imagine.* Bring to mind a valued person in your life or even a pet. Choose someone with whom your relationship is mostly positive and not too complicated.

- *Make Contact*—with how it feels in the presence of this person or pet in positive moments. Feel the positive impact in your body. Perhaps there is a warmth, a subtle filling sensation, or spaciousness.

- *Sense*—that this being is a gift. Sense how this being may not always be in your life; sense how in this moment you get to experience their presence. Sense that this being is a gift in your life.

- *Soak in the feelings*—feel into the experience and sense the energy that runs through your body as you focus on the fact that this person is in your life.

3. REFLECT ON INSIGHTS: Breathe and Reflect

- Come back to your breath.
- Reflect on the insights or benefits you gained during this meditation.

4. MAINTAIN INNER AWARENESS: Soft Gaze and Stay with Awareness.

- Slowly open your eyes and keep your gaze soft, directed downward, and settling on a neutral object.
- Stay with the awareness you gained during the meditation.

GIFT OF RELATIONSHIP MEDITATION WORKSHEET

After you have completed the meditation, jot down observations about what came up during your meditation. Make note of thoughts you had, feelings you experienced, bodily sensations you felt, and/or detours that you took.

1. FOCUS INWARD: Breathe and Center. How well were you able to concentrate inward and turn your attention to your intention in this meditation?

_____

_____

_____

2. DIRECT ATTENTION: *To the ways that a relationship is a gift.*

Imagine. Who did you bring to mind? Why?

_____

_____

_____

Make Contact with how it feels in the presence of this person in positive moments. Did you feel the positive impact in your body? Was there is a warmth, a subtle filling sensation, or spaciousness? Briefly describe the feeling.

_____

_____

_____

Sense that this person is a gift. Did you sense how this person may not always be in your life? Did you sense how in this moment you get to experience their presence? Did you sense that this person is a gift in your life? Briefly describe the sensations.

_____

_____

_____

Soak in the feelings. Did you feel the sense the energy that runs through your body as you focused on the fact that this person is in your life? Briefly describe the feelings.

_____

_____

_____

3. PERSONAL APPLICATION. How can I use this Mindfulness Practice in improving my relationships?

_____

_____

_____

GIFT OF RELATIONSHIP MEDITATION TRACKING LOG

DAY	APPLICATION Who was the focus of my meditation? In what ways is this relationship a gift? What internal or external factors helped me successfully complete this meditation?	IMPACT What was the impact of this meditation on me, my feelings about a situation, or the relationship positivity ratio?
Day 1		
Day 2		
Day 3		
Day 4		

GIFT OF RELATIONSHIP MEDITATION TRACKING LOG

DAY	APPLICATION Who was the focus of my meditation? In what ways is this relationship a gift? What internal or external factors helped me successfully complete this meditation?	IMPACT What was the impact of this meditation on me, my feelings about a situation, or the relationship positivity ratio?
Day 5		
Day 6		
Day 7		

INSIGHTS - What patterns or benefits emerged?

_____
_____
_____
_____

COACHING GUIDELINES

Use the self-coaching process and coaching tools to create long-term change. For maximum effectiveness, focus on one skill at a time. For each skill, take an *assessment* if one is available, complete a *coaching worksheet*, practice high road and low road techniques, and track your application of the skill over a seven day period using a *Tracking Log*.

Select one skill. Consider which skill would make the greatest difference in your current life circumstances if you used it more frequently and effectively. It is easier to build new habits if you focus on one change at a time. Select the *one skill* in this chapter that is your highest priority:

- Bids for Connection
- Identify Conflict Escalators
- Craft Constructive Conflict
- Deep Dive Conversations

STEP 1. ASSESS. Assess the need and benefits of practicing this particular skill. Assess your current mastery level of the skill. Use one of the on-line assessment tools if one is available for the skill. The Coaching Worksheet will also help you assess your need and benefits of using the skill.

Assessments—Questionnaires that assess your current skill level and provide data on your progress.

STEP 2. PLAN. To create an action plan, understand how a technique can help you build greater mastery of a skill. Next, consider how you can apply it to your own situations.

Coaching Worksheets—Tools for learning and creating an action plan for practicing the techniques.
- Bid for Connection Worksheet
- Identify Conflict Escalators Worksheet
- Craft Constructive Conflict Worksheet
- Deep Dive Conversations Worksheet

STEP 3. PRACTICE. During the following seven days, apply the skill daily. Use both the High Road techniques and the Low Road techniques to practice the skill.

Tracking Logs—Habit forming tools to guide your efforts as you practice the techniques for seven days.

- Bid for Connection Tracking Log
- Identify Conflict Escalators Tracking Log
- Craft Constructive Conversation Tracking Log
- Deep Dive Conversations Tracking Log

- Gift of Relationship Meditation Tracking Log

Meditation Guides—Low Road techniques to build the skill at the emotional or non-verbal level.

- Gift of Relationship Meditation

STEP 4. TRACK RESULTS. In addition to systematically helping you to practice the techniques, *Tracking Logs* provide a place to note the impact of the skill on your experience. Tracking Logs help you become more aware of behaviors and patterns in yourself. They are a source of feedback so you can modify a technique to make it more effective.

POSITIVE PSYCHOLOGY AND THE KEYS TO SUSTAINABLE HAPPINESS
Stanford University

Positive psychology research has demonstrated that sustainable happiness is based on a skill set that can be learned. This course sequence assists students to gain mastery in these valuable skills.

• *Choosing Happiness* provides a science-based action plan for enhancing sustainable happiness.

• *Enhancing Emotional Intelligence* focuses on building fundamental personal and interpersonal skills for happiness and success.

• *Thriving at Work: Science-Based Practices To Elevate Success & Fulfillment* applies the skills of positive psychology to the workplace.

• *Mindfulness* focuses on cultivating mindfulness as a way of being, and as a powerful tool in daily life.

CHOOSING HAPPINESS
THRIVE: SELF-COACHING FOR HAPPINESS ® AND SUCCESS

Happy people don't just feel better—they do better than less-happy individuals. Research shows they achieve greater success and wealth, are healthier, are more altruistic, and have more satisfying relationships. The keys to happiness are within everyone's reach—because the keys are actually habits. In this course, students learn happiness-enhancing habits that will help them improve responses to stress and opportunities at work, at home, and in relationships. The tools presented are derived from research in the innovative field of positive psychology, the science of well-being.

The course workbook is focused on *The Habits of Happiness*. The workbook is written for this course and includes case examples, summaries of scientific findings, action plans, and weekly practices. Students apply these principles to their daily personal and professional lives and engage in class discussions, mindfulness practices, and experiential exercises.

This course is part of a series in applied positive psychology, which also includes the courses Enhancing Emotional Intelligence, Thriving at Work, and Mindfulness. The series is designed to help students build a comprehensive skill set in sustainable happiness. While these courses build upon one another, each course can be taken independently as well.

ENHANCING EMOTIONAL INTELLIGENCE
MINDFULNESS BASED STRATEGIES FOR HAPPINESS AND SUCCESS

What is the skill set underlying happiness, success, and overall well-being? Research shows that emotional intelligence, which is defined as being self aware and skillful in managing emotions, leads to benefits in a variety of life domains. Emotionally intelligent people tend to have satisfying relationships, manage stress well, and excel in school and at work. Emotional intelligence predicts professional success more than IQ or experience. It is related to confidence, charisma, optimism, and resiliency. Most important, emotional intelligence can be learned.

The aim of this introductory course is to help students assess and build the skills of emotional intelligence. Students improve their ability to understand and manage emotions, change counterproductive thinking patterns, and leverage strengths. Everyone receives a workbook, written for this course by the instructors, on how to build and apply these skills at work, at home, and in relationships. Activities include self-assessment, experiential exercises, mindfulness practices, and working with personal scenarios.

This course is part of a series in applied positive psychology, which also includes the courses Choosing Happiness, Thriving at Work, and Mindfulness. The series is designed to help students build a comprehensive skill set in sustainable happiness. While these courses build upon one another, each course can be taken independently as well.

THRIVING AT WORK
SCIENCE-BASED PRACTICES TO INCREASE SUCCESS & FULFILLMENT AT WORK

Thirty years of Gallup surveys have found that the most successful companies are ones whose employees believe they get to do what they do best every day. (Only one-third of working people do.) A decade of research suggests that happiness at work—defined as pleasure, engagement, and a sense of meaning—can improve productivity, revenue, profitability, staff retention, customer loyalty, and workplace safety. Many of the studies are preliminary, but they strongly suggest that positive emotions, positive relationships, inspiration, and resilience increase creativity and problem-solving ability and aid in fighting negative stress.

People can take control of certain behaviors and habits of mind that will make them happier and more productive at work. They can focus on positive outcomes, listen mindfully, communicate authentically, leverage their strengths, and live their values. They can add gratitude, hope, and a dose of self-control to each working day. They can challenge their negative perceptions, thoughts, and emotions. They can learn to apply the power of realistic optimism. And it's clear that happy bosses perform measurably better, building productive teams and inspiring loyalty. This course is one in a series in applied positive psychology, which also includes the courses Choosing Happiness, Enhancing Emotional Intelligence, and Mindfulness. While these courses build upon one another, each course can be taken independently as well.

MINDFULNESS
SCIENCE-BASED STRATEGIES TO THRIVE AT WORK AND IN LIFE

Research demonstrates that mindful people enjoy many advantages in wellbeing, vitality, and success. Mindfulness is especially relevant in our fast-paced era with increased demands on attention, productivity, innovation, and energy. This course focuses on cultivating mindfulness as a way of being, and as a powerful tool to use in daily life.

While mindfulness is growing in popularity, its definitions differ significantly. We define mindfulness as a mental state characterized by being present, noticing new information, and revising mindsets. Based on the research of Harvard psychologist Ellen Langer, our approach blends traditional and modern views of mindfulness.

We expand on traditional views of mindfulness and include techniques for challenging mindsets, for considering multiple perspectives, and for systematically applying mindfulness in the workplace, in relationships, and in personal well-being and health.

We also explore mindfulness through a modern lens, and employ skill-building techniques that include but are not limited to meditation. Participants engage in interactive exercises, in-class paired discussions, home practice, meditations, and reflective exercises. The interactive, practical exercises help participants relate differently to experiences, and to see circumstances, themselves, and others more objectively and clearly.

Course Instructors

Laura Delizonna
&
Ted Anstedt

CPSIA information can be obtained
at www.ICGtesting.com
Printed in the USA
LVOW04s0044180817
545458LV00006B/52/P